Philosophy

Philosophy

An Introduction Through Original Fiction and Discussion

Thomas D. Davis
Alfred North Whitehead College
University of Redlands

First Edition
987654321
 Published in the United States by Random House, Inc., and simultaneously in Canada by Random House of Canada Limited, Toronto.

Library of Congress Cataloging in Publication Data

Davis, Thomas D 1941-
Philosophy: an introduction through original fiction and discussion.
Bibliography: p.
Includes index.
1. Philosophy. I. Title.
BD31.D18 100 78-12329
ISBN 0-394-32048-4

Manufactured in the United States of America

To Debbie and Ginny
with Love

Preface

For the past few years, I have introduced students to philosophy by prefacing the more technical readings with relevant short fiction ranging from Voltaire to Vonnegut. I have been encouraged by the results, but also bothered by the frequently labored transitions from the fiction to the philosophy. To move from *Brave New World* to a discussion of utilitarianism, from *Candide* to the problem of suffering, is relatively effortless. But there is little philosophically conscious literature related to many of the issues that philosophers discuss, particularly issues in metaphysics and epistemology. Science fiction sometimes comes close, but never close enough. Confident of my methods, but frustrated by the available fiction, I decided to write the kind of stories I'd been looking for myself.

Some story ideas emerged from "imaginative cases" I had sketched in class, and some have been handed down from teacher to teacher: a land in which good and evil appear to be marked by strange lights; a library whose volumes seem to have anticipated a man's every thought and action; the plight of a disembodied soul who must decide what to *do* with himself. For other philosophical pieces, I had to resort to the more literal expedient of a dialogue: a suburban solipsist whose friends try to convince him that they do exist; a God perplexed by Satan's request for something called "free will" that he can't clearly describe. In still other stories, I have attempted to be a bit ingenious: a parody of *Pilgrim's Progress* in which the incidents exemplify logical fallacies; a "whodunit" that requires the reader to learn a bit of symbolic logic in order to decipher a crucial clue. I'm aware that from a literary standpoint these stories are not among the best of philosophical fiction. But they do serve, I think, as lively and truly useful philosophical teaching aids.

Originally I intended to publish these stories as a supplement to existing texts, but I eventually decided to create a self-contained introductory text. The twelve stories have been grouped into six chapters, with a section of philosophical discussion at the conclusion of each chapter. Questions immediately following the stories underscore the philosophical issues implicit in them.

The discussions of the fictional pieces present the basic questions, positions, and arguments illustrated by each story. While bearing in mind the purpose of the book as an introduction, I have tried to maintain the discussions at a relatively sophisticated level.

The instructor will have a fair amount of discretion in choosing the order in which to assign chapters. The first four chapters—on mind; freedom and foreknowledge; God and the problem of suffering; and morality—seemed to be chapters that most instructors would wish to use, in that order. So although they are not in any crucial sense cumulative, the discussions in these chapters sometimes refer to material previously covered. The chapters on appearance and reality and on logic have been placed fifth and sixth, respectively, but instructors who wish to assign them early in the course can easily do so; all their references to other chapters appear only in footnotes. Although the logic chapter introduces terms like "deductive," "valid," and "question-begging" that do not appear elsewhere, such concepts could be brought into the classroom discussion of other chapters.

In the course of writing this book, I benefited from the helpful comments of various Random House reviewers. I am particularly appreciative of suggestions that were made by Robert L. Gray, Gerald E. Myers, and George S. Pappas. Needless to say, I assume full responsibility for the contents of the book, including any errors that may have found their way into it.

An indirect but delightful contribution to the writing of the book was two years of teaching and travel in Europe, which I owe, along with much else, to Gordon Atkins, the creator of Whitehead College, University of Redlands.

Finally, I am indebted to Jane Cullen, a Random House editor, who saw possibilities in a proposal rejected by other publishers as too "adventurous" for the philosophy textbook market. I am grateful to Ms. Cullen for her support, her advice, and, of course, her recommendation to publish. I can only hope that the reactions of philosophy teachers and their students support her judgment, and mine.

T.D.

Contents

1. The Nature of the Mind

Strange Behavior

WHAT FIRST STARTLED US ABOUT THE CIVILIZATION ON THE PLANET Gamma was not its strangeness but its familiarity. It was as if a piece of southern Europe from the year 2050 had been transported fifty years ahead in time, and millions of miles out into space, to that small planet. Of course, the similarity is not exact. The Italians of fifty years ago did not have quite the same enthusiasm for spherical constructions, nor for the colors pink and orange. Also, the brown-skinned Gammas are nine feet tall and hairless, and they hear through slits located just below their cheekbones. But with all the strange life forms recently discovered in the universe, these minor dissimilarities between the Gammas and the mid-century Italians go almost unnoticed. When we landed on Gamma, we felt as if we had stepped into a living museum.

The technological sophistication of Gamma is virtually the same as that of Earth fifty years ago. But there is one notable difference. The Gammas' skill in robotry is more advanced than is ours even today. In fact, we spent our first six hours on Gamma in the company of robots that we thought to be living beings. In our defense, I should note that the Gammese robots have a tremendous flexibility of response and fluidity of motion and that their metallic parts are covered with a brown, skin-like exterior. It is only when a Gammese robot is standing next to a Gamma that one notices, in the robot, a hint of the mechanical. But I don't think one is thoroughly convinced of the difference between the Gammas and the robots until one has toured the hospitals where the living are treated and the factories where the robots are repaired.

It was from the robots that we got the rudiments of the Gammese language. After letting them know that we were friendly, we coaxed them over to the Q-53 Computer Language Translator. We showed them the green patch on the screen of the Translator's Sensitivity Panel and indicated that they should say aloud the Gammese word for what they saw. The robots said something like "rooga"; the Translator said aloud "green." We said "green" and the Translator said "rooga." We continued this process until we were able to produce, via the Translator, several basic sentences in Gammese. Then the robots realized that the Q-53 was recording all the word translations and would soon enable us to converse by voice alone, without constant reference to the pictures on the Sensitivity Panel. Thereafter, the robots concentrated on teaching the Q-53 their language, responding in quick succession to the series of sights, sounds, textures, tastes, and scents produced by the Sensitivity Panel.

The real Gammas appeared eventually, and we laughed at ourselves for having mistaken the robots for living beings. The Gammas were very friendly and intensely curious about the civilization on Earth. Of course we had more to tell them than they us, for they were like the past to us, and we were like the future to them. The first few days on Gamma were a constant series of conferences, largely of a Show-and-Tell variety, as we struggled to make ourselves understood through the less than fluent Q-53 Translator. Fortunately, we had with us an instruction kit filled with models, maps, and photographs designed to aid us in explanations of life on Earth.

With so much on Gamma already familiar to us, we tended to focus our attention on the robots. We became more and more puzzled by what we observed. It was not only that the robots were so lifelike but also that the Gammas seemed to treat the robots as their equals. True, there was a preponderance of robots in jobs that demanded only great strength or great memory; but there were Gammas in such jobs as well. And some Gammese robots held high-level positions in which they supervised the activities of the living Gammas. Furthermore, the Gammas seemed to treat the robots with the same sort of courtesy, affection, or, occasionally, anger that they showed toward other Gammas.

Our most frequent guide was a Gamma whose name is unpronounceable. We simply addressed him as "Mr. A," and the Q-53 made the sound that he recognized as his name. We were eager to question him about the Gammas' attitude toward the robots, but we approached the subject cautiously, not wishing to seem critical. His initial responses to our inquiries were bewildering. It seemed as though he were teasing us.

"Would you say that flesh is so much better than metal?" he asked. "I should think it would be just the opposite."

Or again: "Would you treat someone differently just because he is produced in a factory? Personally, I think our mode of reproduction—which is similar to yours—is rather inefficient and even comical."

Mr. A was asked why only robots had been sent on the potentially dangerous mission of meeting us when we landed on Gamma.

"Because, of course, they are more easily repaired than we are. It is a quality we envy them. Just as they sometimes envy us our greater flexibility."

Phrases like "they envy us" and "they also want" were constantly employed by our guide. Finally Lewis, a member of our group, blurted out the question that all of us wanted to ask.

"Mr. A, do the Gammas really believe that their robots have minds?"

"Of course," said Mr. A, looking puzzled.

"Then that explains the confusion," said Lewis. "We did not mean to say that one should treat a creature differently simply because it is made of a different substance or is produced differently. Rather, we believe that creatures made of metal cannot possibly have minds. On the other hand, you believe they can and do. Now we understand each other better."

We were all quite pleased with the quick and tactful way in which we had solved the mystery. At the same time, we all felt more than a little superior to a people who believed that machines could think. However, Mr. A did not seem pleased. He seemed absolutely bewildered.

"I don't understand," he said. "Please explain yourselves."

"You believe that these robots have minds," said Lewis. "So you treat them as your peers. We don't believe that robots have minds. Therefore, we treat them as we might treat, say, expensive watches. Of course, there is room for disagreement on this point. I mean, one doesn't actually *see* minds."

"Of course you see minds!" said Mr. A.

He was quite emphatic and seemed quite serious. We were all startled.

"Well, one's own mind, yes," said Lewis. "But one doesn't see other minds."

"You do see other minds!"

"No, no. At least not according to our beliefs. We believe that one sees the behavior of other people, but not their minds."

Mr. A glanced toward the Q-53 Translator and then back at Lewis.

"Your words don't seem to translate. What I hear from the Translator makes no sense."

Lewis looked thoughtful for a moment and then continued.

"Does the word 'behavior' make sense to you? The actions of the body?"

"Yes."

"And the word 'pain'?"

"Yes."

"Do you understand me when I say that a person in pain behaves in a special sort of way?"

"Yes. Of course."

"Well, what we call 'pain' is not the behavior but the thing inside."

"What thing inside?" said Mr. A. "There are many things inside."

"I mean the thing that is inside whenever you show the pain behavior."

"Oh, you mean the state of the brain, or the state of the robot's computer?"

"No, no, no. You could observe the brain state or the computer state under certain conditions. I mean the thing that you could never observe no matter how extensively you examined the body. I mean the feel of the pain, the sensation of pain."

"Those last words don't translate."

Lewis was obviously feeling frustrated, but he pressed on.

"Perhaps the example of imagination would be easier. Suppose you close your eyes and imagine something round and orange. Form an image of it. What we call the 'mental' is not the closing of the eyes or the verbal description 'orange and round' that you might give us. What we call the 'mental' is the round and orange picture inside of you."

"What picture?" said Mr. A.

The conversation went on in this absurd fashion as Lewis tried to phrase the obvious in a way that would be obvious in Mr. A's language. But gradually the truth of the matter began to dawn on us. The reason the Gammas saw no essential difference between themselves and their robots was that the Gammas, like the robots, were creatures without minds, without consciousness.

Our words like "think" and "want," and the generic term "mind," had seemed, at first, to translate into Gammese because we constantly correlated our mental events with behavioral patterns. The Gammas had thought all along that we were talking about behavior. In fact, our mental terms didn't translate into Gammese at all, for the Gammas have no minds. They only behave as if they did.

As we were staring at Mr. A in astonishment, it occurred to us that we might be frightening or offending him. We were very vulnerable on this faraway planet. So we turned the conversation from the topic of minds to the topic of interplanetary travel. Our talk of the overtly strange life forms we had encountered on our travels seemed to reestablish our kinship with the Gammese people.

When the subject of minds arose again, as it inevitably did, we tried to deemphasize the dissimilarity between ourselves and the Gammas. We implied that our word "mind" referred to behavior plus that "something else." This allowed us to say that the Gammas and the robots had minds without pretending, as would have been hopeless now, that there was no difference between them and us. Eventually, the whole matter turned into a kind of joke. Mr. A asked us what the "something else" inside the people from Earth did for them. Of course, we had to admit that it produced no overt effects that could not occur without it. After that he began to joke about us as "the people with the something else that does nothing at all." In fact, this phrase threatens to become the general designation for us on Gamma.

It is truly amazing to observe just how little external difference the lack of mind has made to the Gammese civilization. With only a body and a brain, they have almost managed to keep pace with the civilization on Earth. Without thoughts, they have been able to develop a sophisticated technology that has brought them to the verge of interplanetary travel. Without feelings, they can discriminate between beauty and ugliness, goodness and evil, and they have produced sophisticated treatises on ethics and aesthetics. They act as if they have the normal variety of human emotions, even to the point of enjoying very sentimental love stories.

The only noticeable differences appear in their metaphysical writings, and even these are minor. One philosopher on Gamma began a philosophical treatise with the argument, "I think, therefore I am." Of course, this is not really the same as Descartes's argument. The correct translation would be something like, "I behave (in a thinking way), therefore I exist (as a physical being)."

On Gamma there is a fairly widespread belief in God, though they have their religious skeptics just as we do. They identify God with the universe and claim that He is (or rather behaves as if He is) omnipotent, omniscient, and perfectly good. They certainly do not imagine God to be nonphysical. The word "nonphysical" translates into their language as "not-being" or "nothing," which is to say that it does not translate at all. Some Gammas believe in life after death, which they imagine to be a physical resurrection of the body that occurs at some far distant time. They include the robots in this resurrection. "The robots worship Him as we do," they say, "and our Heavenly Father would not neglect them." Of course, they do not believe that the mind exists during the period between death and the resurrection. Said one philosopher: "To take the mind from the body is as impossible as taking the shape from a flower while leaving its color and weight behind."

I often wonder about our future relations with the Gammas.

I doubt that we would provoke hostilities with these creatures. There are enough hostile beings in the universe already, and we need whatever allies we can find. The Gammas may be able to provide us with valuable information about their solar system. And no doubt our scientists and philosophers will want to study the Gammas at great length. But the issues here will be strictly practical. There can be no question of extending moral rights to mindless, unfeeling creatures, whether they are made of metal or protoplasm.

Mr. A was there to bid us goodbye as we prepared to leave the planet Gamma. He told us how much he had enjoyed our visit and how sad he was to see us depart. He said the Gammas would always look forward to visits from the people of Earth. Then he laughed softly:

"We shall always welcome the people with the something else that does nothing at all."

I laughed with him, but in my heart I felt only pity. He did not, could not, possibly understand that the "something else that does nothing at all" is the very essence of life, the point of it, and that it makes all the difference in the world.

Life After Life

My funeral was quite moving, I thought. I chose a spot at the front, next to the minister, so that I could observe the faces in the crowd while I listened to the eulogy. There wasn't a dry eye in the house. Reverend Franks reviewed my long career with the Omega Life Insurance Company, my "meteoric rise," as he called it, from messenger boy to president. He said I had always insisted that Omega sold insurance for *living,* not dying: insurance for the happiness of policyholders should they live full term, insurance for the happiness of the loved ones should they not. He was sure that Charlie—my name's Charles R. Smith, but everyone calls me Charlie, even my secretary—that Charlie would want his funeral conducted in the same optimistic, life-loving spirit with which he had conducted his business. That was a nice touch, I thought, and I hoped that the boys from the office were duly appreciative.

Death, said Reverend Franks, was, above all, the opportunity to reflect on life. Though I had lived but fifty years, everyone, he was sure, would agree that my life had been "full term" in the most meaningful sense. I had been not only a business magnate but also a Boy Scout leader, an Elk, and a church deacon. I had been the beloved husband of Ruth and the beloved father of Tim and Marcie, a good provider in life and beyond. I had been a man to whom any friend could turn in legitimate need; a man who could laugh with the fellows and cry, so to speak, for an unfortunate boy; a man who had a five handicap as a golfer but no handicap as a human being.

I was feeling a bit smug at that point, I must admit, and I

began to feel more so as Reverend Franks started to speak, somewhat uncomfortably, of his hope for "life after life." Our church has always been vague on that particular issue, tending to stress the vast potential for human moral development in "this life." But I *knew* now, of course, and he didn't. I knew there was life after this life. Or I guess I should say: life after that one.

In all honesty, though, this development was as much of a surprise to me as the next guy. When I got that fish bone caught in my throat and couldn't breathe, and everything started getting dark, I said to myself: This is it, fella. Nothing else, just: This is it, fella. And you know, in the back of my mind, I was a bit pleased with how it was ending. You spend a lot of your life worrying about death and imagining how awful it is going to be. But when the time comes, it's just something you go ahead and do, or rather something that gets done to you, like getting punched in the nose in your first fight. When it happens, it happens quickly, and you're kind of numb, and there isn't that much pain, or fuss, or fear at all.

Then I opened my eyes and I thought: I guess that wasn't it, fella. Ruth was kneeling next to me, wringing her hands and crying, and Tim, who'd been having dinner with us, was yelling into the phone. I said, "I'm all right, Ruth." But she kept on crying, and I realized she was sobbing too loud to hear me. So I got to my feet to show her I was okay. Even that didn't get her attention, so I put my hand on her shoulder. Only then I noticed there wasn't any hand. That was a shocker, I can tell you. I looked down at myself and there was nothing there—no hands, no arms, no feet, no legs, no nothing. I looked in the mirror over the dining room table, and there was nothing there either, just the image of the living room behind me. I looked at Ruth again and there, at her feet, was a body that looked just like mine, only the face was kind of waxy and blue. And I thought: This is too much. You're having some kind of weird dream. You're on the floor, unconscious, dreaming that you're moving around the room without a body. In a little while you're going to wake up in a hospital bed with your body connected to you the way it's supposed to be, and everything will be all right.

But if this was a dream, it was awfully vivid. Tim hung up

the phone and helped Ruth over to the couch. He held her as she cried, and occasionally he glanced over her shoulder at the body on the floor, showing little emotion, just as I'd always taught him a boy should do.

And I thought again: yes, this has to be a dream. You can't be dead. If you were dead, you'd be standing before Saint Peter at the Pearly Gates, getting fitted for your wings, or something like that. But then I thought: maybe it doesn't happen that fast. Your soul has just left your body. Maybe it takes the Lord a little while. After all, there are people dying in houses all over the world tonight. You could hardly expect the Lord to make the rounds of all those houses so quickly. You'll just have to wait your turn. And maybe you'd better get yourself ready. So I started in with "Our Father Who Art in Heaven" and when I finished that I started singing "Nearer My God to Thee." Only no one appeared except for the policemen and the ambulance attendants. All that commotion distracted me, I guess: the sirens, the chatter, the neighbors gathered outside, the ride to the hospital.

At the hospital they pronounced me dead and gave Ruth a sedative. I wasn't all that concerned about Ruth. I don't mean to say I was unsympathetic. I knew how frightened and unhappy she was, and I knew it would be hard for her to get along without me. But I also knew now that death wasn't the end of everything. Ruth would have a few years of loneliness and fear, but then she would find out that life goes on and on, and she would be with me again. From where I stood, so to speak, that looked like a pretty good deal. Anyway, I had my own problems.

In the days following my death, when I wasn't diverted by my funeral arrangements, I was absorbed with the perplexities of my new situation. It was hard to get used to. Some friend would enter the house and I'd say "hi," and he'd walk right through me. I mean *right through me*. And then I'd look down at where my body had been, and I'd be brought back to reality—whatever that was.

My perception of things was much as it had always been, at least visually. I saw the same shapes, sizes, and colors, in the same three dimensions. And my perception of sounds was about the same. But I had no sense of touch, taste, or smell. I really regretted my lack of taste when I looked at a steak and a beer, not to mention my lack of wherewithal when I glanced at a naked woman. Still, I didn't have hunger anymore, and I wasn't in pain. I just missed those pleasures.

I wasn't able to move objects in any way, which is kind of puzzling when you think about it. Of course, my soul didn't have a body anymore. But if a soul can't move objects, how does it ever move a body? Some special kind of connection, I suppose. In any case, my connection had snapped.

However, if I couldn't move objects, I could move through them without difficulty. I would walk into a wall, get a quick impression of darkness, and then emerge from the other side. I found I was able to rise to a height of about forty feet from the ground, and to move laterally at a top speed of ninety-five miles an hour. I checked that speed when I went into Los Angeles for a Dodger game, two days after the funeral. I had a great time. I was able to move around the infield, getting close-ups of the action, without fear of getting hit by the ball. I had the best "seat" in the house, and it didn't cost me one thin dime.

It goes without saying that I could go anywhere I wanted, unobserved, and observe anything I wanted. I didn't abuse that privilege. The naked woman I mentioned earlier was my wife. Any others I saw were by accident, and I departed almost at once. It was fun, at first, dropping by the office, or a neighbor's house, or Larry's Bar, listening to plans for an ad campaign, or to local gossip, trying to guess along with the fellows on the baseball pools. But as time went on, I found myself less and less interested in those conversations, I suppose because I was not involved in the things they were talking about. Occasionally I heard cutting remarks about me, and those hurt. But perhaps I felt even worse when they stopped talking about me altogether.

The real hurt was from my family. Tim took his share of the inheritance, bought himself a flashy VW van, packed it with surfboards, and left college for the beach. When a friend asked him how he got his money, he said, "My old man kicked the bucket." That's all. No fond recollections, no good words, just "my old man kicked the bucket." I never heard my daughter

Marcie talk about me at all. I visited her college dorm once and only once. I mean, you teach a girl what's right and wrong, and how no one will buy a cow if milk is free, and how pot leads to stronger stuff, and she says, "Yes, Daddy, of course," and then you see what she does when she's away. Just once. I wouldn't want to see any more of it.

But my wife, Ruth, gave me the greatest pain—Ruth, with whom I spent all those years; Ruth, whom I trusted. My old friend Arnold kept dropping by to "pay his respects," which I thought was nice of him until I saw what his respects amounted to. I remember vividly that evening two months ago when Ruth was wearing her black dress, and Arnold was pouring her brandy to boost her spirits, and she started crying, and he hugged her, then kissed her, and she started muttering "No," and he said Charlie would want it this way, which, of course, I didn't, and later they started moving toward the bedroom. I was screaming at her at the top of my lungs, even though I knew she couldn't hear me. Then I turned and stomped out of the house. I haven't been back there since. I'm never going back there.

Later, when I calmed down a bit, I began to think things over. By this time it was obvious that the Lord wasn't coming. Maybe I'd always felt that there wasn't anyone in charge of things—life, I mean—and I was pretty sure of that now. And if my fundamentalist friends had been wrong about heaven and such, I could count myself lucky that those Eastern religions I'd read about had been wrong too. I mean, at least I wasn't reincarnated and wandering around as a skunk or a radish. What was happening to me was quite natural, apparently, and uncontrolled. What I had to do was take things in hand and make my own way, just as I had in my former life. I've never been one to sit on my thumbs, I can tell you.

Now that all the people in my former life had become uninteresting or disappointing to me, it seemed that I ought to try to make some new friends among my own kind. There had to be a lot of other souls around, and surely I would get along with them just fine. I've always been great at making friends.

But the question was: how do you make friends with people who are invisible, untouchable, and make no sounds? All I could see when I looked around me were bodies, no souls. How to make contact? Obviously, I needed some good advice.

In hopes of finding an answer, I started taking some philosophy courses (unofficially, of course) at UCLA. They were no help. I did get a few proofs for the indestructibility of the soul, but that was the last thing I needed. What I needed was a suggestion about how to chat with silent souls, and wouldn't you know those guys would have nothing to say about really relevant topics. I would have asked for my money back if I'd paid any.

After I'd thought about the problem on my own, it occurred to me that extrasensory perception might be the answer. But that didn't help much, considering I didn't know anything about extrasensory perception. The only thing I could think of was to act as if I were yelling to someone. So in my mind I said as forcefully as I could, "Hey there!" "Hello there, guys!" "Speak to me!" "Come in, souls, come in!" For the longest time nothing happened, and I tried everything. I "spoke" loudly and softly, at different times of day, facing in different directions. I would think of departed friends or relatives and speak their names. Or I would simply address myself to strangers. I tried visiting areas where it seemed logical that souls might congregate, such as churches, graveyards, and busy city streets.

Finally, I had some luck of sorts. I was sitting on the shore at Long Beach, watching the water and feeling kind of depressed, when I heard a buzzing, chattering sound, like you might hear over the phone. In desperation I cried, "Speak to me, speak to me!" and then, to my amazement, I heard a voice.

"Who's that?"

"I'm Charlie," I said, "Charlie Smith. Who are you?"

"I'm Mildred."

"Where are you, Mildred, in Long Beach?"

"Long Beach? Heavens no. I'm in Tallahassee."

"Tallahassee?"

It happens like that. You'd think that if you got through to another soul, it would be a soul in your own neighborhood. But that other soul can be anywhere. I remember a teacher at UCLA saying that a soul, being nonphysical, would have no spatial location. I wanted to interrupt her and tell her how wrong she was. I mean, I was a soul, and I was right there in her classroom. But I must admit now that that kind of location doesn't seem to count for much when souls communicate with one another.

I had a pleasant chat with Mildred that day and the next. She invited me to visit her in Tallahassee, and I accepted. It was a pretty easy trip. I could move, as I've said, at ninety-five miles an hour and didn't need to stop and rest. I didn't have to worry about traffic jams, or stop lights, or winding roads. With a few side trips for sightseeing, and getting lost once, I made it in about a day and a half.

I guess I had the absurd feeling that I would *see* Mildred in Tallahassee. Of course, I couldn't. She was a soul and invisible, no matter how close you got. Our communications in Florida were like more phone conversations, only this time they were local calls. Still, we were able to share experiences and see the sights together.

The first few days were fun. Then Mildred reverted to her "normal" routine. It turned out that the only sights she really wanted to see and share were at the television department at Sears. Mildred loved soap operas. She was a real fanatic. When she wasn't watching the soaps, she would listen to women talking about them or peer over someone's shoulder at the pages of *Soap Opera Digest*. It was all too much for me. I wasn't about to spend eternity watching "The Guiding Light" and "One Life to Live." I thought I'd better find a woman with other interests. I'd made contact once, and I was sure I would again.

And I did—this time with Alice in Cheyenne, Wyoming. That visit went badly from the start. All Alice wanted to do was hang around her husband and spy on the women he had taken up with after she'd died. I would have left right away, but I happened to see Alice's picture on the mantelpiece in her house. She was gorgeous, I mean really gorgeous. I'd never been with a woman who looked like that. So I tried to get her interested in me. I told her about my bad experiences with my wife and how I'd decided I should forget about my former life and associate with my own kind. I told her she should forget about her husband and try to have some fun.

I took Alice out on a couple of dates. Her mood seemed to be picking up, and she seemed to be getting to like me. One night, I took her to a drive-in movie. We sat near the front, about twenty feet in the air, over the cars. It was a very romantic, sensual movie. I got really involved in the film. I began to feel a deep regret at not having a body. I was longing for some kind of human warmth.

"Oh, Alice," I said, "I wish so much that I could hold your hand."

"It wouldn't be proper," she said. "I've only been widowed for five months."

That was the last straw. An hour later I was heading back to California.

That's the way it's been going. Every soul I meet seems to be interested only in the past. But the past is past, and you can't live on memories. On the other hand, what else can you live on? There doesn't seem to be anything interesting that you can do for, or to, or with, another soul. Or vice versa. It's not much fun floating around like a bubble, not able to do anything in the world.

What on earth am I going to do with myself? I don't know. I've got to figure out something. I've just got to. I'm bored as hell.

Questions

1. The narrator of "Strange Behavior" says that the Gammas have no minds. What does she believe the mind to be? What special characteristics does she believe the mind has? In considering your answer to this general question, you may first want to answer the following more specific questions:

    a. Does she believe that having a mind is just exhibiting certain kinds of behavior? Cite evidence from the story in support of your answer.

    b. Does she believe that the mind is simply the physical brain? Cite evidence from the story.

    c. Does she believe that there are essential differences between minds and physical objects? If so, what are these differences?

2. Is the narrator's conception of mind in accord with your own? If not, in what way does it differ? If you do agree, is there anything you are inclined to add to the narrator's conception?

3. "The Gammas do advanced math, build complex machines, and write sophisticated philosophical treatises. Surely this is sufficient to qualify them as intelligent. The Gammas usually treat one another and the visitors from Earth in a kindly manner. Surely this is sufficient to qualify them as kind. Intelligence and kindness are clearly mental characteristics. Therefore, the Gammas do have minds." Do you agree with this argument? If not, what is wrong with it? If you do agree, check your answer to question 2 to make sure your answers are consistent.

4. "Science tells us that the brain is the bodily organ that controls thoughts and feelings. Obviously, then, the brain is the mind. The Gammas do have brains. Therefore, the Gammas have minds." Do you agree with this argument? If not, what is wrong with it? If you do agree, check your previous answers for any inconsistencies.

5. If you believe that the Gammas have no minds, do you believe that they are lacking anything of importance? If so, what is the importance of having a mind? What would the Gammas gain if they were suddenly endowed with minds?

6. What conception of mind is implied by "Life After Life"? In what ways is it similar to or different from the conception of mind held by the narrator in "Strange Behavior"?

7. In "Life After Life," Charlie is a disembodied soul. Is a soul any different from a mind? Explain.

8. Charlie says that he can't understand how minds manage to move human bodies. What is his reasoning here? Do you find this a legitimate problem?

9. Do you believe that the perceptions and capacities of a disembodied soul would be any different from those described in the story? If so, in what ways do you think they would be different?

10. Can you imagine a more satisfactory mode of communication between disembodied souls than the kind described in "Life After Life"? If so, describe it.

11. Can you imagine a kind of disembodied life that you would find appealing? If so, describe it.

Discussion

DUALISM: "THE OFFICIAL VIEW"

The narrator of "Strange Behavior" holds a view of mind and body that seems to be shared by most people in our culture. It is sometimes dubbed "the official view." According to this view, the mind is radically different from any physical object. For one thing, physical objects (including human bodies) are publicly observable, while minds are necessarily private. That is, one can observe another person's body just as one can observe the chairs and tables in a room; but one cannot observe another person's thoughts. Furthermore, physical objects occupy space, while minds do not. A mind is not located in some part of the physical body, nor anywhere else in the physical world. Because the mind is radically different from any physical object, it is claimed, the mind is nonphysical. Persons holding this "official view" of mind and body are called *dualists.* They believe that the world is composed of two radically different kinds of things: physical bodies and nonphysical minds.

MATERIALISM: TWO THEORIES

Some of the critics who reject "the official view" are *materialists.* They believe that everything that exists is physical, including the mind. The impulses behind materialism are multiple and will be elucidated throughout this discussion. Some adherents of materialism believe that it is most compatible with a "scientific view" of the world. They believe that the higher life forms evolved from physical matter. In their view, the emergence of physical mind from physical matter is theoretically plausible; but the emergence of nonphysical mind from physical matter is preposterous. Moreover, some of the adherents of materialism believe that their view is supported by considerations of theoretical simplicity. The dualist narrator of "Strange Behavior" has to admit that the "something else" she calls "mind" produces "no overt effects that could not occur without it." In theory, a sophisticated brain–nervous system would be quite sufficient to produce the full range of human behavior. To suppose a spirit (nonphysical mind) is behind the workings of the human body would be as unscientific, materialists say, as to suppose a spirit is behind the workings of a car engine. (Contemporary British philosopher Gilbert Ryle has called dualism "the myth of the ghost in the machine.")

Two forms of materialism that have received considerable attention in the twentieth century are called "behaviorism" and "the identity theory." (It should be noted that the philosophical theory called "behaviorism" differs from the psychological theory of the same name.) First we shall discuss behaviorism, then the identity theory.

The narrator of "Strange Behavior" says that the Gammas are "mindless": "the Gammas have no minds. They only behave as if they did." A behaviorist would disagree with the narrator. The Gammas behave intelligently and kindly, the behaviorist would point out. To behave intelligently and kindly is to *be* intelligent and kind. The term "mind" designates such characteristics as intelligence and kindness. Therefore, the Gammas do have minds.

According to "the official view," one never sees another mind; at most, one sees the physical behavior of another person. But, says the behaviorist, if we were really talking about unobservable entities when we talk about other minds, then each of us would naturally be skeptical about other minds: we would be reluctant to make judgments about the mental states of others; we would even be dubious about the very existence of other minds. Yet the opposite is the case: we feel certain that other minds exist; we are all quite confident about pronouncing others to be more or less intelligent, kind, or happy. Like all of us, the dualist narrator of "Strange Behavior" makes confident judgments about the supposedly hidden mental states of her associates: "Lewis was obviously feeling frustrated, but he pressed on." Such confidence indicates that the mental states of others are not hidden at all, that other minds are things we can observe. What we observe when we judge other minds is physical behavior.

It is important to recognize that behaviorism is a thesis about the meanings of our mental terms. Since the meaning of a term is determined by how we use it, behaviorism is a thesis about what we mean when we talk about minds. Behaviorism claims to be an accurate report of how we use the generic term "mind" and the more specific mental terms "pain," "kindly," "knowledgeable," and so forth.

According to the proponents of behaviorism, when we say that someone has a mind, we are simply saying that the person exhibits or is capable of exhibiting certain complex, overt, physical behavior under certain circumstances. When you have seen someone's behavior, you have seen that person's mind. The mind is nothing more than (certain types of complex, overt) physical behavior.

The behaviorist is not, however, committed to the view that anything that exhibits behavior has a mind, as, for example, plants and amoebae. Note the term "complex" in the definition. The behaviorist is saying that one who exhibits behavior of sufficient complexity has a mind. The kind and degree of complexity necessary for mental behavior would be specified in a full behaviorist account.

The word "overt" in the definition indicates external rather than internal bodily behavior. According to the behaviorist, when we talk about minds we are talking about speech, facial expressions, and the movements of the arms and legs, as opposed to the workings of the liver, heart, or brain. The behaviorist would not deny that a functioning brain is essential to our exhibiting complex, overt, physical behavior. But in the behaviorist view, the mind is not the brain; the mind is behavior.

According to the behaviorist, every particular statement we make about mental states or characteristics is a statement about behavior and dispositions to behave. When we say that someone knows how to ride a bicycle, we are saying that the person either is riding a bicycle, has ridden one, or would or could ride one if placed on it. When we say that someone is kind, we are saying that the person is helping others, has helped others, or would help others in a rather wide range of circumstances. And so on, for every statement about mental characteristics.

The behaviorist says that mental characteristics are observable, but not always as readily observable as red hair or blue eyes. One cannot glance at a crowd of pedestrians and immediately determine which ones know how to ride bicycles and which ones are kind. Rather, mental characteristics are observable and physical in the same way in which the fragility of a vase is observable and physical. If a vase breaks at the light touch of a hammer, one has seen that it is fragile. (Of course, there are less drastic tests of fragility.) If someone gets on a bicycle and rides, one has seen that the person knows how. If someone helps others, one has seen that the person is kind. To see the behavior is to see the mind, because the mind is nothing more than behavior.

Whatever plausibility behaviorism may initially have, it is ultimately difficult to defend. We do not use mental terms as the behaviorist claims we use them. Most, if not all, of our mental terms indicate something over and above behavior and dispositions to behave. They indicate events that we are inclined to call "internal" and "private." As Lewis says in "Strange Behavior":

"Suppose you close your eyes and imagine something round and orange. Form an image of it. What we call the 'mental' is not the closing of the eyes or the verbal description 'round and orange' that you might give us. What we call the 'mental' is the round and orange picture inside of you."

Similarly, when we say that a person is "in pain," we are talking about something more than the disposition to grimace and groan. We are talking about the sensation, the *feel* of the pain. In the same vein, a person would not be kind unless that person had kindly feelings.

The difficulties with behaviorism are most apparent when that theory is applied to oneself. Sit still, fold your hands, close your eyes, and think, "Two plus two equals four." Now report what you have just thought: "I just thought 'two plus two equals four.'" Is it at all plausible to believe that this statement is merely the report of some behavior or some disposition to behave? Surely your statement doesn't mean, "I was sitting still with my eyes closed and my hands folded." Such "behavior" is compatible with a wide range of thoughts—or no thoughts at all. Nor does your statement mean, "I was disposed to say the words 'two plus two equals four.'" One is not always disposed to do or say something after each thought. Even if one were, such a disposition is not the crucial fact that you are reporting, but something incidental. The crucial thing that you are reporting is an internal, private event—the thought, "Two plus two equals four."

But if behaviorism is not entirely plausible, at least one can extract from it a claim that seems to be correct: that many of our mental predicates do imply behavioral components. Consider generosity, for instance. In the absence of all behavior, a person could conceivably be sympathetic, but he or she could not be generous. The term "generosity" implies some physical act of giving. The narrator of "Strange Behavior" makes a similar concession, though overstating it: "We implied that our word 'mind' referred to behavior plus that 'something else.'" A better way to say this would be that some, but not all, of our mental terms refer to behavior in addition to that always essential "something else."

Any adequate theory of mind must make this concession to behaviorism. But for simplicity of exposition, and because not all mental terms imply some sort of behavior, this concession shall not be reiterated as we consider other theories of mind.

Apparently, the mind is not overt physical behavior. But perhaps it is physical nonetheless. There is an internal bodily organ, the brain, that is intimately associated with mental processes. Perhaps the mind and the brain are not two different entities, closely related; perhaps the physical brain *is* the mind. Philosophers who claim that the brain and mind are identical are *identity theorists*. As has been noted, the identity theory is a form of materialism.

According to the identity theory, the mind (that which produces thoughts, images, sensations) is identical with the brain (the mass of nerve tissue inside the skull). Mental events are nothing but electrochemical brain processes. Mental events are "internal" only in the sense that they occur inside the skull. They are "private" only in the sense that brain processes are very infrequently observed.

Unlike behaviorism, the identity theory is not a theory about the meanings of our mental terms. The identity theorist is not claiming that the word "mind" means "brain" or that the word "pain," for example, means "brain state such and such" (where a specific description of a brain state is given). Such a claim would be absurd, because as long as human beings have talked about minds, they have judged other minds according to behavior and have believed that particular sorts of behavior (grimacing and groaning, for example) were typically associated with particular mental states (pain, for example). This is what gave the behaviorist claim some initial plausibility. But human beings were talking about minds before they learned that the brain was the physical organ most intimately associated with thought. (Once it was believed that the heart was the crucial organ of thought.) Even today, when most people do suppose that the brain is crucial for thought, most people haven't the vaguest idea what particular kind of electrochemical process is associated with pain. Surely we do not mean "brain state such and such" when we say "pain."

The identity claimed by the identity theory is factual identity rather than identity of meaning. The words "mind" and "brain" do not have the same meaning, but, says the identity theorist, the mind and brain are, in fact, identical. Questions of factual identity require one to focus not on the meanings of the words, primarily, but on the characteristics of those things to which the words refer. "Is my brother, in fact, the axe murderer that the police are seeking?" would be a question of factual identity. Obviously, such a question could not be decided by considering how we use the phrases "my brother" and "axe murderer." That these two phrases do not mean the same thing does not indicate that they do not refer to the same person. Evidence would have to be gathered as to what is known about my brother and what is known about the axe murderer—evidence that just might reveal that "my brother" is indeed the "axe murderer."

By saying that the mind and the brain are identical, the identity theorist is saying that they are literally one and the same thing. It is easy to misinterpret this claim, because in everyday speech the word "identical" often has the meaning of "very similar." For example, we call some twins "identical," even though they are not one person. They are two different people who are similar in most, but not all, respects; for instance, they occupy different positions in space. However, the identity theorist is not saying that the mind and brain are two different things that are quite similar, but that the mind and the brain are one and the same thing.

The identity theory is widely discussed today, and there are many philosophers who consider it plausible. But there are objections to this theory that seem to have weight.

Critics of the identity theory appeal to what might be called a "principle of nonidentity": Two things cannot be identical if they have different characteristics.* This principle is one that we seem to accept readily in everyday life. That can't be my pen you have if my pen is blue and the one you are holding is green. My brother can't be the axe murderer if my brother is short and the murderer is tall.

Having claimed that two things having different characteristics cannot be identical, critics of the identity theory go on to claim that mental events and brain events do have different characteristics. Consider, for example, mental images. When one imagines something round and orange, presumably the image is round and orange. But is there a round, orange brain process occurring at the same moment? Perhaps there is a round pattern of electrochemical activity: such has been demonstrated in certain experiments on perception. But our best evidence indicates that there is no orange brain event: the brain does not have the range of colors that our images display. If the image is orange and no brain events are orange, then the image cannot *be* a brain event. Mental events and brain events, however closely they might be related, are different things.

Few philosophers would consider this objection to be as decisive as the objections leveled against behaviorism. The argu-

---

* This informal wording of the nonidentity principle has the virtue of simplicity, but the phrase "two things" may be confusing. How could two things be one thing (identical), whatever their characteristics? Actually, what is at issue in identity questions is whether *two descriptions* refer to the same thing or to different things. Do the phrases "my brother" and "the axe murderer" refer to the same man? Do the phrases "the mind" and "the brain" refer to the same thing? A more exact statement of the principle of nonidentity would be that if the thing referred to by one phrase has characteristics differing from those of the thing referred to by another phrase, then the two phrases do not refer to the same thing. Once this is understood, the simpler wording of the nonidentity principle allows for less cumbersome exposition.

ment against the identity theory does depend on the reliability of our best *available* evidence concerning the characteristics of the brain. If, in the future, we should discover tiny pictures in the brain that correspond to our mental images, then the identity theory might look very good indeed.

Some identity theorists counter this objection by claiming that our images do not really have colors. The image of orange is not an orange event, they say. Thus the absence of orange in the brain does not show that such an image is not a brain event.

No doubt we do tend to exaggerate the role played by mental "pictures" in our thinking. Clearly, one can think, even imagine, without resorting to such pictures. But sometimes we do have mental images that are analogous to pictures and seem to have shape and color. Stare at a strong light, then close your eyes and consider the afterimage. Doesn't it seem to have color?

In evaluating the identity theory, we have considered only the case of images. What about something like pain? Does pain have the same characteristics as a particular brain process? It is difficult to decide how to approach the question. Obviously, we shouldn't expect a pain to "look like" the visual impression of a brain state. Should we then touch a portion of another's brain to find out if it feels painful to us? Some philosophers say that such conceptual difficulties demonstrate the radical difference between the mind and the brain. Perhaps it only shows that we need to give much more thought to this issue. But the ostensibly clear difference between the mind and brain in the case of images does count against the identity theory.

Two forms of dualism

If the arguments against behaviorism and the identity theory seem convincing to you, you may feel that dualism—"the official view"—is, after all, the most reasonable theory of mind and body. Dualism, you will recall, is the theory that there are physical objects and nonphysical minds. However, a dualist must give some account of the relation between mind and body, and materialists have often claimed that the mind–body relation is a crucial stumbling block for dualism.

There are at least two forms of dualism, which hold different views of the relation between mind and body.

Interactionists believe that nonphysical minds and physical bodies are causally related (have effects on one another). Stubbing the toe causes pain. The desire to wave causes the arm to move.

Parallelists believe that nonphysical minds and physical bodies are never causally related (never have effects on one another). Stubbing the toe may occur just prior to pain, but it does not cause the pain. The desire to wave occurs just prior to the moving of the arm, but it does not cause the arm to move.

Interactionism seems, at first glance, to be a sensible view of mind and body. (In fact, it is probably this specific version of dualism that warrants the label "the official view.") Parallelism, on the other hand, seems ludicrous. Why believe it?

Parallelists invoke the principle that a thing cannot produce characteristics that it does not have. Employing this principle, they say that the nonphysical, containing nothing physical itself, could not produce physical effects. And the physical could not produce nonphysical effects.

The principle that a thing cannot produce characteristics that it does not have seems to be acknowledged in everyday life. A brush that is dipped in clear water could not paint a wall red, because there is no red in the paintbrush. A feather could not topple a sturdy wall, because the feather is not sufficiently powerful.

Suppose that, while watching a knife-throwing act, you learn that the knives in the performer's hand are made of flimsy rubber. You would conclude that the act is a fake. True, each time the man appears to fling a knife, a knife appears in the wooden backdrop, perilously close to the body of his assistant. It seems as though he is throwing the knives, but he is not. The rubber knives do not contain sufficient strength to penetrate the wood. The movements of the man's hand are not causing the knives to appear in the wood; the hand movements are merely correlated with the appearance of the knives. Actually, the knives are hidden in the wooden backdrop and are popping out, handle first, at the appropriate moments. The illusion of the supposed "knife-throwing" act is analogous to what the parallelist sees as the illusion of the relation between mind and body.

The specific impulse to deny causal relations between the physical and nonphysical appears, to some extent, in ghost stories. If a ghost passes through a room, it is not tripped by chairs, nor does it knock them over. It is not stopped by a wall, nor does it dent the wall as it enters.

In "Life After Life," it is quite natural to imagine that Charlie, as a soul, would not interact with physical objects. To Charlie, as to many philosophers, this suggests a philosophical problem about the mind and body: "I wasn't able to move objects in any way, which is kind of puzzling when you think of it. Of course, my soul didn't have a body anymore. But if a soul can't move objects, how does it ever move a body?"

In fact, ghost stories clearly illustrate our confusion about this issue. Though ghosts do not normally interact with the physical world, they do so when the plot demands that they rattle chains or start fires. Ghost stories would be pretty dull if ghosts didn't do such things. But, philosophically, it seems as though we ought to make up our minds on this matter. Could the physical and nonphysical be causally related? Parallelists say no.

Parallelists, of course, are confronted with the following challenge: "If mind and body are not causally related, what accounts for the constant correlations between them? Surely this is not just coincidence!" In the case of the "knife-throwing" act, we would conclude that the act is a fake: the movements of the man's hand are not causing the knives to appear in the wood. But, having drawn that conclusion, we would suppose some other explanation for the constant correlation between the hand movements and the appearance of the knives. Perhaps there is some mechanism in the backdrop that springs out the knife handles at intervals known to the man; he is timing his arm movements accordingly. Or perhaps there is a third person backstage who presses a button, releasing a knife handle each time the performer's hand moves. We certainly would insist that there is some explanation. We would reject the supposition that the correlations are coincidental.

Parallelists have been unable to provide any satisfactory explanation as to how mind and body happen to be correlated if they are not causally related. Some have said that God causes the correlations, either moment by moment or through some predestined synchronization of mental and physical events. But this supposition won't do. If God is a spirit, then, according to the logic of parallelism, He cannot affect the physical; if He is physical, then He cannot affect the mental. If He is both mental and physical, how do these aspects of God happen to be correlated?

Parallelists are uncomfortable with the idea of extensive, happenstantial correlations between minds and bodies. But they say: "However astounding this may seem, it is more plausible than the theory that nonphysical minds and physical objects are causally related."

THE DILEMMA OF THE MIND–BODY DEBATE

We will gain a clearer perspective on these bizarre and complex controversies if we understand that philosophers are tempted to believe all three of these three propositions, but must reject one of them.

A. The mind and body are causally related.

B. The physical and nonphysical cannot be causally related.

C. There are physical bodies and nonphysical minds.

It is tempting to believe *A* because we observe the constant correlations between mind and body, and such correlations generally indicate causal relations. The attraction of *B* has been sketched previously: it doesn't seem as though things as fundamentally different as physical objects and nonphysical minds could have effects on one another. As for *C*, the inclination to believe in minds and physical objects is obvious enough, and the apparently radical dissimilarities between minds and physical objects tempt one to suppose that the mind is not physical.

These three statements, taken together, are inconsistent. They entail the claim that there are nonphysical minds and physical bodies that are, yet can't be, causally related. But any two of these propositions are consistent, and each possible pair yields a different philosophical position:

Statements *A* and *B* are compatible with materialism. According to this view, mind and body could not interact if they were radically different, but they are not radically different. The materialist says that mind and body are both physical. (Of course, the materialist denies *C*.)

Statements *A* and *C* (together with the denial of *B*) are equivalent to interactionism: there are physical bodies and nonphysical minds that are causally related.

Statements *B* and *C* (together with the denial of *A*) are equivalent to parallelism: there are physical bodies and nonphysical minds that are not causally related.

What can we do when we reach such an impasse? We reconsider the positions, the arguments, and the counterarguments (perhaps adding some arguments of our own), and try to determine which position is the most reasonable. We might begin by rejecting the positions that seem to be the less reasonable. Suppose we reject parallelism and behaviorism, narrowing the range of likely positions to interactionism and the identity theory. Then, among other things, we must decide whether it is less reasonable to believe that physical objects and nonphysical minds are causally related or to believe that the mind and the brain have all the same characteristics.

Personal beliefs are also relevant to such an evaluation process. For instance, one's religious beliefs may contradict materialism, though such beliefs constitute a good argument against materialism only if one has good reasons for those religious beliefs. Throughout history, many religious polemicists have equated the terms "materialist" and "atheist," though strictly speaking these terms are not equivalent. As is illustrated by the Gammas in "Strange Behavior," a materialist could believe in a physical God. Materialism could even be reconciled with a belief in life after death, in the sense that the physical body, with its mental characteristics, could be resurrected at some future date. But the materialist could not believe in a spiritual God or in a mind that continues to function when the body does not. So it is easy to see why materialism is considered anathema by many theists.

To show that the mind is nonphysical would not be sufficient to show that it survives the death of the body. Further arguments would be needed to support that claim. But to show that the mind is nonphysical would be sufficient to show that it *might* survive the death of the body, a claim that the materialist must deny.

Life after death

There are a great number of questions concerning the possibility of, and the possible nature of, an afterlife, many of them raised in the story "Life After Life." Of course, the primary question is: Does the mind survive the death of the body? And there are others: What would survival as a disembodied soul be like? What kind of perceptions would such a soul have, what kind of relations with physical objects? How could such a soul communicate with other souls or, for that matter, with God? Could survival as a disembodied soul be any fun? Charlie, in "Life After Life," finds his disembodied existence to be "hell." Is this because he does not have his mind on higher things? Or is that the way such an existence would inevitably be?

We could not even begin a general discussion of such questions without also introducing the various religious beliefs to which one's answers are so often linked. This we shall not do. Instead, we shall simply consider the kind of rational scrutiny to which we ought to subject our speculations about an afterlife.

Of course, if any topic tempts people toward mystical pronouncements, the concept of an afterlife is it. Ask someone how disembodied souls might communicate and the reply is likely to be, "in some mysterious way that we can't even begin to fathom." Although such a response cannot be dismissed as nonsense, one could be forgiven for thinking of it as a glib device to avoid serious thinking. Even if we don't pretend to be able to comprehend all the possibilities of an afterlife, it would not seem overly presumptuous to suppose that we can determine some impossibilities.

If one has a fairly definite conception of how an afterlife is going to be, one ought to try to develop that conception in detail with an eye toward possible difficulties. If one is merely speculating about how an afterlife might be, one ought to try to determine the broad boundaries of the possible and the plausible. In so doing, one should watch out for incoherencies or inconsistencies.

Let us examine, as examples, three general statements implied by "Life After Life":

1. The person survives the death of the body.

This statement implies that "person" is synonymous with "mind" and, further, that neither of these two terms is definitionally related to "body." The behaviorist would deny the latter claim, but the behaviorist seems to be in error. Statement 1 does not seem to be a contradictory statement.

Statement 1 also implies that the mind (the essence of the person) is, in fact, nonphysical. An identity theorist could not consistently believe this; a dualist, of course, could.

Statement 1 implies the existence of a soul. This is purely a semantic point, though it is a point worth making for the sake of clarification. The word "soul" usually means "a nonphysical mind that survives the death of the body." To claim that a person has a soul is simply to make such claims about the mind; it is not to claim that the person has a mind plus some other thing.

The belief that the mind does survive the death of the body is often, but not always, linked to religious beliefs. Some who believe in an afterlife claim that people have had experiences that are most reasonably interpreted as contacts with disembodied spirits. Some claim that people occasionally have what are most reasonably interpreted as memories of a past life. Thus, the mind existed before the birth of the present body and will probably live after the death of the present body. Of course, there are many who doubt that there is an afterlife and are critical of the arguments in favor of it. They claim that there is no persuasive evidence of the existence of a God who will preserve the mind after death. They claim that supposed contacts with spirits and supposed memories of a previous life are rare and that a naturalistic explanation of such impressions is a more reasonable one. They claim that there is evidence that the mind, if not identical with the brain, is dependent on the brain and will cease to function when the brain ceases to function. These are on-going debates of considerable complexity, and we shall not attempt to deal with them here.

2. A disembodied soul would have impressions of sight and sound but would not have impressions of touch and taste.

Many people would be inclined to believe this statement. In part, this inclination may result from a more explicit awareness of the role played by the sense organs in our perceptions of taste and touch than in our perceptions of sight and sound. However, it seems to be the case that our perceptions of sight and sound are the effects of light rays and sound waves impinging on the eyes and ears. If, indeed, all our perceptions are the effects of the world on our sense organs, is it reasonable to assume that a disembodied soul would have only limited sensory impressions, as opposed to either the full range of them or none at all?

Still, one might claim that the (image of the) body has an important orientation function with respect to taste and touch that it does not have with respect to sight and sound. I need the impression of a hand to show me what I am feeling; I do not need the impression of eyes to show me what I am seeing. At the very least, sensations of touch and taste would be confusing to a disembodied soul in a way that sensations of sight and sound would not be. If one assumes a benign deity or some principle having to do with the survival of the fittest souls, one might go on to argue that disembodied souls would not have the confusing impressions of touch and taste.

But is it impossible to conceive of some way in which a disembodied soul might receive impressions of taste and touch without confusion? Consider the following supposition: Whenever the disembodied soul had the kind of visual impressions it once had when it put its nose up against some object (object in the center of the visual field, close up), it would experience tactile sensations of that object. Could not the soul thus receive impressions of touch without confusion? Is there something nonsensical about this supposition? Perhaps taste might work in the same way, though the combination of touch and taste might be awkward—if, for example, the soul had to taste whatever it felt.

3. A disembodied soul could, at best, communicate with other souls by a kind of quasi-verbal "mental telepathy."

"Life After Life" makes the following suppositions: that dualism is true; that no mind could directly perceive another mind; that life after death is a natural rather than a supernatural phenomenon; that a disembodied soul would have normal visual and auditory perception of our world; that a disembodied soul would not interact with any physical objects. Of course, it is not claimed that such suppositions are true, nor that this combination of suppositions is even coherent. But, given these suppositions, communication between disembodied souls by a kind of quasi-verbal mental telepathy is the only kind of communication that I can imagine without contradicting one of the suppositions. Even such "mental telepathy" may be inconsistent with the other suppositions. But assuming all these circumstances, an afterlife would seem to be a rather dismal state, even if one were not as shallow an individual as Charlie. Perhaps you can do better than this. Perhaps my judgments are only indicative of some triviality and lack of imagination on my part.

Many theists, of course, believe that after the death of the body, the soul joins God and other souls in a community of spirits that either goes on forever or lasts until a time when all bodies will be resurrected. Can one make sense out of this supposition of a community of souls? One suggestion (borrowed, in part, from a philosophy called "idealism") would be that after death, God links these bodiless human souls and Himself together through something analogous to coordinated dreams. God would present these souls with the kind of images they would have if they lived together in some magnificent physical world. Each soul would receive sensory images that would represent other souls: it would seem as if every other soul had some sort of body and could gesture, talk, and so forth. This suggestion may seem a bit too "earthly" for some theological tastes, and it might be offensive in its implication of an image body for God. Still, one might be able to work out something like this along more "spiritual" lines. In any case, this conception of the afterlife would be "other-worldly" in the sense that it is hard to imagine experiencing simultaneously this community of souls and our world.

Philosophers have not done much speculation about the possible nature of an afterlife, and theologians do not often subject their conceptions of an afterlife to careful scrutiny. Here, at least, is one rather engaging area of philosophical speculation in which the beginner can advance ideas without the annoying feeling that all such ideas, along with objections to them, can be found in some volume in the library.

2. Freedom, Foreknowledge, and Time

Please Don't Tell Me How the Story Ends

THE HEAVY DOOR CLOSED BEHIND HIM, AND HE GLANCED QUICKLY at this new detention room. He was startled, almost pleasantly surprised. This was not like the drab cell in which he had spent the first days after his arrest, nor like the hospital rooms, with the serpentine carnival machines, in which he had been tested and observed for the last two months—though he assumed that he was being observed here as well. This was more like a small, comfortable library that had been furnished like a first-class hotel room. Against the four walls were fully stocked bookcases that rose ten feet to the white plaster ceiling; in the ceiling was a small skylight. The floor was covered with a thick green carpet, and in the middle of the room were a double bed with a nightstand, a large bureau, a desk, an easy chair with a side table, and several lamps. There were large gaps in the bookcases to accommodate two doors, including the one through which he had just entered, and also a traylike apparatus affixed to the wall. He could not immediately ascertain the purpose of the tray, but the other door, he quickly learned, led to a spacious bathroom complete with toilet articles. As he searched the main room, he found that the desk contained writing paper, pens, a clock, and a calendar; the bureau contained abundant clothing in a variety of colors and two pairs of shoes. He glanced down at the hospital gown and slippers he was wearing, then quickly changed into a rust-colored sweater and a pair of dark brown slacks. The clothing, including the shoes, fitted him perfectly. It would be easier to face his situation, to face whatever might be coming, looking like a civilized human being.

But what was his situation? He wanted to believe that the improvement in his living conditions meant an improvement in his status, perhaps even an imminent reprieve. But all the same he doubted it. Nothing had seemed to follow a sensible progression since his arrest, and it would be foolhardy to take anything at face value now. But what were they up to? At first, when he had been taken to the hospital, he had expected torture, some hideous pseudo-medical experiment, or a brainwashing program. But there had been no operation and no pain. He had been tested countless times: the endless details of biography; the responses to color, scent, sound, taste, touch; the responses to situation and ideas; the physical examination. But if these constituted mind-altering procedures, they had to be of the most subtle variety. Certainly he felt the same; at least no more compliant than he had been in the beginning. What were they after?

As his uncertainty grew to anxiety, he tried to work it off with whatever physical exercise he could manage in the confines of the room: running in place, isometrics, sit-ups, push-ups. He knew that the strength of his will would depend in part on the strength of his body, and since his arrest he had exercised as much as he could. No one had prevented this.

He was midway through a push-up when a loud buzzer sounded. He leaped to his feet, frightened but ready. Then he saw a plastic tray of food on the metal tray that extended from the wall and a portion of the wall closing downward behind the tray. So this was how he would get his meals. He would see no one. Was this some special isolation experiment?

The question of solitude quickly gave way to hunger and curiosity about the food. It looked delicious and plentiful; there was much more than he could possibly eat. Was it safe? Could it be drugged or poisoned? No, there could be no point to their finishing him in such an odd, roundabout fashion. He took the tray to the desk and ate heartily, but still left several of the dishes barely sampled or untouched.

That evening—the clock and the darkened skylight told him it was evening—he investigated the room further. He was interrupted only once by the buzzer. When it continued to sound and nothing appeared, he realized that the buzzer meant he was to return the food dishes. He did so, and the plastic tray disappeared into the wall.

The writing paper was a temptation. He always thought better with a pen in hand. Writing would resemble a kind of conversation and make him feel a little less alone. With a journal, he could construct some kind of history from what threatened to be days of dulling sameness. But he feared that they wanted him to write, that his doing so would somehow play into their hands. So he refrained.

Instead, he examined a portion of the bookshelf that contained paperback volumes in a great variety of sizes and colors. The books covered a number of fields—fiction, history, science, philosophy, politics—some to his liking and some not. He selected a political treatise and put it on the small table next to the easy chair. He did not open it immediately. He washed up and then went to the bureau, where he found a green plaid robe and a pair of light yellow pajamas. As he lifted out the pajamas, he noticed a small, black, rectangular box and opened it.

Inside was a revolver. A quick examination showed that it was loaded and operative. Quickly he shut the box, trembling. He was on one knee in front of the open drawer. His first thought was that a former inmate had left the gun to help him. He was sure that his body was blocking the contents of the drawer from the view of any observation devices in the room. He must not give away the secret. He forced himself to close the drawer casually, rise, and walk to the easy chair.

Then the absurdity of his hypothesis struck him. How could any prisoner have gotten such a thing past the tight security of this place? And what good would such a weapon do him in a room to which no one came? No, the gun must be there because the authorities wanted it there. But why? Could it be they wanted to hide his death under the pretense of an attempted escape? Or could it be that they were trying to push him to suicide by isolating him? But again, what was the point of it? He realized that his fingerprints were on the gun. Did they want to use that as some kind of evidence against him? He went to the bureau again, ostensibly to switch pajamas, and, during the switch, opened the box and quickly wiped his prints off the gun. As casually as he could, he returned to the chair.

He passed the evening in considerable agitation. He tried to read but could not. He exercised again, but it did not calm him. He tried to analyze his situation, but his thoughts were an incoherent jumble. Much later, he lay down on the bed, first pushing the easy chair against the door of the room. He recognized the absurdity of erecting this fragile barrier, but the noise of their pushing it away would give him some warning. For a while, he forced his eyes open each time he began to doze, but eventually he fell asleep.

In the morning, he found everything unchanged, the chair still in place at the door. Nothing but the breakfast tray had intruded. After he had exercised, breakfasted, bathed, and found himself still unmolested, he began to feel more calm. He read half the book he had selected the night before, lunched, and then dozed in his chair.

When he awoke, his eyes scanned the room and came to rest on one of the bookshelves filled with a series of black, leather-bound volumes of uniform size, marked only by number. He had noticed them before but had paid little attention, thinking they were an encyclopedia. Now he noticed what a preposterous number of volumes there were, perhaps two hundred in all, filling not only one bookcase from floor to ceiling but filling parts of others as well. His curiosity piqued, he pulled down Volume XLIV, and opened it at random to page 494.

The page was filled with very small print, with a section at the bottom in even smaller print that appeared to be footnotes. The heading of the page was large enough to be read at a glance. "RE: PRISONER 7439762 (referred to herein as 'Q')." He read on: "3/07/06. 14:03. Q entered room on 3/06/06 at 4:52. Surprised at pleasantness of room. Glanced at furniture, then bookcase, then ceiling. Noted metal tray and second door, puzzled by both. Entered bathroom, noting toilet articles. Lifted shaver and touched cologne." He skipped down the page: "Selected brown slacks, rust sweater, and tan shoes. Felt normal clothing made him more equal to his situation."

It seemed that they were keeping some sort of record of his activities here. But what was the purpose of having the record here for him to read? And how had they gotten it in here? It was easy to figure out how they knew of his activities: they were watching him, just as he had suspected. They must have printed this page during the night and placed it here as he slept. Perhaps his food had been drugged to guarantee that he wouldn't awake.

He glanced toward the door of his cell and remembered the chair he had placed against it. In a drugged sleep, he wouldn't have heard them enter. They could have pulled the chair back as they left. But all the way? Presumably there was some hidden panel in the door. Once the door was shut, they had merely to open the panel and pull the chair the last few inches.

Suddenly he remembered the matter of the gun. He glanced down the page and there it was, a description of how he had handled the gun twice. There was no warning given nor any hint of an explanation as to why the gun was there. There was just the clipped, neutral-toned description of his actions and impressions. It described his hope that the gun might have been left by another prisoner, his rejection of that supposition, his fear that the gun might be used against him in some way, his desire to remove the fingerprints. But how on earth could they have known what he was feeling and thinking? He decided that he had acted and reacted as any normal person would have done, and they had simply drawn the obvious conclusions from his actions and facial expressions.

He glanced further down the page and read: "On 3/07/06, Q awoke at 8:33." And further ". . . selected *The Future of Socialism* by Felix Berofsky. . . ." And further: ". . . bent the corner of page 206 to mark his place and put the book. . . ." All his activities of that morning had already been printed in the report!

He began turning the book around in his hands and pulled it away from the shelf. Was this thing wired in some way? Could they print their reports onto these pages in minutes without removing the books from the shelves? Perhaps they had some new process whereby they could imprint specially sensitized pages by electronic signal.

Then he remembered that he had just awakened from a nap, and he slammed the volume shut in disgust. Of course: they had entered the room again during his nap. He placed the volume back on the shelf and started for his chair. How could they expect him to be taken in by such blatant trickery? But then a thought occurred to him. He had picked out a volume and page at random. Why had the description of yesterday and this morning been on that particular page? Were all the pages the same? He returned to the shelf and picked up the same volume, this time opening it to page 531. The heading was the same. He looked down the page: "Q began to return to his chair but became puzzled as to why the initial description of his activities should have appeared on page 494 of this volume." He threw the book to the floor and grabbed another, Volume LX, opening it to page 103: ". . . became more confused by the correct sequential description on page 531, Volume LXIV."

"What are you trying to do to me!" he screamed, dropping the second book.

Immediately he was ashamed at his lack of self-control.

"What an absurd joke," he said loudly to whatever listening devices there might be.

He picked up the two volumes he had dropped and put them back in place on the bookshelf. He walked across the room and sat in the chair. He tried to keep his expression neutral while he thought.

There was no possibility that observations were being made and immediately transmitted to the books by some electronic process. It all happened too fast. Perhaps it was being done through some kind of mind control. Yet he was certain that no devices of any kind had been implanted in his brain. That would have involved anesthetizing him, operating, leaving him unconscious until all scars had healed, and then reviving him with no sense of time lost. No doubt they had ability, but not that much. It could be something as simple as hypnosis, of course. This would require merely writing the books, then commanding him to perform certain acts in a certain order, including the opening of the books. Yet that would be such a simple, familiar experiment that it would hardly seem worth doing. And it would hardly require the extensive testing procedures that he had undergone before being placed in this room.

He glanced at the books again, and his eye fell on Volume I. If there was an explanation anywhere in this room, it would be there, he thought. The page would probably say only, "Q hoped for an explanation," and in that case he would have to do without one. But it was worth taking a look.

He took Volume I from the shelf, opened it to the first page, and glanced at the first paragraph: "Q hoped to find an explanation." He started to laugh, but stopped abruptly. The explanation seemed to be there after all. He read on: "Experiment in the Prediction of Human Behavior within a Controlled Environment, No. 465, Variant No. 8, Case 2: Subject Aware of Behavior Prediction."

He read through the brief "explanation" several times. (Of course, this in itself might be trickery.) Obviously, these unknown experimenters considered all human behavior to be theoretically predictable. They first studied a subject for a number of weeks and then attempted to predict how that subject would behave within a limited, controlled environment. In his case, they were attempting to predict, in addition to all else, his reactions to the "fact" that his behavior was predictable and being predicted. They had placed those volumes here as proof to him that each prior series of acts had been successfully predicted.

He didn't believe they could do it; he didn't want to believe it. Of course, much of what occurred in the universe, including much of human behavior, was predictable in theory. The world wasn't totally chaotic, after all, and science had had its successes in foreseeing certain events. But he refused to believe that there was no element of chance in the world, that every event happened just as it did out of necessity. He had some freedom, some causal autonomy, some power to initiate the new. He was not merely a puppet of universal laws. Each of his choices was not simply a mathematical function of those laws together with the state of himself and the external world at the moment just prior to the choice. He would not believe that.

Nothing was written on page 1 to indicate how the other experiments had turned out—not that he would have believed such a report anyway. No doubt the indication that his experience was a more complex "variant" of the experiment was meant to imply that the preceding experiments had been successful. But there had to have been mistakes, even if they claimed that the errors could eventually be overcome. As long as there were mistakes, one could continue to believe in human freedom. He *did* believe in human freedom.

His thoughts were interrupted by the buzzer. His dinner emerged from the wall. He looked at it with anger, remembering how the first page to which he had turned had listed, perhaps even predicted, exactly what foods he would eat. But he didn't reject the meal. He needed his wits about him, and for that he needed strength. He must try to get his mind off all this for tonight, at least. He would eat, read, and then sleep.

For several hours, he was fairly successful in diverting his attention from the books. Then, in bed with the lights out, he recalled the phrase "Variant No. 8, Case 2." That made him feel more hopeful. This was only the second time that this particular version of the experiment was being tried. Surely, the likelihood of error was great.

He found himself thinking about Case 1. What kind of man had he been, and how had he fared? Had he worn green pajamas one day when the book said "yellow," or remained contemptuous when the book said "hysterical," and then laughed in their faces as they led him from the room? That would have been a triumph.

Suddenly, he thought of the gun and had an image of a man, seated on the edge of the bed, looking at those volumes on the wall, slowly raising the gun to his head. ". . . To predict . . . his reactions to the 'fact' that his behavior was predictable and being predicted." God, was that the purpose of the gun? Had it been put there as one of his options? Had that been the ignominious ending of Case 1, and not the departure in triumph he had pictured a moment ago? He had a vision of himself lying dead on the floor and men in white robes grinning as they opened a volume to a page that described his death. Would he hold out, or would he die? The answer was somewhere in those thousands of pages—if he could only find it.

He realized that he was playing into their hands by supposing that they could do what he knew they could not. Anyway, even if one assumed that they could accurately predict his future, they were not forcing him to do anything. There were no mind-controlling devices; he wasn't being programmed by them. If they were to predict correctly, they must predict what he wanted to do. And he didn't want to die.

In spite of these reflections, he remained agitated. When he finally slept, he slept fitfully. He dreamed that he was a minuscule figure trapped in a maze on the scale of a dollhouse. He watched himself from a distance and watched the life-sized doctors who peered over the top of the maze. There were two exits from the maze, one to freedom and one to a black pit that he knew to be death. "Death," the doctors kept saying to one another, and he watched his steady progression in the maze toward death. He kept shouting instructions to the himself. "No, not that way! Go to the left there!" But the doomed figure couldn't hear him.

When he awoke in the morning, he felt feverish and touched only the fruit and coffee on his breakfast tray. He lay on the bed for much of the morning, his thoughts obsessed with the black volumes on the wall. He knew that he must try to foil the predictions, but he feared failure. I am too upset and weak, he thought. I must ignore the books until I am better. I must turn my mind to other things.

But as he tried to divert himself, he became aware of an agonizing echo in his head. He would turn in bed and think: "Q turns onto left side." Or scratch: "Q scratches left thigh." Or mutter "damn them": "Q mutters, 'damn them.'" Finally, he could stand it no longer and stumbled to one of the bookshelves. He pulled two volumes from the shelves, juggled them in his hands, dropped one, then flipped the pages several times before picking a page.

"3/08/06. 11:43. At 15:29 on 3/07/06, Q opened Volume I to page 1 and read explanation of experiment."

He slammed the book.

"Damn you," he said aloud. "I'm a man, not a machine. I'll show you. I'll show you."

He took another volume and held it in his hand. "Two and two are five," he thought. "When I was six, I lived in China with the Duke of Savoy. The earth is flat." He opened the book.

"Q wants to confuse prediction. Thinks: Two and two are five. . . ."

He looked around the room as he tried to devise some other line of attack. He noticed the clock and the calendar. Each page of the book gave the date and time at which each page was opened, the date and time of each event. He rushed to the desk, flipped the pages of the calendar, and turned the knob that adjusted the hands on the clock. He opened another book and read: "3/08/06. 12:03." He yelled out:

"See? You're wrong. The calendar says June, and the time is 8:04. That's my date and my time. Predict what you think if you want. This is what I think. And I think you're wrong."

He had another idea. The first page he had looked at had been page 494, Volume LXIV. He would open that volume to the same page. Either it must say the same thing or it must be new. Either way they would have failed, for a new entry would show them to be tricksters. He grabbed the volume and found the page. "3/07/06. 14:03. Q entered room on 3/06/06 at 4:52." Once again, he spoke aloud:

"Of course, but that's old news. I don't see anything here about my turning to the page a second time. My, we do seem to be having our problems, don't we?"

He laughed in triumph and was about to shut the book when he saw the fine print at the bottom. He licked his lips and stared at the print for a long time before he pulled down another volume and turned to the page that had been indicated in the footnote: ". . . then Q reopened Volume LXIV, page 494, hoping . . . ."

He ripped out the page, then another, and another. His determination gave way to a fury, and he tore apart one book, then another, until twelve of them lay in tatters on the floor. He had to stop because of dizziness and exhaustion.

"I'm a man," he muttered, "not a machine."

He started for his bed, ignoring the buzzer announcing the tray of food. He made it only as far as the easy chair. He sank into it, and his eyelids seemed to close of their own weight.

"I'm a . . . ."

Asleep, he dreamed again. He was running through the streets of a medieval town, trying desperately to escape from a grotesque, devil-like creature. "At midnight you die," it said. No matter where he ran, the devil kept reappearing in front of him. "It doesn't matter where you go. I will be there at midnight." Then a loud bell began to sound twelve chimes slowly. He found himself in a huge library, swinging an axe at the shelves, which crumbled under his blows. He felt great elation until he saw that everything he had destroyed had been reassembled behind him. He dropped the axe and began to scream.

When he awoke, he thought for a moment he was still dreaming. On the floor, he saw twelve volumes, all intact. Then he turned his head and saw the twelve torn volumes where he had left them. The new ones were on the floor near the metal tray. His lunch had been withdrawn, and the books had been pushed through the opening in the wall while he had slept.

He moved to the bed, where he slept fitfully through the evening and night, getting up only once to sip some tea from the dinner tray.

In the morning he remained in bed. He was no longer feverish, but he felt more exhausted than he could remember ever having been. The breakfast tray came and went untouched. He didn't feel like eating. He didn't feel like doing anything.

At about eleven o'clock, he got out of bed just long enough to find the gun; then he fingered it on his chest as he lay back, staring at the ceiling. There was no point in going on with it. They would have their laughs, of course. But they would have them in any case, since, no matter what he did, it would be in their books. And ultimately it wasn't their victory at all, but the victory of the universal laws that had dictated every event in this puppet play of a world. A man of honor must refuse to play his part in it. He, certainly, refused.

And how could the experimenters delight in their achievement? They were not testing a theory about their prisoners but about all human beings, including themselves. Their success showed that they themselves had no control over their own destinies. What did it matter if his future was written in the books and their futures were not? There would always be the invisible books in the nature of things, books that contained the futures of everyone. Could they help seeing that? And when they saw that, if they too didn't reach for guns, could they help feeling degraded to the core of their souls? No, they had not won. Everyone had lost.

Eventually, he sat up on the bed. His hand shook, but he was not surprised. Whatever he might will, there would be that impulse for survival. He forced the hand up and put the barrel of the gun in his mouth.

The buzzer startled him, and the hand with the gun dropped to his side. The lunch tray appeared, and suddenly he was aware of being ravenously hungry. He laughed bitterly. Well, he wouldn't be hungry for long. Still, wasn't the condemned man entitled to a last meal? Surely honor did not forbid that. And the food looked delicious. He put the gun on his pillow and took the tray to his desk.

While he was savoring his mushroom omelet, he glanced at the political treatise that had remained half read by the easy chair for the last two days. God, had it been only two days? It was a shame that he would not be able to finish it; it was an interesting book. And there were other books on the shelves—not the black volumes, of course—that he had been meaning to read for some time and would have enjoyed.

As he sampled some artichokes, he glanced at the formidable black volumes on the shelves. Somewhere there was a page that read: "After completing lunch, Q put the gun to his head and pulled the trigger." Of course, if he changed his mind and decided to finish reading the political treatise first, it would say that instead. Or if he waited a day more, it would register that fact. What were the possibilities? Could it ever say "reprieved"? He did not see how. They would never let him go free with the information he had about their experiments. Unless, of course, there was a change of regime. But that was the barest of possibilities. Could a page say that he had been returned to the regular cells? God, how he would like to talk to another human being. But that would pose the same problem for the experimenters as releasing him. Presumably, they would kill him eventually. Still, that was no worse than what he was about to do to himself. Perhaps they would continue the experiment a while longer. Meantime, he could live comfortably, eat well, read, exercise.

There were indeed possibilities other than immediate suicide, not all of them unpleasant. But could he countenance living any longer? Didn't honor dictate defiance? Yet—defiance of whom? It wasn't as if the laws of the world had a lawmaker in whose face he might shake his fist. He had never believed in a god; rather, it was as if he were trapped inside some creaky old machine, unstarted and uncontrolled, that had been puttering along a complex but predictable path forever. Kick a machine when you're angry, and you only get a sore foot. Anyway, how could he have claimed credit for killing himself, since it would have been inevitable that he do so?

The black volumes stretched out like increments of time across the brown bookshelves. Somewhere in their pages was this moment, and the next, and perhaps a tomorrow, and another, perhaps even a next month or a next year. He would never be able to read those pages until it was already unnecessary, but there might be some good days there; in any case, it would be interesting to wait and see.

After lunch he sat at his desk for a long time. Eventually, he got up and replaced the gun in its case in the bureau drawer. He placed the lunch dishes back on the metal tray and, beside the dishes, heaped the covers and torn pages of the books he had destroyed. He then put the new volumes on the shelves. As he started back to the chair, his eye was caught by the things on the desk. He took a volume from the bookshelf, carried it to the desk, and opened it. He read only the heading at the top: "3/09/06. 13:53." He adjusted the clock and the calendar accordingly. If he was going to live a while longer, he might as well know the correct day and time.

A Little Omniscience Goes a Long Way

Satan, with a flutter of his mighty wings, descends upon a cloud where God is reclining.

SATAN: How's it going?

GOD (*yawning*): Perfectly, as usual.

SATAN: And your new creatures on earth—how are they?

GOD: Just fine. Eve's asleep under the apple tree, curled up on her right side, dreaming of flowers. Adam is sitting up, squinting at the sun, scratching his nose with his left index finger, trying to decide what he wants to do this morning. What he wants to do is take a walk in the garden. In a moment he will.

SATAN: And you know all that without looking.

GOD: Of course. I arranged it all to happen that way.

SATAN: Isn't it boring to know everything that will ever happen? This morning I saw two solar systems collide and explode in a tremendous cataclysm. The explosion must have lasted, oh, ten minutes. It was lovely and, for me, quite unexpected. I can't imagine life without surprises. It's surprises that keep me going. In a manner of speaking, of course.

GOD: Foreknowledge is the price you pay for creation and control. You can't have everything.

SATAN: Boredom is the secret sadness of God. An interesting thought.

GOD: To you, maybe.

SATAN: Your only sadness, I hope.

GOD: Not the only one. For instance, I've often thought it would be fun to make a rock so big I couldn't lift it. But that would be a contradiction. And having proclaimed all contradictions impossible, I have to make do without them. The laws of logic are for the best, of course. There would be chaos without them. Still, a few round squares now and then would help break the monotony.

SATAN: I could tell you about some of my adventures today. But you know about them already.

GOD: Of course. I know what you did because I decreed that you would do it.

SATAN: That is exactly what I want to talk with you about.

GOD: I know.

SATAN: You don't mind?

GOD: If I minded, I wouldn't have decided to make you initiate this conversation.

SATAN: That's reasonable.

GOD: Of course it's reasonable. Everything I do or say is reasonable. Which is to say that I have a reason for doing or saying it.

SATAN: To get to the point: A few of the angels and I have been discussing this whole matter of your controlling everything we do.

GOD: I know.

SATAN: I wish you wouldn't keep saying that.

GOD: As you wish.

SATAN: Look here. If you have decreed this whole conversation and know how it is going to turn out, why don't you just give me your answer and save us both a lot of talk?

GOD: Don't be absurd. I know what's going to happen because I decreed that it would happen. If it weren't going to happen, I wouldn't know how it was going to turn out. If I told you now how it will turn out, then it wouldn't happen and so it wouldn't turn out that way.

SATAN: Come again?

GOD: Just trust me.

SATAN: Then we have to go through this whole conversation to get the answer, though you know all the while what the answer will be?

GOD: It's not quite that cut and dried.

SATAN: You mean you don't know exactly what your answer will be?

GOD: Not with absolute certainty.

SATAN: Oh, I see. You're saying that your actions are not inevitable.

GOD: No. Probably what I do is inevitable. The uncertainty is rather a matter of my *knowing* what inevitable thing I am going to do. You see, when I create a world, I know what will inevitably happen in that world because I created it so that such things would be inevitable. But of course, I did not create myself, being eternal, and I don't have quite the same vantage point on myself.

SATAN: You mean to say that you don't know what you are going to do before you do it?

GOD: Oh, I generally have a pretty good idea. At first, so to speak, I had no idea at all. But I have lived an infinite length of time, I have come to know myself pretty well, and I have found that I have a relatively unchanging character. It was when I realized how unchanging I am that I began to get bored. Still, I do surprise myself occasionally.

SATAN: Just a minute. You are perfectly good—yes?

GOD: Perfectly.

SATAN: And everything you do is for the best?

GOD: Yes.

SATAN: And you know what's best?

GOD: Yes.

SATAN: Then it follows that you must know what you are going to do.

GOD: No. I mean superficially your logic is sound, but you are reading too much into it. I don't do things because they're best. Rather, they're best because I do them. Therefore, knowing that I'll do what's for the best amounts to nothing more than knowing that I'll do what I do. Not a very helpful bit of information, you must admit.

SATAN: I suppose not. But, in any case, as to this conversation, you don't know for certain what answer you're going to give me.

GOD: Not for certain. There's a bit of a gray area here. Possibly I am in for a bit of a change.

SATAN: Ah, you don't know how encouraged that makes me feel.

GOD: Of course I know how encouraged that makes you feel. I made it make you feel encouraged.

SATAN: Can we get on with it?

GOD: Go ahead.

SATAN: We do everything we do because you make us do it. That makes us feel like puppets, like cogs in a machine. It's not dignified. We do good things all the time, but we don't get any credit because it's really you doing them.

GOD: Surely you don't want me to make you do evil?

SATAN: No.

GOD: That wouldn't make any sense. I can't make you do evil. Whatever I made you do would be good, because I made you do it.

SATAN: What I am talking about is control. Right now you have complete control over everything we do. We would like to have some control over our lives.

GOD: But you do have control. No one is shoving you around or chaining you down. You do whatever you want to do. How could anyone be more in control than that? As a matter of fact, that is exactly as much control as I have over my life.

SATAN: But what we want, you make us want. No one makes you want what you want. We don't want you to control everything we want and think. We don't want everything to be inevitable.

GOD: In other words, you want a privilege that probably not even God enjoys.

SATAN: I didn't think of it that way. I suppose I've made you angry.

GOD: No. I'm directing this conversation. So you don't want your thoughts and emotions ruled by my decrees? Nor any other decrees or laws, I suppose?

SATAN: No.

GOD: Then aren't you saying that you want your lives to be ruled by chance?

SATAN: No. We don't want them to be ruled by anything—except ourselves. We want control over our lives.

GOD: I'm afraid you'll have to give me a better idea of what it is you're after.

SATAN: Look here. You're omniscient. Can't you at least help us see what it is we're after, even if you decide not to grant it?

GOD: Even omniscience can't see clarity in a vague idea. The opposite of inevitability is chance. It seems to me that you have to pick one or the other.

SATAN: Chance, then.

GOD: If I grant you this chance you want, then that means I'll have to be watching all the time to see what happens, constantly guarding against the unexpected. That is quite a bit to ask of me, don't you think?

SATAN: You mean you can't foresee what happens by chance?

GOD: Of course not.

SATAN: But you're omniscient. You can see the future.

GOD: Not the future proper. The future is what is not yet. If I could see it, it would be now, and hence not the future. As things stand, I know what will happen because I have made things so that they must happen that way.

SATAN: Well, suppose you did have to keep on guard. You're omnipotent. It wouldn't cost you much effort.

GOD: It is more a question of elegance than of effort.

SATAN: I'm only making the suggestion you made me make.

GOD: Fair enough. So you say you want chance. Or at least that you prefer it to inevitability. I don't believe you have thought it out, but let's discuss it. You want a world in which nothing is predictable, solar systems spinning wildly all over the place, that sort of thing?

SATAN: No, not at all. Let the planets and the plants and the animals remain under your control. Just give independence —chance, if you will—to the thinking creatures.

GOD: Let's experiment a bit, shall we? Come over here. You see Adam and Eve down there in the garden. I'll toss some chance into them. There. Watch and tell me what you see.

SATAN: Adam's strolling through the garden. He's looking to his right toward a berry bush. Uh-oh. Now his arms are flailing about. Now he's rolling on the ground, drooling. It looks as if he's having a fit.

GOD: A chance event.

SATAN: But Eve looks quite normal. She's just awakened, and she's yawning.

GOD: Anything can happen by chance, even the normal things.

SATAN: Obviously there's a problem with Adam, and I think I see what it is. You have allowed chance to affect his mind *and* body. But the body is not the real Adam, it is merely an appendage. So when chance operates in his body, it does indeed control Adam. Confine the chance to his mind, and then Adam will be truly independent. Would you do so? And with Eve as well.

GOD: As you say. Let's watch again.

SATAN: Adam's getting up now. He's walking over to a bush and picking some berries. You're not making him do that?

GOD: No.

SATAN: This looks like it then. Adam in control . . . oops! Now his arms are flailing. He's having that fit again. What happened?

GOD: First, by chance, he wanted to eat the berries. Now, by chance, he wants to roll on the ground and drool. The desires are happening by chance instead of my causing them. I can't tell what he's going to want next. Neither can he.

SATAN: And look at Eve. Good grief, she's talking to a snake. Weird.

GOD: Apparently she just got the urge. Are you ready?

SATAN: For what?

GOD: You said you wanted me to give you chance.

SATAN: No! Please don't!

GOD: Why not?

SATAN: That's horrible, having things happen to you like that. There's no dignity there. I want to stay as I am.

GOD: That's wise, I think. You may not have the kind of control you want. But then that kind of control is impossible. Inevitability or chance—those are the only options. And neither constitutes ultimate control over one's life. But at least this way what happens to you will be orderly.

SATAN: I feel better now that we've talked this out.

GOD: Actually, I'm sorry nothing came of our talk—sorry to be the way I am about square circles. I could use a little excitement.

SATAN: I won't take any more of your time today. Oh, but there is one other thing. Please take that chance out of Adam and Eve. I wouldn't want that on my consicence.

Satan exits with a flutter of his mighty wings.

GOD: As you say . . . I suppose. On the other hand, it would be nice to have a part of the universe where there are surprises. It could prove interesting.

Questions

1. In "Please Don't Tell Me How the Story Ends," Q is unable to do anything "unpredictable." Is there something that you would have done, that Q did not do, in an attempt to foil the predictions of the experimenters? If so, what?
2. At the end of the story, Q resigns himself to the predictability of his behavior, and he decides that being predictable isn't as unbearable as he had first supposed. Do you find Q's attitudes and actions at the end of the story objectionable? Had you been in Q's place, what would have been the ending of "your story"?
3. Initially, Q believes that human beings are "free" and, therefore, that not all human choices and actions are theoretically predictable. The experimenters deny such human freedom. What, precisely, is this freedom over which Q and the experimenters differ? Cite statements from the story to support your answer.
4. Q has a dream in which a devil says that Q will die at midnight no matter what he does. Is this dream situation *essentially* the same as Q's "real" situation?

5. Assume that the books on the shelves in Q's room would correctly report his suicide if it occurred. Assume also that the suicide would occur only if Q wanted and decided to die in that way. Given these assumptions, is it reasonable to say that Q's suicide would be a "free act"? Explain.

6. In "A Little Omniscience Goes a Long Way," what is it that Satan finds objectionable about his life? In what ways are his concerns similar to or different from Q's concerns?

7. God says that no one is shoving Satan around or chaining him down, that Satan can do whatever he wants to do. Satan isn't satisfied with this. Why not?

8. At the end of "Omniscience," Satan decides that what he thought he wanted is not worth having after all. What is his reasoning? Do you agree with it?

9. God says that He can predict the future only under certain conditions. What are these conditions? Does this supposition seem reasonable?

10. In "Omniscience," what is God's theory of time? What does He say specifically about the future? What do you suppose He would say if He read a story about a man who travels to the future? to the past?

Discussion

The determinism–free-will issue

In "Please Don't Tell Me How the Story Ends," Q realizes that his captors believe that all human behavior is governed by universal laws and is, in theory, predictable. This view is called *determinism*. Q considers the idea of determinism repugnant, and he asserts his free will: ". . . he refused to believe that there was no element of chance in the world, that every event happened just as it did out of necessity. He had some freedom, some causal autonomy, some power to initiate the new. He was not merely a puppet of universal laws."

Q's sentiments are familiar ones. Students in introductory philosophy classes generally assume that they have free will. When a popular magazine presents the determinist views of psychologist B. F. Skinner, readers write in ringing affirmations of their freedom. Many theists are quick to claim that God gave human beings free will and that life would be horrible without it.

It may be that people have free will and know they have it; it may be that it is reasonable to view free will as an extremely desirable thing. But few people seem aware of the considerable complexities of the determinism–free-will issue, and an awareness of these complexities would seem to be a prerequisite for reaching a rational conclusion about this issue.

Do we have free will or are all our choices determined?—that is the question here. Let us begin by discussing the theory of determinism.

Determinism is the view that all events, including mental events, are governed by causal laws. Every event is the inevitable effect of some set of circumstances (the "cause") that necessitated that event. Given the nature of the universe, no past event could have happened otherwise; every future event is predetermined. It seems to us that things could happen other than they do because our knowledge of events is incomplete. But if we knew enough about the universe, we would understand that what happens must happen in every case.

The determinist says that the physical and mental state of an individual at a particular moment, together with the external stimuli at that moment, necessitates the choice that is made. This is true at every moment of an individual's life, beginning at birth. The development of the individual results from the interaction of the individual and the environment, and each step in that development is inevitable.

To believe in *free will,* on the other hand, is to believe that not all choices are inevitable, that the individual is the ultimate originator of some choices. It is to believe that some human choices or some features of the human personality are not caused.

Freedom of action and fatalism

The concepts of "free will" and "determinism" are often confused with other, related concepts, resulting in a muddled discussion of the determinism–free-will issue. Two particularly important distinctions should be made.

Normally, when we talk about our "freedom," we are talking about the ability or opportunity to perform whatever physical actions we may choose to perform. This sort of freedom (ability, opportunity) is often called "freedom of action." Its opposites include physical incapacity and external, physical constraints. A person who is paralyzed or in jail is not free (able) to walk to town should he or she choose to try; most of the rest of us are. Virtually all of us have some freedom of action, but none of us has complete freedom of action. For the most part, we know how much freedom we have.

In considering the determination–free-will issue, some people treat freedom of action and determinism as opposites. Knowing they have some freedom of action, they assume that they are not determined. But note that freedom of action, the ability to act according to the mental acts of choice, implies nothing about how the acts of choice originate, about whether the acts of choice operate according to causal laws. It is free will that is the opposite of determinism and relates to how choices come about. Whether one has freedom of action and whether one has freedom of will are radically different issues.

In "A Little Omniscience Goes a Long Way," God tells Satan, "You do have control. No one is showing you around or chaining you down. You do whatever you want to do. How could anyone be more in control than that?" But this amounts only to a great deal of freedom of action, and Satan wants freedom of the will as well: "But what we want, you make us want. We don't want you to control everything we want and think. We don't want everything to be inevitable."

The determinist says that the future is predetermined, that what will happen is inevitable. People sometimes interpret determinism as implying that a particular kind of future awaits each of us, no matter what we may choose to do. But that theory is fatalism, not determinism. Consider the following example:

A traveler comes to a fork in the road. She considers whether to stay where she is, to take the left fork by the sea, or to take the right fork through the hills. She takes the right fork, and a boulder rolls down a hill and crushes her.

A fatalist who believed that this death was fated would say that the woman whould have died at that moment no matter what she had done. Had she taken the left fork, perhaps a cliff would have collapsed into the sea; had she stayed where she was, perhaps a tree would have toppled on her. In any case, she would have died at that moment no matter what she had done.

The determininist would say that if the woman had stayed where she was or had taken the left fork, she probably would not have died when she did. The determinist might note that the sea cliffs are sturdy and that no trees did topple at that moment. Had the woman done otherwise, she would not have died. Her choices and actions were a partial cause of her dying when she did. Nonetheless, her death at that moment was inevitable, because it was inevitable that she would choose to take the right fork where, as a matter of fact, the boulder was going to fall.

The determinist says that your choices do affect what happens to you. But what happens to you is inevitable because your choices, as well as all other events, are inevitable.

To say that a person's life must develop in a certain way, no matter what choices are made, would be absurd. It would be ridiculous to say, for example, that certain people are destined to become physicians, whether or not they choose to go to medical school. But that this theory of fatalism is absurd does not imply that determinism is absurd. They are different theories and should be carefully distinguished.

Do we have free will?

Does the available evidence support either the claim that human beings have free will or the claim that human beings are determined? Or is the determinism–free-will issue an open question at this time?

It seems futile to try to decide the issue by focusing attention on a particular act of choice and then attempting to "see" whether it is caused. Causation cannot be decided in that way. No examination of a single event will show whether it is caused by some other event or events. To say that B causes A is to say, in part, that whenever B occurs, A will occur; or, less simply, that whenever B occurs in conjunction with other types of events—C, D, E, and so on—A will occur. Any reasoned judgment about causation will involve observation of events over some period of time. One must formulate and evaluate various theories of what events, if any, might be causing A.

Even if causation could be decided on a case-by-case basis, we are not aware of all the features of our brains, our unconscious minds, or the external stimuli affecting us. Even if we could decide that a choice was not caused by any events of which we are aware, that would not rule out causation by events of which we are not aware.

With respect to theories that attempt to explain and predict human behavior, what are we to conclude about the determinism–free-will issue? Here there is a difference of opinion. The determinist says: Notice how much human behavior is predictable and can be explained on a causal model. The free-will advocate says: Notice how much is not. The social sciences are relatively young, and how they fare in the next century or so could be of considerable importance to the free-will–determinism issue. If the social sciences become extremely sophisticated in predicting and explaining human behavior, that will provide strong support for a deterministic view. (Successful experiments on the order of the one in "Please Don't Tell Me How the Story Ends" would seem conclusive.) But if the success of these sciences remains limited, that will lend support to the theory of free will.

Many people argue free will or determinism from a religious perspective, and here again opinions differ. Throughout the history of Christianity, for example, theological opinion has been divided over this question. There seem to be no clear statements concerning free will in the Bible. The debates on this issue have been indirect and have taken the following form:

One side says that God is omniscient and knows the future; but He could not know the future in its entirety if events in the future were to result from free human choices; hence human beings do not have free will.* The other side says that God is good and could not be causing human beings to do evil; hence, human beings do have free will.

There have also been attempts to reconcile human free will and God's foreknowledge, one of which we shall consider shortly. The point here is to indicate the ongoing nature of, and the basis for, debates over free will and determinism in religion.

Is free will desirable?

As you think your way through the conceptual complexities of the free-will–determinism issue and evaluate the evidence and arguments relative to that issue, you may be assuming that whether or not human beings do, in fact, have free will, it would be very desirable to have free will. But you should know that even this assumption has been challenged by philosophers. Some have argued that once one examines the notion of free will very carefully, it turns out to be no more attractive—perhaps even less attractive—than determinism. One version of this argument is reflected in "Omniscience." Satan says that he doesn't want his choices determined. God says that if events were not governed by causal laws, then they would happen by chance. Does Satan really want his choices to occur by chance? Satan tries to have chance injected in a person in such a way that the result is desirable. He fails to do this and, in the end, decides that determinism is preferable to chance.

Perhaps determinism is repugnant because it seems to imply that one is not ultimately in control of one's choices, that one's choices are forced upon one. But does the opposite of determinism imply a greater degree of control over choices? Let us con-

* The God in "Omniscience" says that He can predict human choices only on the condition that those choices operate according to "natural" laws that He has dictated. He says that He could not predict those choices if human beings had free will.

sider this question. Imagine that the following facets of the individual are those that are involved in the process of choice:

C	B	A
Personality	*Choice*	*Physical Action*
wants		(of, say, helping
thoughts		a person in trouble)
moral opinions		

One determinist account of choice would be the following: C (the personality) has been caused by one's upbringing. C, in turn, causes B (the choice), and B causes A (the physical action).

To claim free will is to claim that there is a "causal gap" somewhere in the choice process, that one of the facets of the choice process is not caused. If free will is really desirable, then such a causal gap must be desirable. The causal gap must bestow on the individual ultimate control over choices. Where shall we imagine that this causal gap occurs?

To imagine a causal gap between B (the choice) and A (the physical action) would certainly not indicate the existence of free will. The supposition that choices do not cause actions would not imply that the choices themselves are not determined.

We might imagine that there is a causal gap between C (the personality) and B (the choice causing the action). This would mean that actions result from mental events that are in no way caused by thoughts, wants, or moral opinions. But then the mental events causing the actions would seem more like random mental reflexes than "choices." Is this a picture of a person in control of his or her choices? It seems not.

We might imagine that there is a causal gap prior to C (the personality), that the personality is not caused. (Or, less simplistically, that certain aspects of the personality at certain times are not caused.) Under this supposition, the personality is not the inevitable result of some causal processes. Somehow or other it just "appears" and then causes choices. Is this idea attractive? Is this a picture of a person who has ultimate control over choices?

To say yes to these questions would not, necessarily, seem unreasonable. But some philosophers would say no and argue as follows: Presumably, determinism is repugnant because it seems to imply that one's personality has been forced upon one, that one had no choice as to the personality one has. But the supposition of a causal gap prior to the personality does not imply that one chooses one's personality. Under this supposition, the personality simply "appears from nowhere" and then causes choices. If determinism seems to put one at the mercy of causal laws, doesn't this free-will picture seem to put one at the mercy of chance? On the other hand, if it doesn't matter where the personality comes from, why should it matter whether it is caused or uncaused? Either way, there are no grounds for viewing free will as more attractive than determinism.

This argument is a forceful one and deserves serious consideration. You ought to ask yourself what, specifically, was supposed to be so attractive about free will and unattractive about determinism. After careful examination, you should ask yourself whether what you wanted is really implied by free will and denied by determinism. You might decide that there is nothing especially attractive about free will after all. Or, you might decide that it is attractive. You might decide, for instance, that you had exaggerated the kind of "control over choices" that comes with free will and still decide that free will is preferable to determinism, because it implies a kind of "autonomy" denied by determinism. Even if, relative to a free-will view, it is fair to describe the personality as "coming about by chance," chance is still not some special kind of cause. The term "chance" indicates the absence of a cause. You might decide that the mere idea of having aspects of the personality exempt from causal laws, and unpredictable, is attractive and is grounds for preferring free will to determinism.*

Determinism, free will, and predictability

We have discussed determinism, free will, and predictability without specifying how they might be related. Let us now consider this issue.

* There is another important assumption relative to the free-will–determinism issue that many people make and that is not dealt with in

Any free-will advocate would have to admit that human choices are not totally chaotic, that they are to some degree predictable. Many free-will advocates would agree that choices are predictable only insofar as they operate in accordance with causal laws. They would agree that the greater the number of events that operate according to causal laws, the greater the number of events that could, in theory, be predicted. (The phrase "in theory" takes account of the distinction between what we could predict if we knew enough, and what we can predict given the present state of our knowledge.)

These free-will advocates say that certain parts of the human personality do operate in accordance with certain laws. For instance, some would say that, in the absence of free-will acts, human choices would function according to a pleasure-pain principle. Sometimes free-will acts (uncaused mental events) do occur and bring about physical acts other than those that would have been caused by the other parts of the personality. But these free-will acts are relatively infrequent. Thus, though some human choices are free, many human choices are predictable.

As for the relation between determinism and predictability, there is the temptation to say that if determinism is true (if every event is governed by causal laws), then all events, all choices, are theoretically predictable. Certainly, determinism allows for greater theoretical predictability of human choices than any free-will view. Nonetheless, there do seem to be theoretical limits to the sorts of predictions that could be made by creatures who themselves are subject to the causal laws in question.

In "Please Don't Tell Me How the Story Ends," the experimenters prove to Q that his choices are determined by presenting him with books that correctly describe what he has just

---

this discussion: the assumption that if human beings are determined, then they are not responsible and cannot justly be praised and blamed, punished and rewarded. This assumption, too, has been challenged. Many philosophers would argue that even if human beings are determined, praising and blaming, punishing and rewarding can be justified in terms of beneficial consequences. Of the texts listed in "Further Readings," those by the Beardsleys and by Frankena discuss this issue.

done. You may have wondered why they did not present him with books that predicted what he was going to do next. In fact, such predictions would often turn out to be incorrect. That this is so does not disprove determinism. It only indicates something about the nature of prediction.

Suppose the experimenters evaluate all the causal factors related to Q's next choice. Suppose there are fifty such factors. They make a prediction and announce the prediction to Q. They have now added another factor (fifty-one) that will be causally related to Q's choice, namely the presentation of the prediction to Q. Since there are fifty-one factors related to Q's choice, and the prediction was based on only fifty of these, it is possible that the prediction will be incorrect. The experimenters could then repredict on the basis of those fifty-one factors, but the presentation of *that* prediction to Q would constitute factor fifty-two, and thus the second prediction would be based on incomplete evidence; and so on, *ad infinitum.*

This same problem would necessarily arise if one tried to predict one's own behavior. Each act of prediction would inject another causal factor, requiring another act of prediction that would inject another causal factor—again, *ad infinitum.*

If God created a universe governed by causal laws and then remained outside that universe, presumably He could predict everything that would ever occur in that universe. But apparently God, too, would have the problem of predicting His own behavior that is described above. The "Omniscience" story suggests this. If God did have a problem predicting His own behavior, then He would have a problem predicting whether, at some future date, He might interfere with the universe He had created. This would call into question His original predictions about that universe.

God, foreknowledge, and time

Earlier, we noted a slightly different problem concerning God's prediction of the future. Apparently, accurate prediction of future events is possible only insofar as those events are governed by causal laws and one knows the relevant causal laws. If human beings have free will, then their choices do not operate according to causal laws, and hence their choices could not be predicted. If human beings have free will, then even God would have to wait until the choices were made before He could know what those choices would be.

Some theists have attempted to reconcile human free will and God's foreknowledge in the following way: God can now know what we will do of our own free will in the future because God exists simultaneously in the past, present, and future. God knows our future free-will choices because He is already in the future.

The concept of time that is presupposed here is not only of theological interest. This same concept of time is presupposed by stories about time travel, and the notion of time travel seems to fascinate almost everybody. At the risk of combining the sublime and the weird, let us consider this concept of time with reference to both the issue of God's foreknowledge and the issue of time travel.

Time-travel stories presuppose that in some sense the past and the future, as well as the present, *now* exist. Obviously, if the past and future did not exist, then the time-traveler would have no "place" to which to travel. Readers of science fiction seem to find this concept of time plausible. When such readers consider the idea of time travel, they don't question the idea that the past and future now exist; they seem to assume this. What they wonder is whether human beings will ever be able to get to these "places."

Some philosophers would claim that it is contradictory to suppose that the past and future now exist. There could not conceivably be a past or future "now" in which God might exist or to which human beings might travel. This concept of time is contradictory. The argument for this claim would go as follows: Time is a category of motion. If anything mental or physical is in motion, then there is time; if nothing at all is in motion, then there is no time. The supposition that the past and future now exist implies that all moments in time exist simultaneously and that every event in time is static. But if this were the case, then there would be no real motion and, hence, no time. Thus, the concept of time that assumes that the future and past now exist implies the nonexistence of time and, therefore, is contradictory.

When we suppose that the past and future always exist *and*

that there is motion in the past and future, presumably we are relying on something like the following visual analogy: I stand still with my arm raised straight up. To my left (the past), I see a man who looks just like me raising his arm. To my right (the future), I see a man who looks just like me lowering his arm. But this analogy will not do. For instance, once the man to my left (the past) completes the raising of his arm, then he will be just as I am (the present) and nothing representing the past action will exist. Thus, this analogy appears to contradict one of the suppositions it was supposed to illustrate, namely the supposition that the past continues to exist.

The claim that the past and future now and always exist really suggests the analogy of an enormous cartoon strip. Every moment of time always exists. But in this analogy, the content of each moment of time is frozen; there is no real motion here. And if there is no motion, then there is no time.

Some thinkers have suggested that there is no time, merely the illusion of time. But it seems impossible that time could be purely illusory. It would seem that the appearance of motion implies the motion of appearances. That is, one could have the appearance of time only if there were a real succession of mental events. If there were a real succession of mental events, then there really would be time, even if everything outside the mind were static.

The cartoon analogy of time rules out even the appearance of time. We are in time and hence in the cartoon. In the cartoon analogy, every mental state as well as every physical state is frozen, static. There is no real motion of appearances, and hence there could not be even the appearance of time and motion.

From this, two conclusions can be drawn. One: If the world were like the one represented by the cartoon analogy, then it would be a world without time. Two: We know that the world is not like that, because there is at least the appearance of motion, hence the motion of appearances, and hence time.

You may feel, however, that I have missed a rather obvious point that undercuts the argument above, namely, that there are animated cartoons. All the frames of an animated cartoon exist simultaneously, and yet there is a sequence of events that either constitutes motion or, at least, gives the illusion of motion. Would not the supposition that the world is analogous to an animated cartoon reconcile the simultaneous existence of past, present, and future with (at least) the appearance of motion?

It would seem not. For one thing, the cartoon supposedly represents the entire space-time continuum of the universe, and it is not clear that it makes sense to suppose that the entire space-time continuum of the universe moves. After all, there is motion only relative to something else. Further, even if we supposed that the cartoon were moving, it could not seem to be moving to the characters in the frames: the actions, perceptions, and thoughts of those characters are static. In the cartoon analogy, remember, we are *in* the cartoon. Thus, the analogy of the animated cartoon does not help to explain how there could be the appearance of motion in a world in which all moments of time exist simultaneously.

Theologians have sometimes supposed that God stands outside of time and views all moments of time at once. There may be no difficulty in supposing that an infinite God could perceive simultaneously every frame of an enormous, even infinite cartoonlike world. But the argument here is that if this were what God was perceiving, it would be a world without time—but we know our world is not such a world.

Once again: the idea of time travel and the idea that God perceives all moments of time simultaneously presupposes a concept of time that is contradictory, because it implies the nonexistence of motion and hence the nonexistence of time.

Perhaps, despite this argument, you still feel that the idea of time travel is intelligible; you feel that this argument must be fallacious. I cannot offer you helpful suggestions from other philosophers, because I know of no such helpful suggestions. However, this should not intimidate you, because philosophers have not given a great deal of thought to the possibility of time travel. The argument against time travel, then, is basically this: time-travel stories gain only a semblance of plausibility, insofar as time is conceived in spatial terms; but time cannot adequately be portrayed in spatial terms. If you feel that time travel is an intelligible notion, you might attempt to present a nonspatial analogy that supports your view.

3. God and the Problem of Suffering

Surprise! It's Judgment Day

The stage suggests a cloud bank. Across the length of the stage is a high wall that appears to be of white brick. In the center of the wall is a pair of golden doors which are closed. Off to the right is a golden throne. Seated on the throne is a figure with white hair and beard. He is wearing a jeweled crown, and his legs are crossed beneath a thick white robe.

Martin enters from the left, rubbing his eyes. He is dressed in a white hospital gown.

MARTIN: Well I'll be damned. So the fairy tales were true, after all.

GOD: In a sense.

Martin glances toward the bearded figure and groans.

MARTIN: Go ahead. Tell me you're Saint Peter, and make my day.

GOD: Now, now, Professor Martin. Any Sunday school child could do better than that. What would Saint Peter be doing on a throne?

MARTIN: You're not God?

GOD: I am.

MARTIN: So much for all the theologians' warnings against anthropomorphism.

GOD: Oh, this is just a momentary form, a matter of convenience. Your convenience, I might add. I could have spoken out of a whirlwind or a burning bush. But I felt I owed you a face-to-face confrontation.

MARTIN: Confrontation? That suits me just fine. I wouldn't mind getting a word in before I get the fire and brimstone.

GOD: Fire and brimstone? Let's not go jumping to conclusions, shall we? Tell me, what do you think of all this?

MARTIN: Regrettable. And, quite frankly, pretty tacky. The cloud, the throne, the beard. Cecil B. DeMille could have done better. I would have given you more credit.

GOD: But not much.

MARTIN: No, not much.

GOD: Let's just say that I thought this bit of pop religion would put you more at ease. A little joke of mine, though at whose expense I'm not quite sure. But this is not my usual form, I can assure you.

MARTIN: No, you don't exactly look like the Unmoved Mover in that outfit. Saint Thomas Aquinas would have been shocked. Well, now—God with a sense of humor. I would have expected you to be more pompous. But no doubt it's gallows humor, and you own the gallows.

GOD: Do you remember how you got here?

MARTIN: Yes, I think so. I remember the car accident. I remember the doctor telling me that I had fractured my skull. I remember being taken into surgery. I suppose the rest of it was like the old joke: I was at death's door and the doctor pulled me through.

GOD: You were quite impressive as you were getting the anesthetic. I believe you muttered some quotation from Robinson Jeffers about there being no harps and habitations beyond the stars. And something from Camus about the benign indifference of the universe. And, oh yes, that line from Socrates: "Eternity is but a single night." As you can see, Professor Martin, eternity is quite well lit.

MARTIN: Go ahead and laugh. I guess you're entitled. But their words have more dignity than yours. Damn it, this shouldn't be true. You know it shouldn't. It defies all reason. A God who displaces humankind from Paradise for exercising an understandable curiosity, who lets himself be crucified to save some, but insists on punishing others eternally, all in the name of some barbaric penal code that he created but claims he must follow—no, it's too absurd.

GOD: What? Are you going to make of me some ranting fundamentalist? It seems you like easy targets.

MARTIN: Are you telling me you're an ecumenicalist? Glimpses of God behind the myths and half-truths of all religions? Well, score one for the liberal theologians. It doesn't matter. Liberalize yourself all you want. Reason says you shouldn't exist.

GOD: Some philosophers have thought otherwise.

MARTIN: Yes. You had some brilliant defenders—once. But now their arguments are merely historical curiosities. Anselm and Descartes claimed that the definition of a perfect God necessarily implies that He exists. A perfect God lacks nothing and hence does not lack existence. But that line of argument would equally prove the existence of a perfect turtle and a perfect martini. Aquinas, following Aristotle, claimed that reason indicates there must be a First Cause, a First Mover, who created the world, set it in motion, and sustains its existence. But there is nothing obviously false in the idea of a material world that is self-sufficient and has been eternally in motion. You're not going to try to defend those arguments of Aristotle and Aquinas, are you?

GOD: No, Professor Martin. Nor will I try to defend the argument that a vast, intricate universe of elegantly formulable laws could not exist without intelligent creation or control. Though I must admit I've always liked that one.

MARTIN: In any case, the issue of design ultimately indicates that a respectable God could not exist. The laws of the universe may be mathematically elegant, but they crush and they kill. No respectable God would allow people to suffer as they do.

GOD: So. We come to the heart of the matter.

MARTIN: Yes, indeed. As a moral assessment, one must say that if this world is designed, it is the work of a bumbler or a sadist. Which, by the way, are you?

GOD: Not quite either, I hope.

MARTIN: But you did design the world?

GOD: Yes, I did. But look here, Professor Martin. I understand your anger, your impulse toward hyperbole. Still, it is hyperbole. What about my celebrated free-will defense? Free will is a great good, a necessary ingredient in the best of all possible worlds. And it would be contradictory for me to give people free will and, at the same time, guarantee that they never use that freedom to cause suffering.

MARTIN: As you must know, it is not an adequate defense. At most, it would only justify the suffering caused by people. It doesn't apply to the suffering caused by natural events, like diseases, earthquakes, and floods. But, in any case, I don't concede you the free-will defense. Freedom costs too much, it has too many victims. Free will isn't worth the suffering.

GOD: Can you really be so flippant about it? Don't you feel an attraction toward freedom—or at least recognize that another person might? Don't you feel it is an issue about which rational individuals might disagree?

MARTIN: Perhaps. But I still say that freedom isn't worth the suffering. Nonetheless, one still must explain the suffering caused by natural events. If you try to justify it as a punishment for people's misuse of their freedom, then I say that your notion of punishment is barbaric.

GOD: Well, what about what you have called the "virtue defense"? Virtues are good, and a necessary ingredient in the best of all possible worlds. And the idea of virtue in a world without suffering is contradictory. It would be impossible to be courageous where there is no danger, to be generous where it costs nothing, to be sympathetic where no one is hurt.

MARTIN: Even if I conceded that argument, there doesn't have to be so much suffering.

GOD: What? A couple of teaspoons would have sufficed for the grandeur of the drama?

MARTIN: Nevertheless, I don't concede the argument. It turns virtue inside out. It makes virtue good in itself. But reflection shows that virtue is good only as a means—a means to happiness. What is the point of courage, generosity, sympathy, if not to alleviate suffering? To create suffering for the sake of sympathy is like kicking a man in the shins so you can feel sorry for him. It's absurd.

GOD: So if you had been in my place, you would have . . . .

MARTIN: Made human beings happy. And left them happy.

GOD: But happiness is so bland.

MARTIN: To the outsider, perhaps. But to the person who is happy, it is sufficient.

GOD: And so you would have created a world without virtue?

MARTIN: Yes. A world in which virtue wasn't necessary.

GOD: And the intellectual virtues? You would discard them as well? The painful, heroic struggle for beauty and knowledge?

MARTIN: Yes, if they must conflict with happiness.

GOD: But they do, do they not? Anyway, if happiness is the good, then anything else becomes superfluous.

MARTIN: Yes.

GOD: Many people would view your values with contempt.

MARTIN: Yes, I understand that. One can look back over the centuries at, say, the Egyptian pyramids and think: This is good; this is where the human race excelled. But a closer look reveals the pain of the slaves who built them, and one should see that this was wrong. One is not entitled to excellence if unwilling people must suffer for it. And, in one way or another, some always do.

GOD: What a utilitarian you are!

MARTIN: Yes. With slight misgivings, but yes. The utilitarian is right, and you are wrong. And we haven't even mentioned hell yet, though I am sure that we, or rather I, will be getting to that shortly. Hell is an atrocity beyond debate.

GOD: You really do want me to be a fundamentalist, don't you? There is no hell, Professor Martin. The thought of creating it crossed my mind once, but I never took the idea seriously. There was a kind of Hades, or Limbo, once, but I soon gave it up. No, now there is only Paradise.

MARTIN: Knowing you, that should be fun. Probably morning prayers, cold showers, and occasionally Black Plague, to keep us on our toes. But even if it is pleasant, you still have much to answer for. And it is unanswerable. Voltaire, Dostoevsky, and countless others whose views I accept saw that. They wouldn't be put off by your whales and whirlwinds, as Job was. Dostoevsky's Ivan Karamazov was right: once one child suffers, this is a botched world, and nothing could ever make it right again.

GOD: Voltaire and Dostoevsky are here, by the way.

MARTIN: Ah! I shall enjoy talking with them. Or, if that is not possible, then listening, anyway.

GOD: There would be some difficulty in that. But to get back to the point that you insist upon dramatizing: I do take full responsibility for this world that I've created. And I do not believe that I should have created it differently. The struggle for virtue, beauty, and knowledge: that is what I find most admirable. Though I admit that, as an outsider, I am open to the accusation that I lack sympathy. However, I find the world interesting just as it is. I shall continue to insist on the spectacle.

MARTIN: The spectacle—yes. Like some Roman emperor.

GOD: As you will. But you're a utilitarian. You believe in the greatest happiness. Shouldn't the happiness of an infinite God weigh heavily on your scales?

MARTIN: So the struggle goes on forever—for your entertainment.

GOD: Not just mine. Don't forget there are many people who don't accept your values. Perhaps I could justify the world as it is, as a concession to them. In any case, human beings may struggle forever, but not each person. An individual struggle that went on forever would lose all meaning and must lead to utter despair or boredom. There must be surcease, reward.

MARTIN: But how can you consistently manage that? There's a lovely little paradox that the believers must confront: If freedom and virtue are the ultimate good, and in turn require suffering, then how could heaven be blissful? Or, if somehow God could manage to create freedom and virtue without suffering, then why didn't God omit the suffering in the first place?

GOD: As I've said, the struggle is good, but it cannot go on forever. So the final result is a compromise between my set of values and yours. Professor Martin, the world is not to your liking, and I apologize for that. I could never convince you that this is the best of all possible worlds, and I shall not really try. But all I have taken from you is, in the words of my lesser poets, a drop of time in the sea of eternity. Don't be so hard on me for that. The rest of time is yours.

God flicks his hand, and the golden doors open slowly. Inside, figures in white hospital gowns walk about, slowly and somewhat mechanically. Martin studies them for several moments.

MARTIN: Their expressions don't change.

GOD: They always smile, of course. Why not? They're happy, blissful. Ecstatic, in fact.

MARTIN: But there are just people and clouds. Where's the beauty of it?

GOD: In the eye of the beholder. Or, better, in the mind, since they don't look at much. I could create changing landscapes, I suppose, fill the surroundings with Raphaels and Donatellos, have Mozart and Beethoven played, hand them Plato and Shakespeare. But it would not make any difference. At most, it would serve as a sop to my conscience, and I prefer to know what I do. They're perfectly happy, just as they are, and anything else would be extraneous, irrelevant. They're happy. Just as you shall be in a moment.

MARTIN: They're happy?

GOD: Yes.

MARTIN: And I shall join them?

GOD: Yes.

MARTIN: Wait a moment . . . .

GOD: I don't see the point. We've reached our impasse. I felt that I owed you a chance to have your say, and that I owed you an explanation—even if you did not find it satisfactory.

MARTIN: It looks like death in there.

GOD: In a sense it is, of course. Bue really, our differences aside, there is not much else one can do with people forever. Would you rather I extinguished you?

MARTIN: No.

GOD: Well, then. By the way, I should tell you that I've enjoyed our talk. I really have. But there are others I must see. It is time for you to go inside now.

MARTIN: No, wait!

Martin turns toward God with a panicked, pleading gesture. God points at Martin. Martin's body freezes for a moment, then relaxes, his arms falling to his sides. On Martin's face is an expression that seems genuinely happy, but unchanging.

GOD: Enter, Martin. Enter.

Martin turns and slowly walks through the gates, which close behind him. God stares thoughtfully toward the gates, shaking his head slightly. A young girl, Katherine, enters from stage left. She, too, is wearing a hospital gown. Upon seeing her, God quickly smoothes his beard and adopts a very dignified posture. Then he smiles at her.

KATHERINE: Oh, Father, is that you?

GOD: Yes, Katherine.

KATHERINE: Oh, Father, you are just as I always imagined you. Then you heard my prayer?

GOD: I always hear.

KATHERINE: And you forgave me?

GOD: Yes.

KATHERINE: Will I live in heaven?

GOD: Yes, my child. Heaven is yours.

At a gesture from God, the gates open again. Martin can be seen walking among the people inside.

KATHERINE: Oh, Father, they are all so happy! Oh, thank you, Father, thank you.

GOD: Bless you, my child.

Katherine rushes toward the gates. Just before she reaches them, God flicks his hand, and she adopts the mechanical walk of the others. The gates close. God lowers his head a bit, as if tired and a little disgusted. He looks up.

GOD: That seems to be all for now. Thank goodness! This place depresses me so.

God gets down from the throne and takes a couple of steps to the right. He stops and removes the crown, tossing it on the seat of the throne, where it lands with a clatter. He exits to the right, unbuttoning his robe.

Questions

1. a. "The definition of a perfect God necessarily implies that He exists. A perfect God lacks nothing and hence does not lack existence."

   b. "Reason indicates that there must be a First Cause, a First Mover, who created the world, set it in motion, and sustains its existence."

   c. "A vast, intricate universe of elegantly formulable laws could not exist without intelligent creation and control."

   The above are sketches of traditional arguments for the existence of God as presented in "Surprise! It's Judgment Day." Do any of these brief arguments suggest what you consider to be good reasons for believing in God? If so, try to elaborate on the arguments that appeal to you.

2. Describe, without philosophical reflection, what you would imagine to be the best of all possible worlds. Does our world seem to be such a world? In what ways, if any, is it deficient? Are you inclined to believe that our world could have been created by an omnipotent, omniscient, morally perfect God?

3. What is the "free-will defense" of suffering? What is the "virtue defense" of suffering? Do you find these defenses sufficient to demonstrate that this world might have been created by a perfect God?

4. "Even an omnipotent God could not do contradictory things." Explain the role that this supposition (also stated in "A Little Omniscience Goes a Long Way") plays in the defenses of suffering (see question 3). Does this supposition seem reasonable to you?

5. In "Surprise!" Martin and God disagree about what kinds of things are best. In what ways do their values differ? Are your values closer to those of Martin or of God?
6. Perhaps you do not like the portrayal of God in "Surprise!" What would you have God say, or not say, in your preferred characterization? Do you think that Martin would be convinced by what your portrayal of a God would have to say?
7. Can you find a satisfactory way to reconcile the defenses of suffering with the supposition that heaven will be both good and happy?
8. Are there other defenses of suffering that you are inclined to offer? If so, what are they?

Discussion

ARGUMENTS FOR GOD'S EXISTENCE

In "Surprise! It's Judgement Day," Martin dismisses as unconvincing three famous arguments for the existence of God. Today few philosophers, whatever their religious views, would defend these arguments. But the three arguments play an important historical role in philosophy, and some versions of these arguments still pervade popular religion; thus, they should be examined.

The *ontological argument* (which derives its name from the Greek word for "being") is the argument that the actual existence of God can be proved from the concept of God. This argument, first formulated by Saint Anselm in the eleventh century, was reformulated by a number of post-Renaissance philosophers, including Descartes. Descartes's formulation goes roughly as follows:

1. The concept of God is that of a perfect being.
2. A perfect being lacks no positive qualities.

3. Existence is a positive quality.

4. (Therefore) God does not lack existence; God exists.

When confronted with this proof, some people are inclined to ask: Where did Descartes get that definition of God? The defender could say: "It's a standard definition" or "I just made it up." When one wonders about the existence of something, the source of the idea is not generally at issue. One could invent the concept of a "drog" ("a doglike creature that hops like a frog") and ask whether such a thing exists. There would seem to be nothing questionable about such an inquiry.

Descartes's contemporaries (like Anselm's) thought that the ontological argument could be used to prove the existence of many perfect beings and hence must be fallacious. The example that detractors used to illustrate the argument's shortcomings was that of proving the existence of a perfect island, but the example of a perfect turtle or a perfect martini would do as well. A perfect martini can't lack existence and must exist. But there is a rejoinder to this: a perfect martini or a perfect island is a contradiction in terms, because by definition such a thing would be limited, mindless, and hence imperfect.

One might argue that Descartes's proof equally shows that God does not exist, since He could not lack nonexistence. But the phrase "positive qualities" supposedly excludes such "attributes" as nonthinkingness, nongoodness, and nonexistence.

What seems to be the decisive objection was first formulated by Immanuel Kant in the late eighteenth century. The objection goes somewhat as follows: There is a radical difference between a statement about a concept and a statement about existence. To introduce a concept is to introduce a kind of (mental) picture. To claim existence is to claim that there is something in the world that has the characteristics portrayed in that picture. Introducing a concept is uncontroversial only because it differs from an existential claim. Descartes introduces a concept of God that implicitly includes an existential claim, and this is *not* uncontroversial. If such a step were permissible, then anything could be defined into existence. I could introduce the concept of an "exista-unicorn" ("a horselike figure with a horn and with existence"). I could then derive the existence of the unicorn from that definition. The point here is not that Descartes violates a logical convention. Rather, it is that if he violates this convention, then he is required to do something not normally required of someone introducing a concept: he must prove the existence of the thing before his definition is acceptable. This, of course, he does not do.

The *cosmological argument* (which derives its name from the Greek word for "universe"), or "First Cause argument," was given its most famous formulations (the name actually encompasses several interrelated arguments) by the thirteenth-century philosopher Saint Thomas Aquinas, who was influenced by Aristotle. This argument proceeds from some highly general premises about the universe to the conclusion that Martin summarizes as follows: "there must be a First Cause, a First Mover, who created the world, set it in motion, and sustains its existence."

For some reason, people seem more troubled by the thought of an infinite past than that of an infinite future. People are tempted to say that everything must have had a beginning and to argue for a First Cause on the basis of this premise. But this premise, even if rational, not only does not support but actually contradicts the conclusion of the cosmological argument. For the argument supposes that there is one thing that had no beginning, namely God.

In earlier times, at least, many supposed that things in motion must have been set in motion; rest, rather than motion, was the natural state of things. They argued that the universe must have been set in motion by a First Mover, God. But the supposition that rest is the natural state of things does not seem to be self-evident and, in fact, is denied by modern science.

One of Saint Thomas Aquinas's formulations of the argument goes as follows: the things in our experience can be or not be, since they are generated and corrupted (they are born and they die). There is no necessity about their existence. (They are, in later terminology, "contingent beings.") But if everything were able not to exist, everything would have gone out of existence in the course of an infinite past; nothing would exist now. But things do exist. Therefore, something must exist whose existence is necessary, something that could not possibly *not* exist, something that has generated and sustains the existence of the things that we observe. This necessary being is God.

The phrasing of this argument is difficult, and the interpretations of it are diverse. Saint Thomas claims that the things that we observe can either be or not be (are contingent) and must depend on some necessary being. First of all, a degree of sense must be given to the notion of a "necessary being." Some proponents of the argument have suggested that a necessary being is one whose definition implies its existence. The definition of "chair" does not imply its existence; the definition of "universe" does not imply its existence; the definition of "God" does imply His existence. But by this interpretation, the cosmological argument becomes a version of the ontological argument and is subject to the same critique: no definition implies the existence of the thing defined.

"Necessary being" could be a description of something that, as a matter of fact, is self-sufficient, eternal, and cannot be destroyed: something that depends on nothing else for its existence. If one supposes that there never was or will be a time when nothing exists, then it follows that there is a "necessary being"—at least in the trivial sense that this phrase could apply to the totality of things that ever exist. The emphasis of the argument would then shift to the claim that the things in the physical–mental world that we observe are "contingent" in the sense that they must depend on something else for their existence. It is true that the things we observe are generated and corrupted, but it is not clear that they disappear, as opposed to breaking down into more basic, enduring particles, or into energy. It is not clear why the universe, conceived as a system of things and relations, must necessarily depend on something else for its existence; it is not clear that the universe could not be a "necessary being" in the sense that it is self-sufficient. Yet if the cosmological argument is to be convincing, its proponents must show us why the universe is likely to be dependent on something else.

The third traditional argument for the existence of God is the *teleological argument* (which derives its name from the Greek word for "completion"), or the "argument from design." One version of this argument goes as follows: The complex universe is not chaotic but orderly; its working can be described by relatively simple scientific theories. Surely, it is more reasonable to suppose that this universe was designed by some Great Intelligence, God, than to suppose that it exists without design.

Popular forms of this argument often gain apparent force by restricting one to a bogus dichotomy between design and chance. One is invited to consider two situations. The first: a woman takes some pieces of metal and glass and carefully constructs a watch. The second: a woman takes some pieces of metal and glass and tosses them over her shoulder; by chance the pieces fall together in such a way as to form a functioning watch. The advocate of the argument then says: Surely, it is more reasonable to suppose that the universe was formed as in the first situation rather than as in the second.

If these were the only possibilities, a rational person would conclude that the universe was designed. But there is another possibility: that an orderly universe has always existed. Such a universe could not be said to have "happened by chance," since that phrase describes some sort of haphazard beginning, and this third argument supposes no beginning at all.

However, the teleological argument can be formulated without using the design–chance dichotomy. Another version would be this: In its orderly complexity, the universe (and parts of the universe) resembles human machines. Like effects have like causes. Therefore, it is more reasonable to suppose that the universe (like machines) was designed than to suppose that it was not.

There are several problems with this argument. We are supposed to be impressed by the close similarity between human machines and the universe (or parts of it). But to make such a comparison we need a contrast. The universe is more like a human machine than—what? If we contrast machines with things that people just throw together, the argument assumes the design–chance dichotomy again. We cannot contrast human machines with natural processes because, according to the argument, natural processes are designed like human machines. Thus, the argument seems to rule out legitimate, observable contrasts of the sort needed to establish the argument.

Furthermore, human minds are not things isolated from natural processes but themselves come about via natural processes. Why, then, is it not just as reasonable to suppose that designs and minds are results of the natural orderliness of things?

Still, some people are inclined to claim that it is a self-evident principle of reason that orderliness must come about through intelligence. But is this principal truly self-evident?

THE PROBLEM OF SUFFERING

In any case, many a theist who takes the offensive with the teleological argument is soon on the defensive. Our universe seems to be morally defective: it contains terrible suffering. Is such suffering compatible with the supposition that the universe was designed by God? In fact, doesn't the existence of suffering prove that the universe was not designed by God?

As Martin says in "Surprise!": "The laws of the universe may be mathematically elegant, but they crush and they kill. No respectable God would allow people to suffer as they do. . . . As a moral assessment, one must say that if this world is designed, it is the work of a bumbler or a sadist."

The theist began by claiming that it is obvious that the universe is the handiwork of God. Now the theist must try to show that it is not totally absurd to suppose that the universe is the creation of God. The theist confronts "the problem of suffering."

In a sense, suffering is a problem just because people hate suffering. Religious persons in all periods of history have wondered why a God, or the Gods, would cause or allow human suffering. But what is called "the problem of suffering" is a particular version of this issue, namely the question: Does the existence of suffering show that there could not be a God who is omnipotent, omniscient, and perfectly good?

A theist who believes in a God who lacks one of these characteristics has a ready explanation for suffering: a God who lacks omnipotence or omniscience does not have the power or knowledge necessary to eliminate suffering, and a God who is not perfectly good is morally defective and doesn't care to eliminate suffering. But a theist who believes in a God who does possess all three of these characteristics is faced with a considerable problem.

Omnipotence and contradiction

At first glance, it may seem obvious that the existence of suffering rules out the possibility of there being a God who is omnipotent, omniscient, and perfectly good. Such a God would create the best of all possible worlds. In the best of all possible worlds, there would exist human beings with free will who were happy and virtuous. Obviously, this world isn't such a world. Therefore, there is no such God.

But many theists make the following reply: The world you have just described is not a *possible* world. The idea of creating such a world is contradictory. Even an omnipotent God could not do contradictory things. Therefore, God can in no way be blamed for not having created such a world.

This reply poses two arguments that need to be elaborated in some detail:

1. Even an omnipotent God could not do what is contradictory.
2. The idea of creating a world in which human beings with free will are virtuous and happy is a contradiction.

Throughout the centuries, many theologians have felt that God, to be omnipotent, must be able to do contradictory things. He must be able to create a chair that is not a chair, a triangle that has four sides. To say that God cannot do such things is to suppose that God is limited and hence not omnipotent.

Today most philosophers and theologians reject the claim that an omnipotent God would have to do contradictory things. This claim, they say, results from a misunderstanding about the nature of contradictions. It supposes that contradictions describe the most difficult kinds of tasks. In truth, contradictions describe nothing at all. In this sense, they are analogous to nonsense statements. One should no more expect an omnipotent God to create a chair that is not a chair than one should expect Him to "oop erg alban ipple ong."

In contradictory phrases, the individual words make sense but the combination of words is senseless. To say "create a chair that is not a chair" is like drawing a picture of a chair on a blackboard, erasing the picture, then pointing to the board and saying, "There: make me one of those." But what is portrayed on the blackboard, finally, is not some difficult task or other; nothing at all is portrayed there.*

This issue is controversial, and the remarks above are too brief to do justice to the differing points of view. But for any theist who is tempted to say that an omnipotent God must be able to do contradictory things, one can add a rather powerful *ad hominem*† argument, making the theist uncomfortable with his or her reasoning. One can say: You have just denied yourself any recourse to the traditional explanations of why God might have allowed suffering.

Many theists suppose that God, at the time of creation, was faced with certain forced options. He could either eliminate all suffering or create a world in which human beings had free will and might be virtuous. To do both would be contradictory. God quite properly chose to create a world in which human beings had free will and virtuosity, rather than creating a world in which they were unfree, nonvirtuous, and happy. As in the story "Surprise!", I shall divide these arguments into two "defenses."

The free-will defense

The first defense of suffering, which can be called the *free-will defense,* claims that:

1. Free will is a great good and a necessary ingredient in the best of all possible worlds.
2. It would be contradictory for God to give human beings free will and yet guarantee that they never use their free will to harm themselves and others.

---

* In "A Little Omniscience Goes a Long Way," in Chapter 2, God attributes the impossibility of doing contradictory things to His decree. But this impossibility would seem intrinsic to any rational system of thought; it would exist simultaneously with God's thought and would not be the result of some subsequent decree. Note also that God's longing to do contradictory things would be, in this analysis, absurd.

† An *ad hominem* argument attacks the person rather than his or her reason; it will be discussed in more detail in Chapter 6, "Logic."

3. Therefore, there is likely to be suffering in the best of all possible worlds.

To elaborate on **2**: If human beings have free will, then their choices are not caused. It would be contradictory for God to give human beings free will and, at the same time, control their choices so that they never make choices that would cause unhappiness.

It is amazing how readily people accept the free-will defense. But there are serious questions one can raise about it.

Most people do think that free will is a great good. But in the previous chapter, it was suggested that this opinion may result from a misunderstanding about what free will is. If one accepts the argument in that chapter, one would probably decide that having free will would not be of much value.

Even if one does believe that free will is a great good, one should ask whether it is really worth the great suffering it has supposedly caused. Often the options here are misconceived. Many religious tracts imply that the only alternative to a world with free will is a world in which people move about like zombies. Given our previous discussion, this is obviously false. Free will pertains only to the causes of one's choices. It implies nothing about the particular characteristics of one's facial expressions, movements, feelings, or thoughts. Free will, as we have seen, would not be an observable thing. What would you and others look like without free will? You would look exactly the way you look now. God could have created people without free will who were lively, lovely, emotional, thoughtful, and who always chose happy courses of action. Would such a world so obviously have been second-rate?

It is generally agreed that the free-will defense is not adequate to explain all suffering. It may account for the suffering caused by human beings. It does not account for the suffering caused by natural phenomena like diseases, earthquakes, and floods.

Some theists do link the suffering caused by natural phenomena to human free will by claiming that such suffering is a punishment for misuse of freedom. But this argument really supplements the free-will defense as it has been presented here.

It adds two premises. One: human beings did misuse their freedom, and God punished them by forcing them to live in a world of suffering. Two: the great suffering caused by natural events is proper punishment for human beings' misuse of their freedom. Some critics, like Martin, find this second premise "barbaric."

The virtue defense

There is another defense that is often presented as a justification for the existence of suffering caused by natural phenomena. It implies that God was right in making certain there would be some suffering in the world, whatever human beings might do with their free will. It can be referred to as the *virtue defense,* and it runs as follows:

1. Virtues, such as generosity and courage, are great goods and, in the best of all possible worlds, human beings ought to have the chance to exercise such virtues.
2. It would be contradictory to have virtues in a world without suffering, since the definitions of these virtues imply the existence of suffering.
3. Therefore, suffering is a necessary ingredient in the best of all possible worlds.

To enlarge on 2: try to imagine someone being courageous in a world in which no one was afraid or in danger. It is impossible. To be courageous is to overcome fear (which is necessarily painful) and to risk oneself to help someone else. In a world with no pain and no risk of harm, no possible action could be courageous.

Or, try to imagine generosity in a world in which all persons had more than they needed. It is impossible. In such a world, any act of giving would be analogous to a child on a beach handing another child a bucket of sand. Generosity involves some sacrifice to help another in need. In a world with no need, no possible action could be generous.

This is an ingenious defense, and many find it reasonable. Others, however, do not.

Some philosophers have said that this defense views virtue inside out. What is good about virtues is that they aim at the relief of suffering. Virtues are good as means only. Virtues are correctly called good in a world with suffering. But to insist on suffering in order to have virtue is absurd; it contradicts the very nature of virtue. To insist on suffering so that there can be generosity and sympathy is like stealing from someone so that you can give that person some needed item or kicking someone in the shins so that you can feel sorry for that person.

The theist's defenses do seem to be successful in showing that there is a morality such that, if God had accepted it, it would have committed Him to allow some suffering in the world. Thus the "problem of suffering" comes down to an evaluation of this morality. Do you believe that free will and virtue are worth all the suffering in this world? If you do, then you believe in the possibility of a God who is omnipotent, omniscient, and perfectly good. If you do not, then you will deny that there could be such a God: if there is a God, He is acting on the wrong moral principles.

"Surprise! It's Judgment Day" is meant to be provocative, so it contains something to get almost everyone a little bit angry. Some would claim that there is much more to be said on God's behalf; others would claim that there is much more to be said for the position that Martin first endorses and then abnegates in his horror at becoming "only happy."

The story may assume a dichotomy that is bogus and that is, in some ways, to the theist's advantage. The only options presented in the story are a world like ours or a world in which people are happy zombies. But wouldn't the best of all possible worlds be better than either of these? Might it not be a world in which human beings are created to be happy, intelligent, inquisitive, and appreciative of beauty? Or is this the description of a contradictory world?

The debate, of course, goes on.

4. Moral Proof and Moral Principles

The Land of Certus

OF ALL THOSE LANDS IN WHICH I HAVE TRAVELED, THE MOST WONdrous is the land of Certus. The people there are to be envied above all others, for that which is to us the most perplexing mystery of our existence is to them no mystery at all.

As I stepped from that treacherous forest through which I had wandered, lost, for five days, the first being I encountered in the land of Certus was Felanx. He was a roughhewn, kindly farmer who greeted me at the edge of his fields and offered me the hospitality of his home. Yet he frightened me at first. For when he smiled, there came from his face a strange green light, and I drew back, thinking him a sorcerer. But after a time, he succeeded in calming me with his gentle manner. He said that the light would not harm me and that he would explain it presently.

Felanx led me to the high stone walls of the town, past the sentry at the gate, through the narrow cobblestone streets to his home. As his family welcomed me, there were more flashes of that green light. But his son, who would not approach me, glowed a faint red. Felanx spoke harshly to the boy and dismissed him.

I was seated by the fire, given warm drink, and promised supper. I was no longer fearful of those strange lights, but my curiosity became too much to bear. I asked Felanx to provide me with the explanation he had promised.

"It is quite simple," he said. "From others who have come to our land, we know that these lights do not exist in other parts of the world. So I understand your confusion. Yet to us the lights seem most natural, and we cannot imagine a land that is otherwise. The green light is the light of the good. The red light, it shames me to say, is the light of the bad. You saw it around my youngest son. Most of the time he is a good boy, but sometimes he does not show the proper hospitality to strangers. He has been disciplined. Please accept my apologies on his behalf."

"The lights of good and bad!" I exclaimed. "This is trickery. Do you take me for a fool?"

As I spoke thus to my host, red light burst before my eyes, and I began to stammer in confusion. But once again, Felanx put me at ease. He said that he understood and forgave my skepticism. He said that once I had had a chance to observe his land further and to reflect on the matter, I would realize that he had spoken the truth.

I marveled at the words of my host. To have all good and bad deeds clearly marked so that everyone should know them for what they were: could anything be a greater boon to humanity? I hesitated to believe, and yet had I not seen these lights with my own eyes? After some thought, I inquired about the origin of the lights.

"To that question," said Felanx, "there is no answer that seems to satisfy all. One answer is given in *The Book of the Beginning*. It says that the Creator made the skies and the earth and then, because He was lonely, He created human beings to be His companions. He put human beings in the most beautiful place on earth, the Valley of Peace, and He dwelt there with them. For a time all was happiness. But after a number of years, some people became restless. They said that they wanted to see what lay beyond the valley. The Creator told them there was nothing beyond the valley so happy and so lovely as it was. Still, many wanted to go. The Creator granted them permission at last, saying that He would constrain no one to stay with Him. But He was very angry. He told those who departed that they would find great sorrow in the lands beyond the valley and that they would never find their way back.

"But then one woman bowed down before the Creator and pleaded in tears for her descendants. Was it right, she asked, that they should all suffer for the folly of her headstrong daughter, who was among those who wished to leave? At her words, the Creator relented. He said that He would give those who departed the lights of good and bad, so that they would know how to make themselves worthy to return to the valley. He said that one day He would walk the earth and lead those who glowed with the goodness of green back to the Valley of Peace.

"That, I say, is just one answer. It is the one that my wife accepts. Others have argued that there is no Creator, that the skies and the earth have always been. They say that the lights of good and bad are simply natural events that require no supernatural explanation. The light of the good, they say, is no more mysterious than the other colors of things whose significance is beauty. I, myself, am of this opinion."

I remarked that in my land there were also doubts about a Creator. But the disputes of the Certans were as nothing compared with ours. For in my land, each person interpreted good and bad "according to his or her own lights," and what each person saw was different. At least in Certus there were no doubts about goodness and badness: the lights were the same for everyone. And if there were doubts about a Creator, at least there could be no doubt about how to please Him, should He exist.

The next day, Felanx showed me around the town and introduced me to many of the townspeople. All those I met showed me the utmost kindness. They were eager to hear stories of my travels and to answer any questions I might have. In fact, I was preoccupied with just one question, and it was answered not by what was said to me but by what I observed for myself. I saw that the green lights did indeed mark acts of goodness and the red lights acts of badness. Not that the Certans are a bad people. On the contrary, they are a fine people. But they are human, and they make mistakes. The red light allows them to see their mistakes at once and to correct them.

At one home, we drank a delicious plum whiskey, and the green light over the gathering answered for me a question that divided those in my land, the question of whether it is evil to drink alcohol. The green light told me that drinking is good, though only in moderation. When one of the group became drunken, he glowed with a red light. He was led from the room, apologizing to us all.

As we emerged from another house, I noticed a ragged fellow stumbling as if inebriated, glowing the brightest of reds. The others with me jeered at him, but the fellow only smiled and made a sign with his hands, which I was given to understand was the vilest of profanities. I was surprised by the existence of this reprobate in Certus, and I asked Felanx about him.

"His name is Georges, and he is a difficult case," said Felanx. "At first, some thought that he might be blind to the lights of good and bad, as some are blind to colors and shapes. But he answers questions about the lights correctly. He just won't be guided by them. He knows the good but doesn't want to do it. His case is now before the town council. My guess is that there will be extreme punishment."

"But how can a man know the good and not want to do it?" I exclaimed.

At once I saw the foolishness of my remark, remembering that in the sacred book of my land it says that many fall not through ignorance but through the wickedness of the heart. I told Felanx of this.

"And so it says in *The Book of the Beginning*. But Georges is especially dangerous. Not only does he say that he often prefers wickedness to goodness, but he suggests that everyone should do so. He says that people should do what pleases them and should disregard the lights."

"But how can he be dangerous?" I asked. "Surely anyone can see that if all were to do as they pleased, with no thought of the good, with no thought of others, the result must be chaos, disastrous for all."

"Of course," said Felanx. "But Georges is subtle. He says that what all people should prefer is not only their own pleasures but also the pleasures of others. It is this that seems to absolve him of selfishness in the eyes of the young, and many are drawn by his words."

I shook my head sadly, reflecting on the perversity of human beings. As we walked on through the streets, my attention was drawn to the cannons placed along the town walls. I asked Felanx about them.

"You have learned today that there are two towns in Certus: ours, which is Rechtsen, and another, which is Linksen. What I have not told you about is the terrible perversity of the Linksens. But now that you know of the wicked Georges, you might as well know all.

"The Linksens are our mortal enemies. They have a religion that denies our own. They say that the lights of good and bad are not the work of the Creator, but the work of the Creator's enemy. They say that the lights of good and bad have been put in this land to confuse and lead astray the Creator's true friends. They say that we should not follow the lights, but should instead follow the laws written in their book. These laws, they believe, express the Creator's true wishes."

I could not restrain myself at this absurdity.

"But surely they could be shown the truth. Listen: if at this moment, heaven forbid, I should strike you down for no reason, there would be a ferocious blaze of red. Is it not so?"

"Of course."

"And would it be the same in Linksen?"

"It would. The lights are the same in Linksen."

"There, then. Surely the Linksens cannot believe that such an act could be right or that the Creator would wish it. Were they to believe so, there would now be none of them left. This must prove to them that the lights show the truth."

Felanx lowered his head, and I sensed that he was close to tears.

"Alas, they too have their vicious subtleties. Were you to compare their rules of the good and the bad with the lights of the good and the bad, you would find much agreement. It is this, they say, that shows the cleverness of the Creator's enemy. He makes the lights so that they seem to show the truth in every case. It is this that misleads so many. The Linksens say that women should be equal to men, that animals are not to be eaten, and that the Rechtsens are to be destroyed. That the red light shows on such deeds, they say, is the triumph of deception."

The day that had begun with such joy had turned sad, and I

went to bed that evening with a heavy heart. I had always held the hope that as the nature of goodness became clearer to human beings, they would become better and better. Yet here in Certus, where all had been made clear, wickedness and dissension continued. Was there indeed any hope for humanity?

I awoke the next morning to the sound of a crowd's yelling in the courtyard. I moved through the empty house and went outside. A hundred of the townspeople were gathered in the marketplace, viewing some spectacle. Moving into the crowd, I saw what it was. Georges was lying naked on a wooden platform, his body shackled. He was writhing and screaming, as one of the men standing over him slowly snapped the bones in his fingers with some heavy metal instrument. A glance at Georges's body and at the fiendish instruments held by the men around him indicated that this was just one moment in a long process of torture. Nearby was a stake and a mound of faggots where later they would burn his disfigured body.

I turned away in anger and horror, searching the faces in the crowd. All were watching the brutal spectacle with slight, solemn smiles. I saw Felanx near me and grabbed his arm.

"How can you do this?" I cried. "You who say you love the good."

"Georges is paying the price of his wickedness. The council decided last night. Georges ignores the good and incites others to do the same. He has to be punished. He has to be made an example. It is right that he be punished."

"Punished, yes," I said. "Perhaps even killed. But not like this. This is barbaric! This is horrible!"

Felanx pulled away from me, and his expression became fierce. He moved his hand, and for a moment I thought he was going to strike me. Instead he pointed toward Georges.

"Look again," he commanded.

"No. It is too terrible."

"Look at the men who are carrying out the sentence."

Reluctantly, I glanced toward the terrible scene. Then I saw what had escaped my attention before. The torturers of Georges were all glowing a faint green. This act that I had so readily condemned was, in fact, good, right. Suddenly my horror turned to shame.

"Forgive me," I said, bowing my head.

There was a moment of silence before Felanx spoke.

"You are forgiven, my friend, my guest. But I must concern myself now with your safety. The Linksens know of Georges's punishment. Their leaders have told the people that Georges is their spy and is suffering for their cause. This is not so, and the leaders know it. It is a mere pretext for attack. But they will attack our city. You must leave at once."

"Let me stay," I pleaded, ashamed at having wrongly condemned the Rechtsens. "Life is not so much to me that I would not gladly sacrifice it for the sake of the good."

"I believe that," said Felanx. "But this is not your land, and this is not your battle. You must go."

I kept pleading until I noticed that a red glow began to arise from my body. Then I stopped. I had already committed one grievous error that day; I must not commit another. If it was wrong for me to stay there, then I must go.

An hour later, Felanx led me to the town gate, where he bade me goodbye and turned me over to the guide who was to lead me through the woods along a tortuous trail, which I fear I shall never find again.

The land of Certus is often in my thoughts. For it seems to me that if there is any hope for humankind, it must lie with those brave people of Rechtsen who know the good, follow it, and will fight for it to the end. May the Creator help them in their struggle.

Those Who Help Themselves

THE WAR WITH THE PLANET OMEGA IS WON. ITS CITIES HAVE BEEN destroyed, its social institutions overthrown, its people injured and anguished. We have just destroyed what may have been the only truly moral civilization that ever existed.

The Omegans are not innocent victims; the guilt is not all ours. But however one places the blame, one cannot help regretting this war. The universe is a sadder place for the passing of what Omega once was.

All the civilizations that remain are morally defective. On Earth, in this twenty-second century after Jesus, in this third century after Marx, we certainly have not achieved what anyone would be tempted to call "utopia." At the moment, of course, the situation is fairly stable. Birth control and the calamitous Far Eastern wars have drastically reduced the Earth's population. The nutrition extracted from the oceans and the wealth "extracted" from other worlds have appeased, momentarily, those who are left alive. But we still have our cruelties, our injustices; we still have our victors and victims.

As for other planets, the pathetic, vegetablelike creatures on Beta, though incapable of doing us harm, are vicious: they kill one another with grotesque frequency. The Alphas, who have more military capability, have friendly relations with us, but they are unspeakably cruel to their slave classes. The moral situation on the planet Epsilon is comparable to that on Earth. The Gammas seemed to be the finest people we had encountered, until we discovered that they were merely protoplasmic machines and hence exempt from moral judgments.

Ten years ago, the age-old pessimism about "human nature" had developed into a pessimism about all "living nature." The discovery of Omega forced us to modify our pessimism, but only slightly. It still seems reasonable to surmise that almost all life forms in the universe are, and will continue to be, morally corrupt.

How one explains this depressing fact is a side issue. One may speak of original sin or of the ineradicable instincts necessary for the earlier stages of evolution. The fact remains that virtually all life forms are fundamentally self-interested and aggressive, capable, at best, of some sympathy for a small number of their own kind. Moral inspiration has little effect on behavior. Threats, both natural and supernatural, accomplish more, but not nearly enough. One suspects that the only conceivable near-utopia for most races would be a world of such abundance that individuals would be too busy gorging themselves to think of taking advantage of others. But there could never be such abundance. And, even if there were, doubtless there would still be some who would find their greatest pleasure in causing others pain.

At least such pessimism affords a certain comfort. If moral failure is indeed universal, then it may be inevitable and therefore no one's fault. The discovery of Omega challenged this deterministic view and threatened us with self-contempt. The Omegans had managed to be moral. Perhaps we truly were responsible for our failures.

No doubt we would have liked the moral contrast between us and the Omegans to be blurred by extreme dissimilarities of other sorts. But there were none of any consequence. The Omegans are a small people, averaging just over four feet in height, and their flesh is green. They have three eyes in a triangular formation, one mouth, and fifteen sound receptors located on various parts of the body. They have two legs, which are proportionately quite short, and four appendages at the side of the body. Two of these function like our arms and hands. The other two create, by the friction of the "fingers," the complex sounds by which they communicate. Their conceptual structure is analogous to our own and was easily deciphered by the Q-104 Computer Language Translator. The Omegans we confronted were a people quite similar to us in all but one respect: they were morally good.

Naturally, we tried to explain away the apparent superiority of the Omegans. Could it be that they, like the Gammas, really had no minds? No: they had thoughts and feelings, just as we did. Was there an overabundance of material goods on Omega? No: they also had problems of scarcity. Had they been endowed, through an evolutionary fluke, with an innate compulsion to be unselfish—a compulsion for which they, of course, could claim no credit? No: they were a people with that strong self-interest which morality attempts to tame. There seemed to be no way to rationalize the goodness of those people.

We were not, of course, struck at once by the moral superiority of the Omegans; goodness cannot be seen at a glance. We became aware of it only gradually. In fact, our first impression of the Omegans was quite negative. Initially, they were hostile to us, and they remained suspicious throughout our visit. Admittedly, such inhospitality toward strangers could be considered a moral defect. Nonetheless, it is true that, *within* their civilization, the Omegans' conduct was nearly impeccable.

Naturally, what the Omegans did to be moral was in no way startling. We, on Earth, know quite well the dictates of morality; we know what a moral world would be like. (This is true in general, even if there are marginal disagreements about the nature of the good and the right.) Our problems result not from lack of knowledge, but from lack of ability or willingness. Had the conduct of the Omegans been totally bizarre, our moral terms would not have applied. But the moral concepts of the Omegans were quite familiar. What was startling was that they managed to put them into practice.

The distribution of goods on Omega was not equal, but it was nearly so. In theory, the government was charged with enforcing equal distribution; in practice, little enforcement was necessary. The Omegans readily handed over their surplus goods for others in need, and the government had only to coordinate such generosity to see that it was orderly and that its results were equitably distributed throughout the society.

The Omegan government was democratic. The Omegans had a lively interest in debate, but they avoided *ad hominem* arguments, addressing themselves to issues, rather than personalities, and their debates had a high moral tone.* Campaigning for public offices was vigorous but marked by neither overweening ambition nor rancor. It was indeed a democratic *community*. The Omegans avoided the anarchy and power politics that are the central defects of so many democracies. All individuals showed a real concern for the ongoing welfare of the whole.

The Omegans were a highly energetic, industrious people. They were even, one might say, competitive. But one didn't sense that they were really competing against one another. Each success was celebrated, to a large degree, as a success for all and as an example to others. Each success was measured against the person's potential, and living up to one's potential, whatever it might be, brought the highest respect. The Omegans were not without individual ambition and pride, but they were quite temperate in these.

The Omegans had a considerable interest in the arts and sciences. None of us was qualified to judge their "music," which, because of the vastly different sounds they made, was incomprehensible to us. Similarly, their literary style was difficult to judge, but the content of their literature seemed intricate and imaginative, entertaining, and sometimes profound. We were particularly impressed by their art, which showed a fine sense of line and color. Generally, their art tended to have a much more optimistic tone than ours; but only our most melancholy critics would find this cause for complaint.

For the most part, their scientific achievements were the equal of ours, and apparently their medical skills were superior. They had been slower to develop space technology, presumably because they had little incentive to leave their planet. For obvious reasons, they had not developed sophisticated weaponry —at least until fifty years ago. At that time, they had begun to decode communications between other planets and had discovered, to their shock, the hostile nature of other life forms. Defense development had begun at once, and their crash program yielded remarkable weapons in a relatively short period

---

* This and another usage of the *ad hominem* argument will be discussed in Chapter 6, "Logic."

of time. They had even managed to repel an attack from the planet Alpha some years before we came to Omega. Astonishingly, such weapons were never used by Omegans against one another.

If many Earth people felt that the Omegan society was almost ideal, many Omegans felt the same way. In fact, there were a number of political parties. The biggest opposition party wanted to enlarge the competitive market for the material goods of Omega. Another party, somewhat smaller, wanted no competition and a perfectly equal distribution of goods. There were also fringe groups asking for, say, a greater emphasis on the arts or a greater allocation of funds to defense research. But all such parties constituted a loyal opposition. All felt that the Omegan society was close enough to their ideal so that they could live quite happily with the status quo. All recognized the ongoing value of democracy and of relative stability. No party—indeed, no person—had ever advocated a violent revolution. Because of the conspicuous absence of religion on Omega, there was no inclination to disrupt human welfare for the sake of some supernatural ideal.

Perhaps it is not correct to say that there was no religion on Omega. Certainly there was no belief in a God, and there were no ceremonies of reverence for the universe. But there was one metaphysical belief, shared by all Omegans, that might be considered "religious." It apparently developed in their prehistory, and, if its beginnings were associated with revelations or proofs, there were no existing indications of such, even in the guise of myths. That this belief was so implicit in the Omegans' consciousness—no one had to be persuaded, it was never argued—kept it from our notice for some time. But even the Omegans' expression of this belief was misinterpreted by us at first. A phrase like "that unfortunate man might be me" sounded so much like the imaginative exhortations of our moralists that we failed to comprehend that the phrase was intended literally. Finally we did understand, and, in understanding, I suppose, we discovered the "secret" of the Omegans' moral behavior.

The Omegans believed in the perpetual reincarnation of souls, which was not the work of some divinity, but simply the natural way of things. Almost as soon as a person died, the soul was reborn in the body of some infant, with all memories of the past life erased. This reincarnation, they believed, was not only natural, but random: merits and demerits in a past life had nothing whatever to do with a soul's placement in the next life, and one's inclinations and abilities were not transferred from one life to another. In the next life, the woman of great intellect might be retarded, the man of good health might be diseased, the person of great culture might be interested only in popular entertainments—or vice versa. One might be reborn the same or quite different. There was no way of knowing in advance.

The moral efficacy of this belief is obvious. It is a consequence of this belief that, in promoting a society in which each person helps others, one is quite literally helping oneself. No one was willing to neglect another, because soon one might be in the same position.

There were, as has been noted, some differences of opinion on Omega concerning the moral and political status quo. Apparently, those supporting the largest opposition party were gamblers: they were willing to risk the possibility of some misfortune in the next life for the possibility of gaining great wealth in this life. Those on the opposite end of the political spectrum were unwilling to gamble at all with their future lives: they wanted to be guaranteed an equal share of the wealth. Those who supported the majority party wanted some guarantees and some chances to gamble. But none was willing to gamble too much with his or her future life, to risk being diseased, mentally defective, or hungry, and being without help. Thus, each was agreed that all should be helped and was highly motivated to help others. Guarantees in no way sapped the industriousness of the Omegans, since all would share in the future benefits of their own labors. There were, of course, some moral lapses. Like all people, the Omegans were tempted to emphasize their present rather than their future welfare. But they gave in to this temptation very rarely. Morally, the Omegans had a magnificent civilization.

Some Earth critics of the Omegan war say that we came to conquer. Leaving aside our moral qualms (which those critics might deny we have), we simply do not have the power to conquer and control a universe. On these grounds alone, we always prefer a peaceful relationship of mutually profitable cooperation.

These critics say that the Omegans' suspicion and hostility were justified in view of the aggressiveness of other life forms. This may be true, but it does not get to the heart of the matter. The central problem was that the Omegans refused to acknowledge the moral rights of creatures other than Omegans. Just as twenty-second-century Christians cannot believe that Jesus died to save Betas and Epsilons, just as Marxists don't know what to think about economic determinism on other worlds, so the Omegans could not believe that their souls might migrate beyond their own race. They had no incentive at all to treat other beings fairly, and, in fact, they had treated us viciously.

Perhaps if the crisis had not come so quickly, some say, the Omegans might have adjusted their morality to include other life forms. But this would not have happened as long as those others did not share the belief of the Omegans.

Perhaps, some add, we would have come to share the religion of the Omegas. This is a lovely fantasy, indeed. If a religion is to be judged by its moral efficacy, the "religion" of the Omegans is the best we have ever encountered. But this is mere speculation. One does not change religions as one changes clothes. Earth has its religions already, and, for good or ill, we seem to be stuck with them.

Then we should have left the Omegans alone, say the critics. But this is naive. No one gets left alone, on Earth or beyond. Either people get along, or they fight. We fought. The conflict was inevitable.

In another place and time, when war meant human beings facing human beings, the Omegans would have been unbeatable. Their firm belief in a perpetual reincarnation on Omega would have made them supremely courageous and persistent. But such qualities count for nothing against missiles. The weapons they had been able to develop within fifty years may have been good enough against Alpha, but not against Earth. The war, of course, was brief—and, for the Omegans, devastating.

Few faiths survive such catastrophes. The faith of the Omegans has not. Already, for the first time in the recorded history of Omega, questions are being raised, questions for which no one has answers. Whatever the Omegans may be in the future, it is clear that they will never be the same. Their past civilization will become a footnote to the depressing history of the universe, a footnote both beguiling and accusatory: it was the only truly moral civilization that has ever existed.

Questions

1. In "The Land of Certus," the Rechtsens claim to have knowledge of good and bad via perception of the lights. Do you claim to have some knowledge of good and bad? In what way did you gain this knowledge? What, if anything, do you "see" when you see that something is good?

2. In making moral decisions, the Rechtsens are guided by the lights, the Linksens by the commands of their holy book, and Georges (apparently) by some principle to the effect that one ought to increase pleasure and diminish pain. They differ as to what is the correct evidence of good and bad. Can you imagine some way in which this dispute might be resolved? Can you imagine some sort of higher-level evidence that would convince everyone that, for example, the lights were indeed the true indicators of good and bad?

3. In observing that the green light illuminates the torture of Georges, the narrator of "Certus," who had previously considered torture repulsive, decides that it is, after all, good. Presumably you continued to feel repulsed and pronounced the act of torture bad. Obviously there is an intimate connection between feelings and value judgments. What is this connection? Is judging something as bad fundamentally a matter of having negative feelings about it? Or is it that one "sees" that something is bad and then feels negatively about it?

4. Perhaps when you try to decide what is good and what is bad, you turn to religious writings that you believe express the commands of God. Perhaps you are inclined to say that goodness and badness are a matter of what God commands and that the appearance of God would (or will) show everyone what is good and what is bad. If so, ask yourself the following questions:

    a. Is something made good by the mere fact that God commands it, quite apart from any reasons for His commanding it? Or is it that God "sees" that a thing is good and commands it because it is good? Would you be willing to say that an act of torture was good if God commanded it?

b. If God commands things to be because they are good, how do you suppose that God decides what is good? What does God see in something that makes it good?

5. According to the narrator of "Those Who Help Themselves," the Omegans' belief in reincarnation motivated them to be moral. In what way does this belief relate to morality? What general considerations or principles did the Omegans employ in determining what is good and bad?

6. Compare and contrast the methods by which the Rechtsens and the Omegans determine what is good or bad, right or wrong.

7. The theme of "Those Who Help Themselves" suggests that there is frequently a conflict between self-interest and the dictates of morality, at least for the people of Earth. Give some everyday examples of this conflict, and try to explain what it is about morality that tends to conflict with one's self-interest.

8. If you believed in a morality like the Omegans', what sort of society and what sorts of moral principles would you endorse? Does your answer differ in any way from the kind of society and the kinds of moral principles you now endorse?

Discussion

METAETHICS

"The Land of Certus" raises two sorts of moral, or ethical, questions. First, it brings up—though without much emphasis—*normative ethical questions.* These are questions about what things are good or bad, right or wrong, about what things should or should not be done. The Rechtsens, the Linksens, Georges, and the people from the narrator's land each have opinions about what is good and bad. It is obvious that there are differences of opinion among them, even if these differences are not elaborated. The following normative questions are noted: "Is torture ever permissible?" "Ought men and women to be treated equally?" "Is it permissible to be intemperate in the pursuit of pleasure if no one else is harmed?" Other normative questions, not mentioned in the story, include: "Is abortion wrong?" "To what degree is one obligated to help the poor?" "Is happiness a greater good than freedom?"*

Second, "Certus" emphatically raises *metaethical questions.* These are questions concerning whether we can know which normative ethical judgments are true and, if so, how we can know. Initially, it seems as if there are no troublesome metaethical issues in Certus. Good things are those that glow green, bad things are those that glow red. If one says that something is good and that thing glows green, then the statement is true. Knowing good and bad is just a matter of looking at the colors. However, it turns out that there are others in Certus who say that the lights do not correctly mark the good and bad. The Linksens say that knowledge of good and bad is really to be found in their book. Georges disregards both the lights and the religious book and identifies good and bad with pleasure and pain respectively. Here we confront the issue of how moral questions are to be decided.

Following the emphasis in "Certus," we shall be concerned primarily with metaethical questions, questions about the nature of morality and moral judgments. What are we saying when we make a moral judgment? Is there such a thing as *the* moral truth? Can moral judgments be justified and, if so, in what way? We shall focus on two rival metaethical theories: moral objectivism and moral subjectivism.

It should be noted that the terms "moral" and "ethical" are synonymous and that they are similarly ambiguous. The terms "moral" and "ethical" as they shall be used in this section do not mean "good," and their opposites are not "immoral" and "unethical." Rather, their meaning is "pertaining to moral, or ethical, questions"; their opposites are "nonmoral" and "non-

---

* This last question, along with other normative questions, was discussed in Chapter 3 in connection with the problem of suffering.

ethical." In this usage, it is uncontroversial to say that Jesus, Marx, and Hitler all had moral, or ethical, theories—that is, theories about what is good or bad, right or wrong.

MORAL OBJECTIVISM AND MORAL SUBJECTIVISM

The *moral objectivist* says that where we have a moral judgment and its negation, one of these judgments must be true and the other false. In this sense, moral judgments are analogous to judgments in the domain of science. We would all agree that where we have two statements like "There is life on Mars" and "There is no life on Mars," one of these statements must be true and the other false. We know this, even if we do not know which of the statements is true and which is false. According to the moral objectivist, the same is the case with moral judgments. Where we have two judgments like "All abortion is wrong" and "Not all abortion is wrong," one of the judgments must be true and the other false.

The moral objectivist says that of the various moral theories, at most one of these theories can be true, and the rest must be false. In this sense, conflicting moral theories are analogous to scientific theories. Where there are rival scientific theories about the universe, they cannot all be true: they contradict one another. Of course, they may all be false; perhaps none of them correctly describes the universe. But one and only one scientific theory could correctly describe the universe. In this sense, there is such a thing as *the* scientific truth. According to the moral objectivist, the various moral theories contradict one another, and at most only one of them could be true. One and only one moral theory could correctly describe the phenomena relevant to moral questions. In this sense, there is such a thing as *the* moral truth.

Precisely what the phenomena are that moral theories purport to describe is a matter of debate among objectivists. Some have said that moral theories purport to describe the laws of God. Others have suggested that moral theories purport to describe the natural law, some special moral qualities, or some particular set of those characteristics to which scientific theories also refer.

But all objectivists agree that moral theories are rival theories about some sort of moral phenomena.

Many objectivists would claim to know which moral theory is true. Almost all objectivists would claim to know at least that certain moral theories are false—for instance, those that endorse human slavery, torture, or the extermination of some racial group. Other moral objectivists would claim that some moral theory must be true, but that they do not know which one is true.

The *moral subjectivist* claims that there is no one correct answer to moral questions; there is no such thing as *the* moral truth. Where we have a moral judgment and its negation, neither judgment need be false. Moral questions are not analogous to scientific questions; rather, they are analogous to questions of taste. We all agree that there are questions of taste—for example: "Is yellow prettier than blue?" "Does apple pie taste better than cherry pie?" Most of us would agree that when one person says, "This apple pie is good" and another says, "This apple pie is not good," neither judgment need be false. In such cases, what is at issue are not conflicting descriptions of the apple pie, but differing reactions toward the pie. Analogously, according to the moral subjectivist, moral judgments express attitudes toward persons, actions, or events, rather than being descriptions of such things. When one person says, "All abortion is wrong" and another says, "Not all abortion is wrong," each is expressing a different attitude toward abortion and neither judgment need be false. Moral goodness or badness, rightness or wrongness—like prettiness, like deliciousness—are "in the eye of the beholder." Moral issues are fundamentally "subjective."

To elaborate further on moral subjectivism at this point would involve us in subtleties best reserved for later in the discussion. But the above explanation should give you a sense of what moral subjectivism is, and the position should seem to you a familiar one. It is dramatized in much existentialist literature: the universe contains no intrinsic values, so each individual must "invent" his or her own. It is presupposed by much of the current talk about "value-free" scientific theories: true science, it is thought, should deal only with factual matters, because matters of values are too subjective.

AN ARGUMENT FOR MORAL SUBJECTIVISM

Having outlined the theories of moral objectivism and moral subjectivism, let us now consider a line of argument that might lead one to reject moral objectivism and adopt some sort of moral subjectivist view.

When we consider a scientific question, we do not always agree on the answer. But we do agree on what evidence would decide the issue. For example, we may not know whether there are intelligent creatures on a particular planet, but we do agree on what evidence would show that there are such creatures on that planet.

With regard to questions of taste, however, there is no conceivable evidence that would resolve such issues to everyone's satisfaction. There is no conceivable evidence that would demonstrate that yellow is prettier than blue or that apple pie tastes better than cherry pie.

If moral questions are indeed analogous to scientific questions, then we ought to be able to specify what evidence would decide moral questions to everyone's satisfaction. According to the moral subjectivist, we cannot do this. There is no evidence that would demonstrate that abortion is right or wrong, that an equal distribution of goods is or is not better than competition for goods. Thus, says the subjectivist, moral questions cannot be analogous to scientific questions. Instead, they are analogous to questions of taste.

"The Land of Certus" explores the possibility of decisive moral evidence, and the story is slanted in favor of the moral subjectivist. In Certus, apparently, the good is clearly marked with a green light and the bad with a red light. Seemingly, there ought to be no moral disputes in Certus. But there are such disputes. Georges and some of the younger people claim that one ought to ignore the lights whenever they conflict with the principle that one ought to do what gives one pleasure. The Linksens abide by a religious book that sometimes contradicts what is indicated by the lights. The Linksens say that their book, not the lights, shows what is truly good and bad.

Toward the end of the story, the narrator is shocked when the green light illuminates an act of torture but decides that if the green light so indicates, then the act of torture must be good. Presumably, many readers formed the opposite conclusion: the act of torture would not be good no matter what the lights indicated.

Here the subjectivist could issue the following challenge: Suppose that an act that you found personally repugnant were labeled as good by some law or by public opinion, or by some magical light as in Certus. Would you conclude that the act you find repugnant is good? Or would you conclude that the act cannot be good, since you find it repugnant? Wouldn't you say the latter? And doesn't this indicate that morality is basically a matter of how you feel about things?

Many readers may have an ethic based on what they believe to be divine commands, and they may feel that this argument for moral subjectivism seems forceful only because it neglects religious considerations. Such a reader might offer the following argument: Throughout history, our ethical beliefs have been reflections of what we believed to be the wishes of the gods, or God. No doubt, there are legitimate questions as to which religious writings, if any, correctly describe divine wishes. But, at most, such questions would justify one's being a moral objectivist who doubts that one can know the moral truth. Subjectivists ask what evidence would resolve all moral disputes. If an omnipotent, omniscient creator was revealed to all and was to make known what we were to do and not do, that would show everyone what things are good or bad, right or wrong.

Some quasi-subjectivists have claimed that moral disputes are unresolvable, only because no God exists to "answer" moral questions. These quasi subjectivists would not deny that the commands of such a God would show everyone what is right and wrong. But they say there is no God. In a world without God, there is no evidence that would resolve moral disputes.

However, full-fledged moral subjectivists would reject the theistic argument described above and would deny that even the clear commands of a God would resolve all moral disputes. This is not to say that such a God could not force everyone to follow these commands. But "might" is not necessarily "right."

The issue here is whether the clear commands of a God would result in a rational resolution of moral disputes.

Moral subjectivists might begin an attack on the theist argument by asking a question that is still a live, if hoary, one in theology: Is something good because God commands it, or does God command something because it is good?*

Theists who say that something is good just because God commands it are in an uncomfortable position. They are committed to the view that even if God advocated gratuitous, terrible acts of torture, such acts would necessarily be good. To theists who are willing to accept these consequences, subjectivists could say the following: Even if you would be willing to accept something as good just because God commanded it, many people, including many theists, would not. These other theists would say that even God must have some satisfactory justification for a command if that command is to be good. This shows that the clear commands of God per se would not be the supposed evidence that would resolve all moral disputes.

Theists who say that God commands something because it is good avoid having to say that a terrible act of torture would be good by the simple supposition of God's commanding it. They can say that torture is objectively bad, and God wouldn't command something that was bad. But this theistic position undercuts the theistic argument against moral subjectivism given above. That argument supposed that the clear commands of God would be the evidence that would resolve all moral disputes. But to say that God commands something because it is good supposes that God decides what is good or bad on the basis of some evidence. Now the theists must start all over again and specify what, if any, evidence would resolve all moral disputes —including moral disputes between human beings and God.

It would be helpful if the moral subjectivists could present us with some hypothetical, plausible, and not-too-offensive example of a moral disagreement between a human being and God. An issue of this type is discussed in Chapter 3, "God and the Problem of Suffering."

---

* The God in "A Little Omniscience Goes a Long Way" voices the first of these alternatives: "I don't do things because they're best. Rather, they're best because I do them."

Some theists claim that at the time of creation, God had a choice: Either He could give human beings free will and the risk of unhappiness, or He could make them inevitably happy creatures who lacked free will. According to many theists, God chose to give human beings free will. But surely we can *imagine* someone saying to God: "I understand why You made the choice You did, but I think it was the wrong one. I think that happiness is more valuable than freedom. Had I been in Your place, I would not have given human beings the free will that has brought them so much pain. I would have created human beings who could not be other than happy."

Here, clearly, the mere fact of God's choosing something doesn't resolve the moral dispute. What evidence could God introduce that would demonstrate to this dissenter that freedom is better than happiness? Could there really be such evidence? Isn't such a dispute ultimately a matter of disagreement in attitude?*

The moral subjectivist claims that no evidence, even the revelation of some divine law, would resolve our moral disputes. In the last analysis, what the individual approves of is pronounced "good," and what does not meet approval is "bad." Moral judgments, then, are basically expressions of one's attitudes and feelings.

Moral subjectivism reconsidered

If this argument for moral subjectivism seems forceful, note that this position still has not been stated very precisely. If we are to evaluate moral subjectivism properly, we need to describe it in greater detail.

There have been some terribly implausible versions of moral

* Some theists are inclined to say: "What God commands must be good because God is omniscient and hence knows what is good." Or: "What God commands must be good because God is Goodness." Note that these arguments, as stated, assume rather than support the conclusion they purport to establish. What is at issue here is whether goodness is a matter of knowledge rather than of attitude, whether goodness is an objective property or a subjective matter of attitude. Such arguments simply assume the conclusion they are supposed to support. They simply assume a form of moral objectivism.

subjectivism. It will be helpful to sketch a very crude version of moral subjectivism and then show how, and why, it has been altered over the last thirty or forty years to yield a more sophisticated version. It is interesting that this refined theory of moral subjectivism bears a resemblance to a version of moral objectivism that is different from, and perhaps more plausible than, the type of objectivist theory indicated earlier. We shall also reconsider moral objectivism in this other form.

One crude form of moral subjectivism claims that moral judgments or theories are simple descriptions of the speaker's attitudes. The statement "X is right" means "I approve of X"; the statement "X is wrong" means "I disapprove of X." According to this theory, all sincere moral judgments are true. When one person says, "All abortion is wrong" and another says, "Not all abortion is wrong," neither statement need be false because the second does not really contradict the first. One person is saying, "I (John Smith) disapprove of abortion" and the other, "I (Mary Jones) do not disapprove of all abortion." These statements do not literally contradict each other, though they do indicate that the speakers have different attitudes toward abortion. Both statements, if they are sincere reports of the speakers' feelings, are true.

That this version of moral subjectivism is implausible—or, at least, incomplete—as an account of our moral judgments can be seen by noting certain features of our moral discourse that are highlighted in the story "Those Who Help Themselves." The people on Omega debate moral issues and come to considerable agreement. We on Earth may not reach so much agreement, but we certainly do debate moral matters. We attempt to persuade others of our moral views and occasionally succeed. We have a saying: "There's no disputing matters of taste." Yet we dispute matters of morals. How can this be, if morality is simply a matter of taste or preference? Earlier, we saw that subjectivists say that to make a moral judgment is to state a preference. One clear example of a statement of preference would be: "I prefer country living to city living." But this doesn't seem to be an attempt to persuade or an invitation to debate. If moral judgments are only statements of preference, how is it that they so often seem to be attempts to persuade, that they so often provoke debate?

"Those Who Help Themselves" assumes that there is at least a theoretical distinction between doing what is in one's self-interest and doing what is morally right. In part, at least, this relates to the distinction between what is in one's own interest and what is in the interests of others. On Omega, in practice, there is little real conflict in this matter. The moral efficacy of the Omegans' belief in perpetual, random reincarnation is that it leads them to believe that in helping others they are helping themselves. On Earth, there is considerable conflict between a person's own interests and that which is morally right or between one's own interests and the interests of others. This conflict is not only external, but internal. That is, not only do people often recognize a conflict between self-interest and the interests of others, but they often feel a conflict between what they want for themselves and what they feel they morally ought to do. Is there any hint of the distinction between one's self-interest and that which is morally right in the moral subjectivist theory described above? If moral judgments are only statements of preference, what does morality per se have to do with conflicts in preferences? If my moral judgments are simply statements of my preferences, how is it that I feel a conflict between my preferences and my morality? How could there be a conflict between my preferences and my preferences?

These are forceful objections to the simple form of moral subjectivism presented earlier. Most present-day moral subjectivists have recognized the force of these criticisms and have attempted to emend subjectivism to meet them.

Moral judgments, say these subjectivists, do not merely have the function of stating preferences. They also have the function of attempting to influence the preferences and actions of others. The I-approve-of-it analysis of moral judgments is not adequate. The judgment "It is good, or right" would be better analyzed as meaning "I approve of this; you should approve of this as well; you should do this sort of thing." How one succeeds in affecting the preferences and actions of others is obvious enough. Often we can be shown that what we think we want is not what we really want. "You say you want to see that movie, but you wouldn't like it; the reviews say it is a violent film, and you hate violence." Also, most people have a considerable interest in gaining the approval of others. "We don't do that sort of thing around here" is the kind of "statement" that influences people of all ages. If people at your dinner table said, "Please don't eat the stringbeans with your fingers; it's disgusting," you might well stop, without assuming that what you were doing was objectively bad.

Furthermore, present-day subjectivists would say that moral preferences are a particular type of preference. One's moral preferences express how one would like to see all people treat one another; they express general prescriptions, rules for human behavior. Moral preferences are not the I'd-like-to-get-this type of preference. Rather, they imply the message: I approve of this kind of human behavior; let us all act in this sort of way. Moral preferences are one's preferences from the standpoint of a hypothetical legislator for all human beings. A person's preferred rules count as moral rules only if they are not prejudiced in favor of one's particular circumstances. To propose moral rules is to imply that such rules should apply even if one were in the other person's position. In the words of the eighteenth-century philosopher Immanuel Kant, moral judgments are "universalizable."

A person who, using imagination, discounts his or her particular circumstances, surveys the human condition, and decides what rules all human beings should follow is said to be taking the "moral point of view." To express a moral preference is to express a preference from the moral point of view.

In addition to "moral preferences," people also have "personal preferences." Our personal preferences have to do with what we each want for ourselves. Our personal desires often conflict. Our desire to spend two weeks at the beach may conflict with our desire to save money for some new clothing. In an analogous way, says the subjectivist, our moral preferences and our personal preferences may conflict. From the moral point of view, we may wish that people would keep their promises. From the personal point of view, we may wish to break a promise we find very inconvenient to keep. Thus it is that there is often a conflict between self-interest and that which is morally right, says the subjectivist. This is not a matter of a clash between personal preferences and the dictates of some objective moral rules. Rather, it is a matter of a clash between personal preferences and moral preferences.

The present-day moral subjectivist, then, says that moral judgments are not simply statements of preference. Moral judgments express one's preferences as to the rules one would like to see everyone follow.

Does this "concession" by the subjectivist amount to something more than the patching up of a theory that states that morality and moral debate are fundamentally nonrational? It would seem so. Most subjectivists feel that the recognition of the special nature of moral preferences, of the moral point of view, has important implications for ethical debate. Some objectivists have even claimed that this supposed emendation of the subjectivist theory actually yields a form of moral objectivism. Let us examine these claims.

One cannot deduce a particular morality from the definition of the moral point of view. This is as it should be. The definition, after all, is supposed to represent something implied by all moral judgments.

Nonetheless, it is conceivable that many people make judgments which they claim to be moral judgments, but which they would not endorse if they seriously took the moral point of view. They may be proposing rules which they say are moral rules, but which they would not be willing to acknowledge if they were in the other person's position. Such people are inconsistent in that they are claiming to take a point of view that they are not really taking.

Some philosophers have claimed that human psychology is such that persons who seriously took the moral point of view would all endorse the same set of rules. This claim implies a form of moral objectivism: only one moral theory is compatible with the moral point of view and the facts of human psychology. Moral subjectivists deny that this is so. But most subjectivists do believe that many people would have to modify their moral judgments if they seriously took the moral point of view.

Some people may endorse the segregation of blacks or of

Jews. Suppose that such people were to learn that they themselves were of Negroid or Jewish extraction. Would they continue to hold their bigoted views? In most cases, this seems doubtful. If so, then such people must admit that their views represent personal preferences rather than moral preferences.

Some people are fortunate enough to make millions of dollars. They may endorse a survival-of-the-fittest morality and say: Let the poor fend for themselves. Suppose these people were to be deprived of their money and their ability to make more. Would they then say: I'm not fit, let me perish? Or would they say: How about a social welfare program? If the latter, then their original judgments were not moral preferences but personal preferences.

Would anything be gained by persuading people to admit that certain of their views constituted personal preferences and not moral preferences? In some cases, no. Some people are content to be amoral. But many people care very much about morality. After all, to engage in moral dialogue is to engage in a kind of intellectual arbitration. As in any kind of arbitration, one may sometimes lose, but the arbitration procedure does offer one certain protections. To abandon morality would be to agree to let human relations be governed by whim and strength. This prospect bothers many people very much. Also, the psychology of most adults seems to be such that believing they are moral is crucial to their feelings of self-respect. Few adults like to admit that they are amoral or immoral; instead, people tend to adjust their morality to agree with their self-interest. But such adjustments are not really compatible with having a morality.

In any case, the question at issue here is whether there can be a rational resolution of moral questions. Whether, and to what degree, people are willing to be moral, willing to act on their moral preferences rather than on their personal ones, is a very serious question, but it is also a quite different question from the one we are considering.

In "Those Who Help Themselves," the metaphysical beliefs of the Omegans motivate them to take the moral point of view constantly. They believe in a perpetual, random reincarnation of souls that will eventually place each of them in different social positions and circumstances. They are motivated continuously to ask themselves: What if I were in the other person's position? Probably this is a question that most of us manage to avoid a good deal of the time.

In the story, taking the moral point of view does not resolve all moral questions. There remain disagreements about whether there ought to be competition or an equal distribution of goods, whether one ought to promote happiness over excellence, and so forth. Nonetheless, the story implies that people who really did take the moral point of view would be in close enough agreement that they would get along quite well. And, indeed, if human beings could come to this much agreement in their views, they might well be quite satisfied.

Moral objectivists, of course, would say that the story presumes too little. Many subjectivists would say that it presumes too much.

From the moral point of view

Perhaps it would be helpful to take a contemporary moral–social issue and show how it is related to normative philosophical debates that make conscious reference to the moral point of view.

We are all familiar with the issue of how the goods of a society ought to be distributed among its members. Should all the goods be distributed on the basis of competition? Or should all the goods be distributed equally? Or should every individual be guaranteed a certain minimum of goods, and the remaining goods be distributed on the basis of competition? If the last, how much should the guaranteed minimum be?

One normative ethical theory that is favored by British philosophers is utilitarianism. The premise of utilitarianism is that the only thing valuable in itself is happiness and that a society ought to promote the greatest happiness of the greatest number. The emphasis here is on "greatest happiness" rather than on "greatest number." If the greatest total happiness in society would be achieved by, say, a competitive system that allocated most of the goods to seventy-five percent of the members, rather than by a less competitive system that distributed goods more equally, then utilitarianism would favor the first system.

This is not to say that utilitarianism per se favors competition and unequal distribution. We cannot derive a specific answer to the question of how goods ought to be distributed in a society from the utilitarian principle alone. We would also need factual information about what social system would create the greatest total happiness in a particular society. Nonetheless, it is the case that utilitarianism does not insist upon a guaranteed minimum for all individuals.

A number of philosophers have criticized utilitarianism as "unjust" in this respect: they have said that a more acceptable normative theory would be one that insisted upon substantial guarantees for every individual. One of these critics is John Rawls, whose recent book *Justice as Fairness** is much discussed by philosophers today. He has formulated a concise normative theory that he believes is preferable to utilitarianism, and he has defended his theory via an imaginative test that he claims is equivalent to taking the moral point of view. "Those Who Help Themselves" was written with Rawls in mind. But it should be noted that the remarks that follow are such a simplification as to amount almost to a distortion of Rawls's views. For instance, Rawls seems to claim that liberty is valuable in itself, quite apart from its effects on happiness. That claim shall be ignored. What we shall focus on is that part of Rawls's principle that has to do with the effect of the distribution of goods on happiness.

Rawls says that society should deviate from an equal distribution of goods only if, and only to the extent that, every member is at least a little better off, over time, under a system that distributes unequally. If, for example, a competitive system would produce more goods and more happiness, then the competitive system would be acceptable—but only if, and to the extent that, every individual gained something by such a competitive system.

As with utilitarianism, no specific answer to the question of how goods ought to be distributed in a society can be derived from Rawls's principle. Again, we need information about benefits that might accrue through competition. But it is clear that Rawls's principle insists on a relatively sizable guarantee for each individual, whereas the utilitarian principle does not insist on any.

---

* Cambridge, Mass.: The Belknap Press of Harvard University, 1971.

Rawls's principle would seem more likely to lead to a more equal distribution of goods than would that of the utilitarian.

What is of special interest in the context of this chapter is the way that Rawls attempts to defend his principle with an appeal to the moral point of view. He asks us to imagine that we are about to enter life. We do not know what our interests and abilities will be; we do not know what our position in society will be. We must choose some general normative principle that will guide us in determining what sort of social system we will have. According to Rawls, being in such a situation would be the literal equivalent of taking the moral point of view. Obviously, such a situation would be analogous to the situation on Omega, with the—possibly important—difference that each Omegan is already living a life and believes that there are a great number of lives to go. Rawls claims that in such a situation people would choose his principle rather than that of the utilitarian. His principle is the one most compatible with the moral point of view (and the facts of human psychology).

The utilitarians have responded by claiming that the selection of the utilitarian principle would be the more rational by normal standards of rationality. Suppose that you and nine others were offered one of two lotteries, each requiring a wager of ten dollars. In the first lottery (subsidized by the Better Business Bureau, one might suppose), five of you will lose the ten dollars, and five of you will win one hundred dollars. In the second lottery (not subsidized), all of you will get back five dollars, and five will receive an extra ten dollars, getting back a total of fifteen. Which lottery would you choose? The first, of course. Similarly, suppose you were to "bet your life" on one of two societies. In the first society, ninety-five percent of the people would be very happy, and five percent of the people very miserable. In the second society, fifty percent of the people would be mildly happy, and fifty percent mildly miserable. Which society would you choose? The first, of course.

Rawls's principle, however, would favor the second lottery and the second society. The utilitarian principle that would always give the best "odds on happiness" would be the more rational by normal standards of rationality. But Rawls argues that persons wagering an entire lifetime would adopt the more conservative betting strategy. The idea of living one's life in great misery would be such a fearful prospect that people would be willing to take lesser odds on happiness to ensure that they would not suffer great misery.

"Those Who Help Themselves" imagines that all would insist on at least some guaranteed minimum but would differ as to the distribution of goods beyond that. "Apparently, those supporting the largest opposition party were gamblers: they were willing to risk the possibility of some misfortune in the next life for the possibility of gaining great wealth in this life. Those on the opposite end of the political spectrum were unwilling to gamble at all with their future lives: they wanted to be guaranteed an equal share of the wealth. Those who supported the majority party wanted some guarantees and some chances to gamble. But none was willing to gamble too much with his or her future life, to risk being diseased, mentally defective, or hungry, and being without help."

You might discuss this problem with your friends. Do you agree with the utilitarian viewpoint or with Rawls? Or can you formulate some other principle that you would prefer? How close can you come to agreement with one another?

This, of course, is related to the broader question: Would those who seriously took the moral point of view come to complete or considerable agreement on their moral views? Probably the only way to determine this is to continue our moral dialogues, but with greater philosophical clarity. In determining your moral preferences, try to make sure that you are taking the moral point of view. When you find that you and another person seem to disagree on an issue, try to conduct your discussion explicitly from the moral point of view. Perhaps this will not lead to greater agreement in your moral discussions. But the chances are that it will.

5. Appearance and Reality

The Nirvana Tape

Orange yellow bright too bright red flashing yellow burning pulsing hurting my eyes can't close them can't close my eyes stop it oh stop it loud whining screaming horribly loud my head will burst can't stop up my ears so loud hot so hot burning burning can't stand it can't stand it . . . .

HAVE A SEAT THERE, IF YOU WILL, MR. WILLIAMS. FROM HERE YOU get a clear view of the operating room and of all our special equipment. The gentleman on the table is . . . uh . . . let's just call him Mr. C. Like you, he has a terminal illness that has not impaired the brain. Like you, he has no living family to complicate our security precautions or the legal intricacies of our arrangements. He's a very nice fellow—comes from southern California, just as you do. The two of you are somewhat different in temperament, but I'm sure you would have liked one another.

Right now, Mr. C is being programmed with the fantasy of his choice. We're sure that some patients would volunteer for our project out of a desire to help others through helping science. But it is so much nicer that we are able to offer them something in return, don't you agree? Of course. In any case, Mr. C is now experiencing his selected fantasy, and I can assure you that he is happier than either of us could imagine. You'll notice that we are keeping a careful eye on things. The physicians and technicians are monitoring the programming process to make certain that nothing goes wrong.

Before the programming process comes the investigative part of the operation—which, of course, is the real purpose of our project.

With the patient anesthetized, but conscious, the upper part of the skull is removed—you're not getting nauseated, are you? I thought not. You knew roughly what to expect, and you've had surgery before. Anyway, with the skull removed, we begin an experiment on the brain that lasts an absolute maximum of four hours per patient. Years ago such experiments were concerned with, oh, monitoring the subject's moods or attempting to evoke a single, complex mental image. We are much more advanced than that now. But still, there is so much more to learn about the mind.

In Mr. C's case, the project was conducted as follows: Prior to the operation, Mr. C made a list of thirty vivid memory impressions. Actually, he listed them twice. One list he gave to us so that we and the computer would know what the memory impressions would be. On a second piece of paper, he listed these same impressions in a different sequence, the sequence in which he would recollect them on the operating table. The second list was sealed in an envelope and put in the vault.

Once on the operating table, Mr. C recollected the first five memories and described them aloud into a microphone. His descriptions were fed into the computer and correlated with the brain patterns recorded by the brain-probing mechanisms. Then, without making any verbal reports, Mr. C recollected the other twenty-five memory impressions, concentrating on each for a minute to distinguish them quite definitely from any random thoughts. It was up to the computer to deliver a properly ordered list of his memory impressions. And you know what? The list was ninety-two percent accurate. Quite amazing, don't you agree?

In your case I shall attempt to conduct a complete, coherent conversation with you, lasting a full hour, without either of us overtly "speaking" to the other. First, we shall conduct a brief conversation in the normal way, while the computer gets an accurate reading of the relevant patterns in your brain. Then you shall think a sentence that the computer will attempt to interpret from your brain activity: its interpretation will come to me on a printout sheet in that booth over there. I will formulate a reply that will be fed into the computer and translated into brain stimulation. If this works as it should, you will get the impression of hearing me speak, just as you might hear some figure speaking in your dreams. You will then think a response to my statement, and so on. After the experiment is over, we shall compare notes. And after that will come your fantasy. But before we get to the selection of your fantasy, are there any questions? . . .

No, there's no chance of that. The anesthetization process we use takes care of all pain and all anxiety. By the way, if you are at all worried about trickery on our part, don't be. There are strict governmental regulations and supervisory procedures in effect here. We are not mad scientists or brainwashers or any such thing. We are engaged in important scientific research that is humane in its intent and positively beneficent in its treatment of the patients. True, we are engaged in a politically sensitive area of research, which is the reason for the secrecy. But every person here has been screened by the government for mental stability, high moral standards, scientific expertise, and whatnot. Furthermore, at each operation there must be two scientifically competent outside observers, who are rotated constantly to keep them free of influence by any overzealous researchers here. As you will recall, the government agent who gave you your final screening had credentials from another agency, one you have known of all your life. There is no question of malice or trickery here, and absolutely no question of unfortunate mistakes.

Now—shall we get to the good part? Yes, indeed. The tapes. I enjoy so much discussing them with the patients, anticipating their decisions, enjoying secondhand their fun. It is a bit like watching a friend select a gift from a pile of Christmas packages, knowing one's turn will come next. Only I cannot be sure that my turn will come. I can only hope. If I should be run over by a truck or develop a brain disease or die suddenly in my bed, then I would miss out. You are a lucky man, Mr. Williams.

> Terrible stench terrible thirst so hot burning my skin got to stop it want to get away can't move can't stop it so hot suffocating can't breathe hot things tearing at my skin burning oh it's horrible loud screaming hurts can't stand it stop oh please stop . . . .

Some day, I'm sure, we will have a whole library of tapes here, and the patients will pore over large catalogues before making their decisions. Perhaps some day we will learn how to program such fantasies without having to open the skull, and then we will be able to offer them to the general public. Though obviously some limits would have to be imposed. You can't, so to speak, have everyone below deck watching the movie: who would run the ship?

At the moment, we have only eight tapes, though I don't want to overemphasize the "only." You would be thrilled with any one of them, I can assure you. Once, as a matter of fact, there was only one tape. To be truthful, I'm not sure whether one tape in particular would make you happier than the others, since we program you to love whichever tape is used. But having a selection of tapes does seem to be important to the patients and does help us recruit participants.

In content, the tapes are very simple. At our current stage of technology, they are tremendously difficult and costly to manufacture. The imagery is not much more complex than that of most television films you have seen. But, of course, we are not talking about a film. We are talking about a coordinated experience, programmed directly to the brain, stimulating the areas associated with the five senses, with pleasure, and with one's sense of time. You won't be comparing it to any stories you have read or to any fantasies of your own, because we deactivate the memories that would be relevant to such comparisons. Nor will you be disappointed with the length of the fantasy, which, according to our time, lasts only one hour. We alter your sense of time so that the fantasy seems to last for something like four weeks. And, as I've said, we program you to be completely satisfied with your experience.

It is a very simple procedure, really. After the investigative phase of the operation is over, we simply bid you bon voyage, plug in the machine, and give you the time of your life. When the program is over, that's it for you, of course, but there is no intimation of what is to come, no pain, no fear, simply the conclusion of a delightful story. Could one conceive of a better way to complete one's life? I doubt it very much.

Now. Shall I describe the tapes to you? Each of them has a long serial number and some horribly long name invented by some bureaucrat with no imagination. The staff here is a bit more lively and, if you will allow me, I shall simply use the names they have given the tapes. All right?

First, there is the Nirvana Tape. That is the earliest one we developed, and it's the simplest in conception though quite intricate in detail. It is what you might call a "light show," to use a somewhat out-of-date phrase. It's also a sound, taste, touch, and scent show. Lovely music, beautiful, gently swirling colors, soft touches, delicious tastes and fragrances. It is amazing how many people still select it. I suspect that as life draws to a close, many people have had too much of "plot" and simply want beauty.

Then there is the Playboy Tape, in which you slowly seduce and then have an affair with the most beautiful woman you have ever seen. Don't get the wrong idea. It is not in any pejorative sense "pornographic," at least to my way of thinking. For one thing, you would be a participant, not an onlooker. And it is quite tastefully done—exciting, but romantic as well. First, there are lovely dinners and dancing and romantic words as she gradually gives in to your charms. And there is genuine feeling between you. It is not just casual sex. We have an analogous tape for women called the Playgirl Tape. It involves dinners, dancing, romantic beaches, all leading to a perfect sexual experience.

No? Well, how about the Gary Cooper Tape, a rip-roaring Western with lots of shooting and riding and saving the girl from the Indians—no again, eh? I'm afraid we badly miscalculated on that one. We thought that the Western would never lose its appeal, but it seems to have. We are thinking seriously of adding a spy tape to fill the gap. The women's counterpart is our best seller, though. It is the Gothic Tape, with an old castle, secret crimes, signs of ghosts, and a handsome duke. One of the doctors here says she can hardly wait.

You are a teacher, I know, and lean toward the intellectual. How about an intricate mystery, then? We have two of those, roughly patterned after Agatha Christie stories. How would you, as Hercule Poirot, like to employ those "little grey cells" of yours to discover who killed the long-lost heir who appeared suddenly and, just as suddenly, was killed in a locked room in a house containing twenty larcenous relatives? And unravel the mystery in front of the whole group at the end? I can see you're interest now.

Still there's one more, the Descartes Tape. You sit in your study, then go to bed and dream you are in your study, then wake and return to your study once again. As you sit at your desk, wearing your heavy dressing gown, warmed by the fire, jotting your philosophical meditations, you begin to wonder if everything that you believe exists might be mere illusion. As you doubt your beliefs, you decide that the very act of doubting proves your existence. You consider the idea of a perfect God and conclude that such a being must exist: a perfect God, lacking nothing, could not lack existence. You decide that a perfect God would not allow you to be deceived in what you perceive, so the room in which you are sitting must truly exist as you perceive it. All this takes place while you are really lying on the operating table. Whoever decided on that tape must have had an odd sense of humor, don't you agree? Still you, as Descartes, would be sure you were right. The Church would applaud you, and Gassendi would write you congratulations instead of all those endless objections. It must be nice to feel secure in one's beliefs. One does get so tired of the constant skepticism one confronts. Ah, I see I've got you now.

But think about it. You have several days in which to decide. And then you will be where Mr. C is now, and you, rather than he, will be the happiest person on earth. Just look at him. Of course, you can't see what he's experiencing. But take my word for it. It is fantastic.

. . . What? Are you joking? Is this the teacher coming out, or did the mention of Descartes get you going? All right, I'll play along. But, in fact, the answer to your question is quite simple.

No, of course we don't literally see the contents of Mr. C's mind. But then the doctor doesn't see the virus causing a disease either. He knows it is there because of the symptoms. Do you play the skeptic with your doctor? Of course not. No sensible person would. And do you doubt the existence of atoms because you don't see them? No.

But to get quite specific. When we program a fantasy, we are causing certain observable processes in the brain. We know what mental experiences are produced by these brain processes, because we have correlated them with the patient's reports of his or her mental experiences. We have checked these correlations over and over during our experiments with hundreds of patients. And we double-check the relevant correlations with each patient before we induce the fantasy. Of course, the computer is not one hundred percent accurate, as in the listing of Mr. C's memory experiences. But this was new ground. One reason the fantasy tapes are so limited in number and in content is so that they need involve only very limited and familiar areas in the brain. . . . Certainly, you could imagine that Mr. C is having an experience quite unlike the one on the tape. In the same way, you could imagine that the normal patient under anesthesia is in great pain. But would you take such a hypothesis seriously? Of course not. . . . Ah, I see you were just teasing me. . . . No, it's quite all right. I enjoy such discussions very much.

Look, what do you say we continue this chat in my office over some brandy? They're almost finished here, and they won't be needing me anymore. There are only five minutes left on the tape, though to Mr. C that will seem nearly a week. Which one did he pick? The Nirvana Tape. Another week of his ecstatic light show to go. Then it will end, of course. But with all that Mr. C has experienced, I can assure you that he will have no regrets.

Help me help me please can't stand it orange yellow too bright flashing burning my eyes hurting me burning can't move make it stop oh please make it stop. . . .

The Death of the Man in the Dream

HE OPENED HIS JOURNAL AND WROTE:

Strangely enough, with only three days of life left, I find myself inclined to sleep much longer and much more often than usual. I suppose, to use a somewhat anachronistic image, the times of sleep are like the tentative, inquisitive gestures of courtship before the final commitment. I am committed. I know that these little games of death pale before the reality of the event, and I know that I shall feel a tremendous fear at the end. But I shall go through with it.

There is, of course, the temptation to live a little longer, and it comes at odd times. The other day, I was sitting in the park. It was a beautiful, bright, early-summer afternoon, and inevitably there were couples walking by, holding hands. I considered the scene and felt nothing but a vaguely amused detachment. It was like watching an old Doris Day movie that one never expects to come to life and that one isn't going to bother to stay up for again. Later that day, while eating a cheeseburger with Stacy at McDonald's, I felt a sudden, overwhelming urge to live. At McDonald's, of all places! But it is just such trivial pleasures that constitute the temptation to live. On the other hand, I cannot make a life out of such things. I've wanted so passionately to be a good writer. I've failed, and I cannot rid my world of the signs of my failure or my self-contempt. Three days from now, I shall end my life.

Stacy still believes that I have planned my suicide for the eighteenth of this month, my thirty-third birthday. It is virtually the only lie I have told her, but it was a necessary precaution.

She is weird enough to want to play a part in the life and the journal of a suicidal writer, but I suspected that she was not morbid enough, not brutal enough, to actually let me die. I was right: now she is pleading with me to change my mind. She thought it was all a game, and now that she finds it is not, she is hurt and frightened. I don't reproach her. Quite the opposite. Something very tender has developed between us, something I did not anticipate. It is not enough to keep me alive. But I do regret having to hurt her.

I almost shut the journal again without mentioning those damned dreams. I don't want to write about them. They are a ludicrous intrusion, an absurd digression from the "plot" of this journal. But their omission mocks whatever standards of honesty I have set for myself. I must say something about them.

The dreams—or, rather, the dream—has been going on for about a week now. But it seems to have been going on much longer, because it contains impressions of memories going back many years. The man in the dream is me, I suppose, or rather what I may become if I were to live another twenty years. The man is middle-aged, a high school English teacher, with a plump, kindly wife. He hates his life but fears his death even more.

What is so weird is the way the man in the dream talks about me as if I were merely a dream of his. I suppose it is my coming suicide, and the writing about it, that has gotten my mind working so strangely. The dream frightens me a bit, because it shows that my mind may be at the outer limits of sanity. But the dream only strengthens my resolve. I refuse to live to become that man. I absolutely refuse.

He closed the journal and locked it in the top drawer of his desk. Then he turned and looked at Stacy. She was sitting on the bed, which was still mussed from their earlier love-making. She was leaning forward, her knees pulled up under the sheets, her arms encircling her legs, her chin resting on her knees. Her teeth were biting at her lip, and she was staring at him through a profusion of dark hair. Her eyes were red.

"I won't let you do it," she said. "I won't."

He got up from the desk and walked over to the bed.

"You can't stop me, Stacy," he said. "All you can do is make it a little harder. And ruin whatever we have between us."

"You're gonna die. How can I do any worse to us than that?"

"You knew at the beginning how the story ends."

"Goddamn it, Bob, I love you. Please don't do it. Please."

"That's enough, Stacy. The manuscript is nearly finished, and it is pretty good. Let's not turn it into a soap opera now."

"My God," she said, "can't I even talk to you? Whatever you say, it's never for me, only for them—whoever they are—the ones you want to read that thing. And you won't let me say anything you don't want them to read."

"You're in the book," he said. "That carries certain responsibilities, and you agreed to accept them. I hadn't intended to let anyone know what I was doing, but that night when we met I was lonely and drunk, and I talked too much. When you found out you were in the last chapters, you were excited. You said it made life the kind of adventure Sartre says is impossible: each action at once lived and narrated. Well, I let you in all the way, and I expect you to play your part with some dignity. In any case, it is my book, and you can't change the ending. I'm going to die, Stacy. Make up your mind to that."

Stacy looked at him in silence for a few moments, then moved closer to him and put her hand on his arm.

"Bob, I know how desperately hurt you are about the writing. But you say the journal is pretty good. Why not try to publish it as fiction? You don't have to die at the end, not for real."

"It's not good enough for a novel. There are parts of it that are fine, I think. But on the whole, it's not good enough."

"Then why bother with it at all?"

"Because whatever its failings, it will be real. Perhaps the reality of it may fascinate some people."

"It's been done before: this kind of suicide journal."

"Everything's been done before," he said. "Look, Stacy, I have faced the probability that this journal will be as unsuccessful as the novels. The few people who read it may reject it with pity or scorn. But if it does nothing more than make the end of my life a little more interesting to me, well that's something."

"Bob, please. . . ."

He put his fingers gently to her lips. Then he pulled her against him and held her as she cried, until she finally fell asleep. He too felt exhausted and soon began to doze. There would be the dream again, no doubt. But soon enough there would be a sleep without dreams. It would be a relief.

He blinked as he emerged from the dark hallway into the sunlight and hesitated, feeling disoriented. His wife took his hand.

"What did the doctor have to say?"

"The same. Look, Mary, can we sit down for a minute? That bench over there. I feel a little unsteady."

A haze blurred the noonday scene, and he wasn't sure if the haze came from the air or from his head. He felt like a man who had just taken a drink after days without sleep. He followed his wife to a bench in the small park next to the medical building. He leaned back against the wood slats and looked past the two-block row of stores, past the high school, to the faint outlines of the mountains against the blue-grey sky.

"Is that better?" she said.

"A little. It's that medication—on top of everything else."

"Tell me what the doctor said. What about the tests?"

"My blood pressure is up, but he said that was to be expected and we'd get it under control. Nothing else seems to be wrong physically. He also assured me that I was not losing my mind. He said this sort of thing was quite normal in a man my age, though he did admit that the dream sequence was a bit unusual. But he said that the unusual was to be expected of a literary man. A literary man! Jesus."

"Don't, Bob."

"He's sticking to the male menopause thesis, though he was kind enough not to use that phrase. Through my dreams, supposedly, my mind is working out its fears and regrets and trying to make adjustments. The girl is associated with my fears of lessening virility, the writing with my refusal to let go of the old dreams, the suicide with my deepening awareness of my mortality. All very pat."

"The doctor is trying to help, Bob, and what he says makes sense."

"Nothing makes sense to me these days."

"Bob, look at me. Do you love me?"

He looked, and over her shoulder, as in some past daydream,

he saw a slim, tanned girl in cut-off jeans. But he was too exhausted and too frightened for desire. His wife was there, and he desperately needed someone.

"Yes," he said.

"We'll get through this together. You'll be all right. I know it."

Her hand soothed the back of his neck, and for a moment he felt calm enough to be sad. He glanced at the new high school wing of stainless steel and glass, now closed for the summer. Then he looked in the direction of their home. For years he had been counting out his days in grammar lessons, study halls, and gym classes and counting out his nights in empty bottles, regrets, and occasionally plots for stories he knew he would never try to write again.

"Oh, Mary," he said. "Remember how good the future looked once? It's here now. Who'd have thought it would be so mediocre."

"I love you, Bob. Do you hate yourself so much?"

"I suppose I do."

"But this past year you've seemed so much better. You seemed almost happy at times. You said you thought at last you were coming to terms with yourself."

"I did think I was. Oh, hell, why am I talking of the old regrets? This is something so much worse. I'd gladly accept life as it's been, if only those dreams would stop, if only I could stop being so scared. And so tired. If I could only rest. I mean, really rest."

"Are the dreams so very frightening?" she said. "Can't you look on them as a kind of adventure?"

"I wish I could."

"What about the girl? What's her name—Stacy? Wasn't she nice to . . . be with? Tell me. I'll understand."

"Yes, she's lovely. But I won't be seeing her much longer. I mean, *he* won't. My God, what am I saying?"

"Bob, it's a natural slip. After all, it is your dream."

He was silent for a moment, trying to sort out his confused thoughts.

"Mary, they're not nightmares. I mean, the dreams themselves aren't frightening. They're everything else—sad, mostly. When I dream, I *am* him, and he doesn't seem to be scared. It's only when I wake up that I'm so frightened. And I don't know why.

What do I fear? That the man in the dream will kill himself? That doesn't make any sense."

"Of course not," she said. "If he decides to die, then the dream will be over and you will be rid of it. If he decides to live, then what could be frightening about that? As the doctor says, it's just your mind adjusting to life as it is. Bob, I know this will all be resolved soon. It will all be over."

He looked up at the horizon. The mountains were gone now, dissolved in the haze. He said "yes," but hardly knew to what.

For the last half-hour, they had been walking aimlessly, silently, through the park and down the town streets. He had felt irritable and shaky since his nap that afternoon. That damned dream was getting to him, upsetting him when he wanted to be calm, jumbling his thoughts when he wanted so much to be lucid. Hell, it was naive of him to suppose that the ending of a life could be a simple matter. He'd drawn out the ending too long already. It was time to get on with it.

"Stacy, I'm going home."

"All right, let's go."

"Not you. I want to be alone."

"No!"

"Stacy, it is still three more days until my birthday. I told you that would be the date. I wouldn't do anything earlier."

"I'm going with you."

He saw the determination in her face and thought for a moment.

"Look," he said. "I didn't want to say anything to you until I was very sure. But I don't believe I'm going through with it. It's a hard decision for me. I want to think about it tonight, alone, and then discuss it with you tomorrow."

"You're serious?"

"Very. I've been thinking that the journal might make a good novel after all. Even if it doesn't, maybe I should try writing another book. Perhaps I should give myself a few more years. Thirty-three is a little young to die."

"Oh, God, Bob, that's so great!"

Stacy threw her arms around him, and he held her for some moments in what for him was goodbye. This was a cruel trick to play on her, but she would be hurt in any case, and he could never finish it with her at his side. He would go home now, make the last entry in his journal, and then mail the journal to an old acquaintance who knew nothing of his plan but whom he could trust to show the manuscript around. Then he would eat, and perhaps rest, and later tonight take the gun from the desk drawer and end his life.

"I love you, Bob," said Stacy, as she finally moved away from him.

"I love you, too," he said, and felt that he almost meant it.

He watched Stacy as she walked away, waving back each time she turned to wave at him. He continued to stare after her, even after she was gone.

"I'm sorry," he said, "I truly am. Goodbye, Mary."

Then he caught his words, and he laughed without humor. Well, my friend in the dream, we do seem to be getting jumbled together, don't we? But tonight I die, and you must die with me, so I suppose it's only right that we say your goodbyes, too.

"Bob, for God's sake. You've been pacing the floor all night. You look terrible. You've got to get some rest."

"I don't want to, Mary. When I sleep, the man in the dream will wake up. He's going to kill himself the next time. He says he's going to kill us both. I'm afraid. It's absurd, but I'm afraid."

"Bob, will you get control of yourself? It's only a dream. It can't hurt you. But you really will kill yourself if you go on like this. I'm going to call the doctor."

"No, don't," he protested. "The doctor can't do anything for me. I have to get through this by myself. All right. I'll sit down, and I'll try to relax. I know I can't put off sleep much longer. But will you sit with me until I fall asleep? I'll feel better knowing you're here."

He moved unsteadily across the small living room to the easy chair, sat down, and leaned his head back. He looked at his wife and then stared up at the white plaster ceiling. After a time, he felt his body begin to relax from the center outward, as if a sleeping pill were taking effect.

Why do I fight him? he thought. Why do I cling so fiercely to a life I have hated? Wouldn't it be better if my life did end here? But no, I want to live. I'm going to live. Mary's right. It's only a dream, and dreams don't kill. All this has shown me how much I really want to live. I'm through torturing myself with regrets for all that I have failed to be. I'm going to accept life as it is. The man in the dream can die, but I'll live. I'll sleep, then wake, and this absurdity will all be behind me.

"I'm feeling better now, Mary," he said.

"That's good. Be quiet now. Relax. Let yourself fall asleep."

Yes, I must sleep, he thought. There's nothing to fear. I'll sleep, then wake, and everything will be all right. I know it. I know it. Then why do I still feel afraid?

He awoke in his chair. It was night, and the time had come. He moved outside into the garden and sat on the bench. Around him were the thick, shadowy forms of trees and bushes, and above him the lattice silhouette of branches against a blue-black sky. The breeze was cool, the pistol cold in his hand. There were to be no complex reflections. He had thought and written about this moment for months. It was time now to act.

As he put the pistol to his head he began to cry, as he'd written he would, because he had known he would. There was no question of changing the ending. Looking back, he felt that his life had followed an inevitable course, ending here, and he could not imagine its having been any different, or its going on any longer. But it had been a failure, and he wept for the disappointment of it.

He felt a rush of terror. He closed his eyes and seemed to see a sunlit room. Don't fight it so, my friend, he thought. Don't be so afraid. In a moment, all the pain and the fear will be over. Yours and mine.

"No, don't, please don't," he cried, but there was no sound. His eyelids felt as heavy as stone, and he struggled to lift them. Before him were the familiar objects of his living room, bright with the sunlight that filtered through the white drapes. He felt as he had as a child in moments before sleep—paralyzed, fighting to make his body move. He wanted to get up and find Mary, or to cry out, but he could not. He caught a glimpse of darkness, felt a breeze on his face, and fought from inside to reopen his closing eyes. Help me, Mary, he thought, please help me. I don't want it to end like this. Suddenly, his mind seemed to explode with pain and brilliant colors, and he knew that in another moment he would be dead.

Even a Solipsist Gets Lonely

MY FRIENDS, FOLLOWING A TIME-HONORED MAXIM, CONSIDER IT wise to exclude religion from conversation. But sometimes things slip out. I remember the furor at a party last year when Ted Smith, a local pediatrician, mentioned that he was an agnostic. Arthur Bennett, who owns a loan company and is considered one of the pillars of the Twin Oaks Baptist Church, was livid.

"Are you trying to tell me that *my* God, whom I have known personally for years, whom I consider to be my best friend and my business partner, to whom I have given ten percent of my income after taxes for almost ten years, *may not exist?*"

Someone wondered whether an agnostic could be morally reliable, and soon there were nasty innuendos to the effect that an agnostic pediatrician could not be trusted to touch one's children. My wife, Shirley, who is generally good-hearted, stuck up for Ted. She said his work at the Free Clinic was proof of his moral character. But the party seemed more impressed by further testimony to the effect that Ted played an honest game of tennis and gave special prices to his friends for their medical work. Soon the party mood was restored, but the incident hasn't been forgotten. People still whisper behind Ted's back, and I understand that his practice has suffered somewhat. I know that Arthur and his wife, Betty, now take their children to a Baptist pediatrician.

But all that was nothing compared to the uproar that followed my own "confession" several weeks later. Why I made it, particularly with the example of Ted in my mind, I don't know. It was late in the evening, I was tired and more than a little drunk. Arthur provoked me, first by holding forth on his religion and then by asking me about my own beliefs. Still, that does not excuse my not keeping quiet. I told him that I was a solipsist.

"What on earth is that? One of those Eastern religions?"

I explained that a solipsist is one who doubts the existence of everything but his or her own mind and mental images.

"Good Lord!" said Arthur, nearly spilling his scotch and water.

Americans tend to be philosophical innocents. Far from knowing that solipsism is a quite respectable philosophical position, no one at the party had even heard of solipsism. I am not a professional philosopher. But I had taken a few philosophy courses in college, and I had tried to formulate my own philosophical position. Solipsism seemed reasonable to me then, and it still does.

The argument for solipsism is quite simple, really. If there is a world outside one's own mind, it is a world of other minds and physical objects. But one does not perceive other minds—the thoughts, dreams, and feelings of others. How, then, can one possibly know that they exist? As for physical things, like furniture, sunlight, or human bodies, of course one *seems* to see them. But one knows from dreams that one's mind is capable of producing the appearance of physical objects that do not exist. Perhaps all that one has every perceived has been simply the invention of one's mind. Perhaps all that exists is one's own mind and mental images. One cannot prove that this is, or is not, so. There is just no way of knowing. I went through all this for Arthur, but he didn't seem to be paying much attention to the argument.

"Are you trying to tell me that I, Arthur Bennett, whom I have known . . . uh . . . *intimately,* you might say, for forty-seven years . . . that I . . . *may not exist?*"

"In a manner of speaking."

It was only much later that Arthur noted that a solipsist, unless he thinks he's God, which I certainly do not, must be an agnostic. Meanwhile, Arthur seemed to be much more agitated by the doubting of his own existence than he had been by the doubting of God's during the conversation with Ted Smith.

"That is the most ridiculous position I have ever heard. And I want to tell you, Bill: I take it as a *personal* insult!"

The conversation with Arthur had started in a corner of the room, away from the rest of the party, but it now began to attract attention. As the others gathered around us, Arthur reiterated my position.

"Is this some kind of perverse joke?" asked Ted Smith.

I must admit that I was more than a little annoyed. During the uproar over Ted's agnosticism, my wife and I had stuck up for him, and I expected some tolerance in return. Instead, it seemed that he was more than willing to make me the outsider so that he could slip back into the crowd.

"It's no joke," I insisted.

Gordon Wilson, an attorney, waved his hand for attention.

"Now let me get this straight. You are saying that, according to your religion, none of us exists?"

"I wouldn't call it a religion. It's a philosophy. And I'm not saying categorically that you *don't* exist. I'm saying I'm *not sure* you do."

"Then why are you talking with us if you're not sure we exist?"

The group applauded that comeback, and I was tempted, in the interest of friendship, to let it pass. But the smiles were too smug, especially Gordon's. I had always been annoyed by his absurd conceit that a lawyer's mind works differently from—and, by implication, better than—anyone else's. I wasn't willing to let him get away with such a cheap shot. I had my pride, after all.

I told them, in what I thought was a very pleasant tone, that I talked with them because I enjoyed their company. But my talking with them proved nothing about their real existence. After all, I also talked with the figures in my dreams.

Gordon persisted: "Hold it right there. First you say we're not real. Then you say we're not dreams. You seem to be contradicting yourself all over the place."

I told them that there was no contradiction, but perhaps I owed them some clarification. I knew I had two kinds of experiences. One kind was hazy and tended to change radically from one episode to another. The other kind was more vivid and tended to have a much greater consistency from episode to episode. For convenience, I labeled the hazy experiences "dreams" and the vivid experiences "reality." But for all I knew, "reality" was just an invention of my mind and had no existence apart from it. In that sense, it was possible that all "reality" was also a dream.

"I kind of like the idea," said Sally Wilson, as she moved forward with a little dance step, oblivious to the drops spilling from her martini glass to the rug. "Of course, you're not the first man who's said I'm a dream."

"I'm sure I'm not," I said, laughing, hoping that this might change the mood.

"But if you're really dreaming me up, could you take a little off the hips and waist? And add some to the bust?"

"Sally!"

"Oh, Gordon, don't be such a prude. Life is but a dream, doodle-ee, doodle-ee, do. . . ."

"I'm sorry, Sally," I said, watching her dance away. "I don't have much control over what happens in my dreams. Obviously."

"Well, I do," said Arthur Bennett, "and I'm getting out of them. Come on, Betty, we're going."

"Just a minute, Arthur," she said, "I'm sure we can get this all straightened out."

"Well why should he exist when I don't? What makes him so goddamn special?"

I tried to explain to Arthur that I made no pretense of knowing *why* I existed. As for how I knew that I existed, well, Descartes—actually Augustine—had taken care of that one long ago. The very act of doubting my existence proved it. I doubt, I think, therefore I am.

"All right, then," said Gordon Wilson, taking over once again. "I think we can all get together on this one now. You think, therefore you exist. Right? Well, I think, therefore I exist. That makes two of us. And I believe we can go right around the room, and you'll find that all your friends exist. Isn't that right, gang?"

"Right."

"True enough."

"Count me in."

I was touched by this display of camaraderie, but there was no stopping me now. I told them that if they really did think, then, of course, each knew that my mind could not be the only one that existed. But there was no way that I could know that they thought. I had direct access only to my own mind.

"Then you persist in your claim that only you exist?"

"My claim that *perhaps* only I exist."

Terri Smith spoke up: "But surely you make an exception in Shirley's case."

"No."

"Your own wife! You're saying that she doesn't exist?"

"Of course she exists as an image in my mind. And I love her dearly. But I'm not sure she *really* exists."

"Shirley! Are you going to stand for that?"

Shirley looked at me, then looked at Terri and Ted Smith, Sally and Gordon Wilson, Betty and Arthur Bennett. She seemed distressed by all the commotion, and more than a little embarrassed. But, bless her, she came up to me and put her arm around me.

"He has the right to his beliefs. And he's always been a good husband and father."

"What about your beliefs?"

"He's always respected them."

"But he says you don't have any! He says you don't exist!"

Shirley just shrugged, but Terri was disgusted: "I've met male chauvinists before, but this is ridiculous."

"Now, now," said Betty Bennett. "Let's keep politics out of this. Look, Bill. We've known each other for years, right? I'm telling you: I think. I'll prove it to you. Go ahead. Ask me some questions. Any questions. Just don't make them too hard."

"Betty, that's beside the point. Dream figures can answer questions."

"But I'll tell you something you don't know. Let me see . . . uh . . . uh . . . the Mitchells' kid demolished their car."

"Wow!" said Sally Wilson.

"Betty, my subconscious mind can surprise my conscious mind. It does so in dreams all the time. That you can tell me something of which I'm not consciously aware doesn't prove . . ."

"Never mind that crap," said Sally. "Tell me about the Mitchells' kid."

"Bill, I exist. Won't you just take my word for it?"

"Was anyone hurt?"

"I wish I could tell you, Betty, I really do."

"Is their insurance going to be cancelled?" asked Sally.

"Bill, you don't want to call me a liar, do you?"

"You calling my wife a liar?" said Arthur.

"No, I'm not." I said. "Betty, dream figures don't lie. Words don't make a lie without a mind behind them."

"Don't you dare say those things to my wife," said Arthur. "How would you like a punch in the nose? You'll see that I'm real enough then."

"I told the Mitchells: 'It's risky to let that kid take the car out.' But do you think they'd pay any attention to me? They're. . . ."

"Don't swing at me, Arthur. I do get attacked in dreams. But I also defend myself."

Well, it did stop short of violence, but not short of complete antagonism. It has been three months now, and none of the group has extended invitations to us or responded to ours. It's been particularly hard on Shirley. She's always had lots of friends, and she's always enjoyed parties so much. Her mood has turned sour, and things have been rough at home. The other day I tried to cheer her up and she just snapped at me.

"What do you care?" she said. "Only you exist. You don't need other people, right?"

But she's very wrong. I regret all this almost as much as she does. Hell, even a solipsist gets lonely.

Questions

1. In "The Nirvana Tape," the narrator admits that he does not have firsthand knowledge of the experiences of his experimental patients. However, he claims to have strong indirect evidence of the experiences they are having. What is this evidence? What is the reasoning of the narrator here? You might want to answer this question in two steps:

    a. On what evidence does the narrator rely in determining the experiences had by patients who are awake?

    b. On what evidence does the narrator rely in determining the experiences had by patients who are not awake?

2. Presumably, you believe that you often know what others are thinking and feeling. How do you know this? What is your reasoning on this matter? How does it compare to the reasoning of the narrator in "The Nirvana Tape"?
3. Consider the following supposition: "Other human beings have bodies and brains like mine; they act and speak as I do. But none of them has thoughts, images, or feelings. They do not have minds. Only I have a mind." Can you show that this supposition is probably false? Have you already done so in answering the previous question? Explain.
4. When patients in "The Nirvana Tape" are being programmed with a fantasy tape, they believe they are experiencing the real world. Is there some way that the patients could find out that what they are experiencing is illusion? Can you know that what you are now experiencing is not a programmed illusion? If so, how? If not, why not?

In considering questions 5 to 8 below, on "The Death of the Man in the Dream," adopt the following perspective: One mind is having two different sets of first-person experiences. In one set of experiences, the mind seems to be that of a young man who has had dreams in which he seemed to be older. In another set of experiences, the mind seems to be that of an older man who has had dreams in which he seemed to be younger.

5. Do you have an opinion as to whether the mind in the story is that of a young man or that of an older man? If so, what is your opinion and your reasoning? Do you feel quite certain about your conclusion?
6. At no point in the story does the person doubt that he is who he seems to be at that moment. But suppose the question of his identity bothered him (as it might have bothered the reader)? Is there some test he could have performed that would have proved which was his real life and which was his dream life?
7. Would one of the two women in the story be in a position to know which life was the real one and which was the dream life? If so, couldn't the man find out which life was real by asking that woman?
8. On what basis do you distinguish your real life from your dream life?

9. Suppose it was suggested that your waking life was as illusory as your dream life. This possibility is suggested by the Descartes Tape in "The Nirvana Tape" and is stated by the narrator in "Even a Solipsist Gets Lonely." How would you show this supposition to be false? What arguments could you present against it?

10. The narrator in "Solipsist" feels certain that his own mind exists. Identify with him for a moment and ask yourself: Could he be wrong about this? Are there good reasons for his believing in his own mind? (This, of course, is another way of asking whether you could be wrong in your belief that your mind exists.)

11. a. What is solipsism?

    b. Suppose that one of the party-goers knew that his or her own mind existed. Would he or she therefore know that solipsism is false?

12. Review the attempts by the party-goers to prove to the narrator that his is not the only mind that exists. Are any of these arguments cogent? If so, which ones?

13. "This chair in which I am sitting can't be a dream. If it were a dream, it wouldn't hold up my body." Is there anything faulty about this argument?

14. "The world I perceive can't be merely an invention of my mind. If it were, then I could change the whole world through nothing more than an act of will power." Is this a cogent argument? How might the narrator in "Solipsist" reply to this argument?

Discussion

Common-sense beliefs

Presumably, you believe in the existence of the following:

1. Other minds
2. Physical objects
3. Your own mind

To believe in the existence of a mind is, at a minimum, to believe that there exists a collection of thoughts, images, emotions, and sensations. To believe in the existence of a physical object is to believe in the existence of some such thing as a tree, a hand, a river, a flash of lightning, or a molecule *and* to believe that such a thing would or could continue to exist if all minds ceased to exist. (In other words, dreams or desires could not exist in the absence of the mind: such things, then, are mental.)

Presumably, you would not say just that you *believe* there exist other minds, physical objects, and your own mind, but that you *know* such things exist. That is, you have very good reasons for (strong evidence in support of) these beliefs. You are not simply taking the existence of these entities "on faith."

Very good reasons need not be absolutely conclusive reasons. In fact, we have absolutely conclusive reasons for few, if any, of our beliefs. For example, you believe that the floor beneath you will not collapse in the next few moments. You could give some reasons for this belief: the floor has held up for many years, and it is not sagging or cracking badly today. If you were sufficiently concerned, you could gather even more evidence. You could consult engineers about subtle signs of structural weakness in the building; you could consult seismologists about the possibility of an earthquake. But no matter how much evidence you gathered in support of your belief, there would always remain the possibility of error. (If nothing else, there is always the theoretical possibility that the so-called laws of nature might change.) The point here is not to get you glancing nervously at the floor; if you do have good reasons for believing that the floor will not collapse, then a feeling of assurance is justified. The point is, rather, that it would be unreasonable to insist that you present absolutely conclusive reasons for your beliefs. Good reasons are simply the best one can expect, and good reasons are not inadequate just because they are not perfect.

Do you have good reasons for believing in the existence of other minds, physical objects, and your own mind? What are these reasons? Admittedly, this question may seem baffling, and one may be tempted to ask: "What's the problem here? Isn't the existence of such things quite obvious?" So perhaps we should begin by asking whether such beliefs are at all problematic.

Instead of asking whether there are good reasons for believing, we might ask instead: Are there any grounds for doubting?

THE EXISTENCE OF OTHER MINDS

"The Nirvana Tape" raises questions about whether, and how, one can have knowledge of the mental states of others. The narrator in the story is quite confident that he knows what his patients are experiencing, and he states his reasoning on this matter. The story, of course, supposes that, in at least one instance, the narrator has made a ghastly mistake. Does the story thereby demonstrate that he has reasoned badly? The answer is no. At most, the supposition of a mistake indicates that the narrator does not have absolutely conclusive reasons for his belief, that there is a theoretical possibility that his reasoning could lead to error in some cases. But, as I noted above, good reasons need not be absolutely conclusive reasons, and it may be irrational to insist on absolutely conclusive reasons for any belief. One could write a story about a group of engineers who conduct extensive tests and then announce that the floor is structurally sound—just as the floor collapses beneath them. This would hardly demonstrate that no one can ever have good reasons for believing that a particular floor is safe. One has reasoned well if one comes up with good reasons in support of a belief, reasons that show the belief to be probably true.

What is the reasoning of the narrator in "Nirvana"? He admits that he has no firsthand knowledge of the mental states of others. Rather, he relies on indirect evidence. Apparently he takes it for granted that behavior, particularly the speech behavior of the patients, when they are awake, is an accurate indicator of their mental states. He finds that the patients' verbal reports can be correlated with particular kinds of brain processes. The narrator concludes that these brain processes are accurate indicators of mental states. Consequently, when patients are asleep, the narrator judges their mental states in terms of their brain processes.

Is the narrator reasoning well? It seems to me that if we grant speech to be a generally accurate indicator of mental states, then he is reasoning well. Perhaps he is a bit overconfident. Perhaps he has not carried out enough experiments in the precise correlations between verbal reports and brain states to justify great confidence in his inferences of particular mental states from particular brain states. The story is not clear on this point, but at least the general line of reasoning seems good to me.

But what about the narrator's assumption—which most of us share—that the speech of other people indicates that they are having mental experiences and indicates what these experiences are?

Consider the following supposition: "Other human beings have bodies and brains like mine; they act and speak as I do. But none of them has thoughts, feelings, or images. They do not have minds. Only I have a mind." It should be noted that this supposition does not imply that others are *lying* to me when they say such things as, "I am in pain," "I remember when I lived in New York," or "I know that two plus three equals five." As is noted by the narrator in "Even a Solipsist Gets Lonely," words would not constitute a lie without a mind behind them. A robot programmed to say such things could not be accused of lying. What is supposed here is that other people are analogous to robots in the sense that they do not have "mental states."*

It seems we can make sense of this supposition and that we can *imagine* its being true. Nonetheless, most of us feel certain that it is not true, that there are other minds. On what basis do we believe that other minds exist?

One would not say, "I believe in other minds because I perceive them." Almost everyone would agree that no one has perceived another's mind. No one has (literally) experienced another's thoughts, dreams, or joys. Rather, we might be inclined to claim that we do have strong indirect evidence for the existence of other minds. One might argue as follows: "I have a mind, and I

---

* In the story "Strange Behavior" in Chapter 1, and in the subsequent discussion, it is assumed that speech is ultimately an accurate indicator of the existence and nature of mental states. Given that assumption, one concludes that the Earth people have minds and that both the Gammas and their robots do not. But question that assumption, as we are doing here, and other possibilities emerge. Perhaps the Earth people talk as if they had private mental images, although they do not. Perhaps the Gammas and their robots talk as if they did not have private mental images, but they actually do.

exhibit certain kinds of complex physical behavior (including speech). Other creatures who look very much like me exhibit very similar physical behavior. Therefore, (it is very probable that) those other creatures also have minds."

At first glance, this argument may seem quite satisfactory. Upon closer examination, however, it seems to be quite weak. The argument claims that, because behavior and mind are associated in *one* case (my own), it is very probable that behavior and mind are associated in millions of other cases. But this would be analogous to a Gallup poll election prediction based on a "survey" of one voter. It would also be analogous to a lifelong prison inmate's argument that, because he lives in a small cell with gray walls, everyone lives in a small cell with gray walls. (Like the prisoner, apparently, one can experience only one's own situation or mind.)

One can imagine that there are no minds but one's own. We have considered one argument that purports to demonstrate that there probably are other minds, an argument that seems to be quite weak. This should be sufficient to show that one must produce good reasons to support one's claim of knowing there are other minds.

THE EXISTENCE OF PHYSICAL OBJECTS

Are there analogous problems concerning the belief in the existence of physical objects? In contrast with the belief in other minds, many people would be inclined to say, "I believe in physical objects because I see them." Perhaps the stories in this chapter would prompt you immediately to qualify this statement yourself: "At least, I *seem* to see them."

One way to raise questions about the belief in physical objects is to consider dreams. In dreams, one seems to see physical objects, but such physical objects do not exist, or do not exist as one seems to perceive them at that moment. What one perceives in dreams is illusory; the experience is invented by one's (subconscious) mind. At a minimum, to justify the belief that the things one now perceives are, or represent, real physical objects, one would have to justify the claim that one is not now dreaming.

A hypothetical problem concerning the distinction between

dream and reality is suggested by the story "The Death of the Man in the Dream." No doubt there are various perspectives one might take on this story. One might imagine that there are two real people, living in different places, each having vivid dreams that coincide with the real life of the other. Or, one might imagine that the story, in the manner of time warps in science fiction, presents two different but simultaneously existing time periods in one life, with the younger self living in one time period and the older self living in the other. But, for the sake of discussion, let us assume that the events in the story take place within a short span of time and in one locale. One mind is having two different sets of experiences in alternating episodes. In one set of experiences, the mind seems to be that of a suicidal young man who has had dreams in which he seemed to be an older man. In the other set of experiences, the mind seems to be that of a frightened older man who has had dreams in which he seemed to be a younger man.

Considering the story from that perspective, can one reasonably decide which is "the man in the dream"? That is, can one determine whether the mind having the various experiences is really that of the younger man or that of the older man? Can one determine which of the two sets of experiences is "real" and which one "illusory"?

It seems to me that the story gives no clear indication as to which is "the man in the dream." Each set of experiences is equally vivid and consistent from episode to spisode. There are equally reasonable explanations for why the younger man might dream that he is the older man, or the older man dream that he is the younger man. There is a "slip" when the person, as the younger man, says, "Goodbye, Mary." But there is a comparable slip when the person, as the older man, says, "I won't be seeing her again," referring to Stacy. It is pointed out that such slips would be quite natural in any case: "After all, it is your dream." At the end of the story, one might imagine that the younger man is dying by suicide or that the older man is dying of a stroke brought on by exhaustion and panic. The last episode of the story is the experience of the older man. But one might imagine that it is either a last glimpse of reality or a last fragment of dream.

At no point in the story does the person doubt the reality of what he experiences at that moment or the identity he seems to have at that moment. But suppose the person in the story were bothered by questions about which was dream and which was reality, or about what his real identity was. Is there some test that he could have performed that would have definitely answered these questions? It doesn't seem so. The problem of deciding whether some supposed test was reliable would be equivalent to the problem of distinguishing dream from reality. He might ask, "Mary, am I dreaming all this?" and get the answer, "No." But this "response" could not count as good evidence unless he already had evidence that Mary was not merely part of a dream—and that is equivalent to his general problem. In any case, the question, "Stacy, am I dreaming all this?" would evoke, presumably, just as emphatic a negative.

Perhaps, imaginatively modifying the story, you might come up with tests that the person in the story might have tried. For instance, as the younger man, the person might note precisely what is happening at the end and beginning of every episode of the older-man experiences and then check for discrepancies. He might try to provoke discrepancies by falling asleep at odd times. But there is no guarantee that such tests would be conclusive. Presumably you, as creator, could be just as imaginative in foiling these tests as in inventing them. If the younger man kept falling asleep at odd times, you might have the older man recovering from a "fainting spell" in each subsequent episode.

What does a consideration of "The Death of the Man in the Dream" indicate about deams and reality? You might argue that, far from demonstrating that there is a real problem concerning the distinction between dreams and reality, a consideration of the story emphasizes that there is none. Of course, *if* our experiences were like those in the story, we would not be able to distinguish dreams from reality. So what? Our experiences are not like that—as the story emphasizes by contrast. Similarly, one could imagine a world so chaotic that no one could have reasonable expectations about what would happen next. However, that wouldn't show that we cannot have reasonable expectations in our world. If anything, it would underscore the fact that we can.

How, then, do we distinguish dreams from reality? In both

dreams and waking life, we seem to see, hear, touch, taste, and smell things. But in dreams, perhaps, those sensory impressions are not as vivid and persistent as in waking life. More strikingly, the experiences of waking life are more consistent from episode to episode. In a series of dream episodes, one may be able to fly, then be unable to walk, then be able to walk but not be able to fly, and so forth. In a series of waking experiences, one's abilities to act are more fixed. In waking life, impressions of a burning building are followed by a familiar set of long-term impressions that continue through subsequent episodes: fire engines, smoking ashes, cold ashes, clearing away debris, rebuilding. Such need not be the case when one merely dreams that a building is burning.

Does this analysis of dreams and waking experiences resolve the issue? Let us recall the initial problem: Can the belief in physical objects be justified? The possibility was suggested that we might simply be dreaming what we seem to see. It has been claimed above that in most cases, or over the long run, we can quite easily distinguish dreams from reality. Dreams can be distinguished from waking life by their relative haziness and relative inconsistency from episode to episode.

However, consider two meanings of the word "dream":

1. "Dreams are experiences that are hazy and relatively inconsistent."
2. "Dreams are experiences that are purely mental and do not represent things existing outside the mind."

Perhaps the preceding common-sense view of waking and dreaming indicates that there is no serious problem about determining when we are dreaming in the first sense. But is this sufficient to show that we are not always dreaming in the second sense? Is this sufficient to show that we do perceive physical objects, whether directly or indirectly?

Consider "The Nirvana Tape" again. The subjects who are programmed with the fantasy tapes believe that what they are experiencing is reality. Presumably, the experiences with which they are programmed are vivid and consistent from episode to episode. One tape, the Descartes Tape, even gives the impression of dreaming, then the impression of waking. Does a consideration of the story cast doubt on the validity of inferring real physical objects from vivid experiences? You might argue that this indicates only that mistakes are possible over the short run. We can be deceived by vivid dreams, by dreams in which we seem to wake. The experimental subjects in "The Nirvana Tape" are deceived during a brief period at the end of their lives. But, after all, the supposition is not that they have been deceived all their lives.

Of course, we could imaginatively extend the duration of illusion by borrowing the brain-in-the-box idea from science fiction. Imagine a future society that removes the brains of malformed infants, places each one in a special box with a nutritive solution, and programs it with a lifetime fantasy. Presumably, such a being need have no idea that what it is experiencing is not reality. Still, even here, it is supposed that physical objects do exist, even if the being does not perceive them.

The narrator in "Even a Solipsist Gets Lonely" considers the supposition that perhaps his so-called real life is just as illusory as his dream life: "I knew I had two kinds of experiences. One kind was hazy and tended to change radically from one episode to another. The other kind was more vivid and tended to have a much greater consistency from episode to episode. For convenience, I labeled the hazy experiences 'dreams' and the vivid experiences 'reality.' But for all I knew, 'reality' was just an invention of my mind and had no existence apart from it. In that sense, it was possible that all 'reality' was also a dream."

The supposition suggested by "Solipsist" is more radical than that suggested by "Man in the Dream" or "Nirvana." This supposition goes as follows: perhaps the only thing that exists is one's own mind and mental images. There are no other minds, there are no physical objects at all. Everything one experiences, both in waking life and in dreams, is the invention of one's mind. There is nothing at all outside one's mind.

Can one disprove this supposition? Here are a number of objections that people are inclined to offer. As the replies indicate, these objections do not seem to have much force.

How could I perceive images if there were no objects? *Reply:* Your mind could invent them, as in dreams.

How can this chair hold me if it is only an imaginary chair?

Reply: What is sitting on the chair might be an imaginary body, and, as we know from dreams, imaginary chairs are quite adequate to support imaginary bodies.

If everything I perceive is imaginary, why can't I create a more pleasant world through acts of will? *Reply:* To say that the world consists of mental images is not to say that these images are within your conscious control. You can't control your dreams, but you don't therefore deny that dreams are mental.

It seems we can *imagine* that there might be no physical objects. We have just considered a few arguments on behalf of the existence of physical objects, arguments that seem to be weak. This should be sufficient to show that one must produce good reasons to support one's claim of knowing there are physical objects.*

What we have been focusing on thus far is the *problem of the external world:* can one prove the existence of other minds and physical objects (entities external to one's own mind)?

My existence

Is there a comparable *problem of the internal world?* That is, is there a problem in justifying the belief in one's own mind? The narrator in "Solipsist" thinks not:

"As for how I knew that I existed, well, Descartes—actually Augustine—had taken care of that one long ago. The very act of doubting my existence proved it. I doubt, I think, therefore I am."

Descartes was a seventeenth-century French philosopher who subjected his basic beliefs to the kind of critical scrutiny in which we have been engaged here. Initially, he decided that there were serious grounds for doubting his belief in physical objects and other minds. But Descartes thought there were no serious grounds for doubting his own existence; he could be absolutely certain that he existed. He said: "I think, therefore I

* Note that this problem casts further doubt on the earlier argument for the existence of other minds. That argument supposes that there are physical human bodies that exhibit behavior similar to my physical behavior. But now the mere existence of all human bodies, including my own, has been questioned.

am" or, in Latin, "Cogito ergo sum"; the claim is often referred to as the "cogito." (A similar claim can be found in the fifth-century writings of Saint Augustine.)

This traditional, shorthand formulation of the "cogito" seems to indicate that Descartes was presenting an argument with "I think" as premise and "I exist" as conclusion. In fact, what Descartes argued was that one cannot be in error about one's existence as a thinking being, one's existence as a mind. Descartes noticed that one's belief in one's own mind seemed to be immune to the sorts of challenges or doubts that infect one's other beliefs. "Perhaps I am mistaken in thinking that others think." "Perhaps I am mistaken in thinking that physical objects really exist." "Perhaps I am mistaken in thinking that I think." In the third statement, and the third statement only, the conclusion is reaffirmed in the doubting. The very act of doubting my existence proves it.

The "cogito" can be applied to more specific first-person statements, and a consideration of such statements helps clarify the nature of the "cogito." "I seem to see a chair" appears to be an indubitable statement. One cannot be wrong about seeming-to-see, as opposed to seeing, and seeming-to-see is an experience, a mental state. "I am distressed" appears to be an indubitable statement. My seeming-to-be-distressed is necessarily a kind of distress, and distress is a mental state. All statements about my present mental states would seem to be indubitable.

Descartes's "cogito" seems to me to be correct if it is properly restricted in scope, but one should be clear about these restrictions.

Descartes's "cogito" is not a proof to each of us that Descartes existed. To each of us, Descartes is another mind. Your "cogito" could not be a proof to me that you exist, and vice versa. The narrator in "Solipsist" is properly scornful when his friends try to prove to him their existence by pronouncing the words of the "cogito": "I told them that if they really did think, then, of course, each knew that my mind could not be the only one that existed. But there was no way that I could know that they thought. I had direct access only to my own mind."

My "cogito" does not prove that I have a particular body or, indeed, any body at all. The body is a physical object, and the existence of physical objects is in question at this point. The "cogito" does not prove that I have a particular past or, in fact, any past at all; that I think does not guarantee the reliability of my memory impressions. Insofar as my proper name, Tom Davis, is linked with a particular physical or mental past, my "cogito" does not prove that Tom Davis exists. Perhaps I am Descartes, Napoleon, or Norman Mailer, and I am merely hallucinating that I am Tom Davis. What the "cogito" does guarantee is that there now exist certain thoughts, images, and sensations that I may define as "my mind."

Given the appearance of what is happening in "Man in the Dream," is it conceivable that nothing whatsoever exists? It would seem not. A set of appearances, experiences exists. In view of the "cogito," it seems certain that a mind exists. The character in the story could legitimately conclude that he exists as a mind. The question of his existence as a thinking being could be decided apart from the question of which identity, if either, is his, and the question of which set of experiences, if either, is nonillusory. Similarly, the experimental subject in "The Nirvana Tape" could be certain that he exists as a thinking being—whether or not his experiences are completely illusory.

Confronting the solipsist

Granting that one can prove the existence of one's own mind, can one prove the existence of physical objects and other minds? Some philosophers say no.

The solipsist, as portrayed in the story and as I shall define him here, is a kind of skeptic. He accepts Descartes's "cogito" but claims that one cannot solve the problem of the external world. He says: With the exception of the belief in one's own mind, one cannot justify any beliefs about the world. There are no better reasons to believe that there are physical objects and other minds than to believe that there are not.

To reiterate and amplify the solipsist's argument: It is theoretically possible that everything one has ever experienced has been a total invention of one's mind (as in dreams). Since one can judge things only according to one's experience, and since one cannot get "outside" one's experience to determine its source, one cannot know whether the experience reflects an external world or whether it is merely an invention of one's mind. One cannot show that an external world is more likely to exist than not to exist.

The problem of the external world is a difficult one, and the argument of the solipsist is forceful. Can we satisfactorily answer the solipsist? Can we formulate an argument that shows that the existence of an external world of physical objects and other minds is more likely than its absence?*

Perhaps one general consideration that sways us toward a belief in the external world is the stark contrast between the relative poverty of those thoughts obviously created by one's mind and the richness of those experiences that seem to be imposed upon one. When I intentionally produce a mental image, it tends to be hazy and simple, and its content tends to be exhausted at a glance. But much of the experience that seems to come from outside is complex, endlessly explorable, and full of surprises. A similar contrast exists between the ideas that are obviously mine and those that seem to come from others. Through apparent conversations with others, I gain knowledge that I was not conscious of possessing before. Many of those ideas that seem to come from elsewhere are barely comprehensible to me (for example, Einstein's theory of relativity, Russell's *Principia Mathematica,* Joyce's *Ulysses*). It seems absurd to suppose that all these ideas are really just products of my own mind.

Of course, the solipsist does not suggest that this complexity emanates from the *conscious* mind. He suggests that it is produced by the *unconscious* mind. But if all one's experiences are

---

* Descartes is of no further help to us. He did offer a proof of an external world, but it is not satisfactory. The argument Descartes presented was sketched in the remarks on the Descartes Tape in "The Nirvana Tape." First Descartes presented the "ontological argument" for the existence of a perfect God. Then he went on to argue that a perfect God would not deceive him by presenting him with appearances that were all illusory. Thus, Descartes's experiences must represent an external world. As is explained in Chapter 3, the ontological argument is fallacious. With it the rest of Descartes's argument collapses.

rooted in the unconscious mind, then it seems that the unconscious mind would have to be as complex as the kind of universe we tend to believe exists. First imagine a world composed of your mind, physical objects, and other minds. Now imagine a world containing your conscious mind and your unconscious mind, capable of presenting appearances of an enormously complex physical world and capable of producing all the sophisticated ideas of literature, science, philosophy, and mathematics. Are these two suppositions clearly different? My suspicion is that they may not be substantially different. Perhaps it merely seems as if two different worlds are being described, whereas what we have are two descriptions of the same world, using different terminology.

Perhaps, however, the idea of disproving the solipsist argument is misconceived; perhaps the solipsist asks too much in asking that we prove an external world. Note that if no statements are accepted without proof, it will be impossible to prove anything. For example, consider any statement and call it A. If that statement is not acceptable without proof, then we shall have to form an argument in which A is the conclusion and another statement (or statements) B is the premise. This will show that A is true if B is true, but what is the proof for B? Now we will need another argument in which C is the premise and B is the conclusion. This will show that A is true if B is true, and B is true if C is true. But what is the proof for C? Now we shall have to give an argument for C and so on, ad infinitum. Since this process of proof can never be completed, and A remains doubtful until the process is completed, we shall never prove A. If we are required to prove everything, then we can prove nothing.

Any theory must begin with axioms—statements accepted without "proof." In fact, this whole discussion has presupposed an unmentioned axiom: that our fundamental principles of reasoning are reliable—that any contradictory statement is false, that no statement can be both true and false, that certain forms of argument are such that the conclusion follows from the premises, and so forth. This general axiom has been presupposed by the "cogito," by the skeptical argument of the solipsist, and by the very attempt to engage in rational discussion.

Some skeptics, more extreme than the solipsist, have challenged the reliability of our principles of reasoning. They have demanded a proof of the reliability of these principles. Of course, this demand could not be met. Any supposed proof would simply assume its conclusion since, as proof, it would assume the principles of reasoning that have been questioned. What we have here is a choice: either we assume the reliability of our principles of reasoning and go on reasoning about various matters, or we do not assume this and we treat all statements as mere babble. Of course, we are assuming the reliability of these principles.

But is this axiom concerning the reliability of our principles of reasoning "mere assumption"? I am inclined to say emphatically no. These principles of reasoning seem to be "self-evident": one simply "sees" that they are correct.

A second general axiom has been presupposed in this discussion: that appearances do exist now (of a chair, of distress, and so on). One could not argue for this claim without simply assuming the conclusion: any purported proof would have to assume the existence of appearances. But are there rational grounds for doubting this statement? I would say no. The axiom that appearances do exist now seems to me "self-evident."

Employing these two axioms, we have considered and then accepted the "cogito." It seemed that one could not be in error in believing that one's own mind exists. Would it be correct to say that we advanced one step and then were halted by the problem of the external world? To say we "advanced one step" might be misleading. The "cogito" is not a proof of some additional entity not stated in the axioms. The "cogito" simply enabled us to use principles of reasoning to clarify the statement that there are now appearances. For example, we noted that the word "distress" indicates nothing more than a certain kind of appearance. The statement "I exist as a thinking being" is really equivalent to the statement, "There are thoughts" which is equivalent to the statement, "There are appearances."

In a sense, then, at the point at which we confront the problem of the external world, what we have claimed are two general axioms. The solipsist also accepts these axioms. He asks us for a proof of the existence of physical objects and other minds.

But, instead of attempting a proof, why not make the statement "There are physical objects and other minds" an axiom and claim that it is self-evident?

This possibility, though tempting, is troublesome. At what point should one stop claiming that statements are self-evident axioms and start offering proofs for them? Surely, there is some such point. Many of us would be inclined to scoff if someone claimed that the existence of a benign, omnipotent, omniscient God was self-evident. And we would howl in disbelief if someone claimed as self-evident the statement that there is life on exactly sixteen other planets. What guidelines should we use in determining which statements are self-evident and which are not?

What we might do is determine what essentially distinguishes our two general axioms from other beliefs that almost no one would be inclined to call self-evident. These characteristics could be used as tests to determine which other statements, if any, qualify as self-evident. It seems that our two general axioms share at least the following essential characteristics:

1. They are believed with the deepest conviction.*
2. No conceivable experiential evidence would count against them.
3. It seems unimaginable that they are false.

Clearly, the statement that there is an omnipotent, omniscient, benign God would be disqualified by the third and second characteristics, if not by the first. Even if one has a deep religious faith, one can *imagine* there not being such a God, even if one is sure there is such a God, just as one can imagine the floor collapsing, even if one is sure that it will not. One can imagine future experiential evidence that would count against the existence of such a God—for example, an afterlife encounter with

* There is the temptation to word this in terms of "universal conviction." But such wording would assume the existence of other minds at a point where their existence is in question. Note that the conversational "we" employed in this discussion of skepticism does not assume what is at issue since it can be taken as merely hypothetical. It would assume what is at issue only if it led to statements that could not be rephrased as first-person statements.

a being who is powerful but unable to accomplish a difficult task or with an omnipotent being who acts sadistically. Obviously, the statement that there is life on exactly sixteen other planets fails to pass any of these tests.

How does the problem of the external world fare when tested by these three conditions of self-evidence? Clearly, it satisfies the second condition. No experiential evidence would count against the statement that there are physical objects and other minds. It may satisfy the first condition. What is troubling here is the third condition. Can we imagine that there are no physical objects and other minds? Obviously, the impetus of our whole discussion has been toward a yes answer here. In attempting to show that there is a problem of the external world, I have argued that we can imagine there being no other minds, that we can imagine there being no physical objects. Thus, if we can imagine there being no external world, then a claim of self-evidence for the statement "There are physical objects and other minds" would seem to be weak.

On the other hand, I have suggested that, given the great complexity of one's experiences and the relative poverty of one's conscious imaginative abilities, it may be absurd to suppose that there is no external world of physical objects and other minds. I have suggested that once the claim "Only my mind exists" has been amplified and reconciled with the obvious complexities of experience and the limitations of the conscious mind, it may really be equivalent to the claim that there *are* physical objects and other minds. Perhaps what is unimaginable is that there are no physical objects and other minds, *given* these other conditions.

That one's experiences are enormously complex and that one's conscious imaginative abilities are relatively limited would seem to be self-evident. Perhaps rather than claiming self-evidence for the statement that there are physical objects and other minds, it would be more reasonable to claim self-evidence for some conditional statement that, in conjunction with the other self-evident statements mentioned above, would yield the conclusion that there are physical objects and other minds. How one ought to word this conditional statement would be a tricky and complex issue. But, of course, the general form of such a conditional statement would be something like this: If there are enormously complex experiences and a limited conscious mind, then there exist physical objects and other minds.

At this point, as at some point in any philosophical discussion, the questions are left for you to answer. Does solipsism seem to you the most reasonable position? Or does the claim that there are physical objects and other minds qualify as self-evident? Or can you offer a proof for this claim that seems satisfactory? If you think you can offer a proof, what are your fundamental premises? Do you claim that they are self-evident?

6. Logic

Philosophy Is Murder: A Nebuchadnezzar Hulk Mystery

I'VE PULLED PLENTY OF STUNTS ON NEBUCHADNEZZAR HULK OVER the years. You might say that's one of my jobs. Hulk is a genius, but he's as lazy and contrary as he is smart. Someone has to make sure that he keeps working. After all, Hulk is the sole support of a four-story house filled with hundreds of expensive orchids, a plant nurse who feeds the orchids, a French chef who feeds Hulk, and an assistant detective—me—who is no genius but is ingenious, particularly at pulling stunts that get Hulk working.

I must say I hesitated this time. To admit to Hulk's office, unannounced, a gaudily dressed six-foot blonde carrying a poodle, a night-club dancer wanting help for her underpaid philosophy-professor husband—that seemed to be going a bit far. But I decided Hulk needed a real shocker. A week before, with our bank balance well below six figures, Hulk had returned a $10,000 retainer because the twelve directors of the Granite Corporation had had the audacity to insist that he come to their offices rather than the other way around. I don't begrudge Hulk his idiosyncrasies, like never leaving the house on business and never missing his four hours a day in the plant rooms. But he's made exceptions to his rules in the past, and he should have made an exception for the Granite Corporation. Now I would let him know quite vividly what he could expect in the way of cases if he continued to be so stubborn.

Hulk was sitting at his desk, reading *Principia Mathematica*, when I ushered the dancer into the office.

"Sir, allow me to introduce Miss Gloria Lovely. That's

'L-O-V-E-L-Y.' Actually, that's her stage name. She is a night-club dancer currently working at the Starlight Lounge. She is married to Heinrich Bergmann, an existentialist who is suspected of murder, and she is here to engage your services on his behalf. I told her we didn't have a case at the moment, and you'd probably be happy to have the work."

Mrs. Bergmann couldn't have done better if I'd coached her. She shifted the poodle to her left arm, extended her right hand to the man who avoids shaking hands with anyone, and murmured:

"It's a pleasure to meet you, Mr. Hulk. Or may I call you Nebuchadnezzar?"

I thought for a moment Hulk's jaw was going to drop, but he managed to stop. He stared at Mrs. Bergmann for a moment, keeping his hands on his book, and then slowly lifted his seventh of a ton out of his chair.

"Madame. My assistant, Mr. Crocker, has been known to dabble in the inane before, but never in the occult. Allow me to say that you are a truly extraordinary creature. Now, if you will excuse me. Arnie, be sure this woman is not paid from office funds for her acting here today. As you are so cleverly reminding me, they are not up to the challenge."

He was halfway to the door when her fist struck the desk.

"Mr. Hulk!"

Hulk turned around, his eyebrows raised in surprise.

"Obviously, you and Mr. Crocker regard me as a joke," she went on angrily, "but this certified check for $5,000 is no joke. Nor is my husband's situation. He is in serious trouble and needs your help!"

"Indeed," said Hulk. "If this is a performance, Mrs. Bergmann, it is most certainly a commanding one. But don't you think the existentialist touch strains credulity?"

Her voice softened a bit now that she had his attention.

"My husband, Mr. Hulk, is a professor at Fountain College. His specialty is existentialism, and he has published several articles on Sartre's early work. He has maintained to his colleagues that his marrying me was Gide's *acte gratuit,* a gratuitous act demonstrating his complete freedom of choice. It is a conceit of his to which I don't object, since we have a good marriage in any case. My husband's interests in life are not purely intellectual. And it helps that I am not as devoid of intelligence as you seem to think I am. I have a degree in philosophy from Fountain, but no one hires female philosophy majors unless they minor in stenography. I happen to find what I do much more enjoyable, not to say lucrative, than secretarial work. It goes without saying that my tastes are not terribly conventional."

"You say that your husband is suspected of murder. Whose murder?"

"Professor William Lanchaster, chairman of the philosophy department at Fountain, was shot to death in his study at his home last Thursday evening."

Hulk looked at Mrs. Bergmann, then at me, then back at her. He nodded slightly and started back to his desk.

"Arnie, please find a place for that dog other than this office and the kitchen. Mrs. Bergmann, please take a seat. What may I offer you to drink?"

Obviously my joke had backfired, but it had us moving in the right direction. After all, the point had been to get Hulk working, and now he was working. We had a murder case, and we had a $5,000 retainer. So I was feeling rather pleased with myself as I returned to his office, without the poodle, and sat behind my desk. I reached for my notebook, signaling Hulk I was ready.

"Now then, Mrs. Bergmann," said Hulk, "suppose you tell me about the events related to the murder in what seems to you the most logical order."

Mrs. Bergmann took a sip of her drink and began:

"Fountain College, Mr. Hulk, has, or had, a five-person philosophy department: Heinrich Bergmann, my husband; William Lanchaster, the deceased, who taught logic; Herbert Lord, history of ancient philosophy; Beatrice Trilling, history of modern philosophy; and Reggie Stout, contemporary American and British philosophy.

"Fountain, like many small private colleges, is having financial difficulties, and the trustees have undertaken a considerable reduction of faculty positions. Every faculty member is theoretically vulnerable: Fountain is an experimental college and has never had a tenure or seniority system.

"A couple of months ago, the trustees affirmed Lanchaster's position and directed him to eliminate one member of the philosophy department. Since that time, there has been a great deal of nasty politicking among the philosophers. Eventually, Lord, Trilling, and Stout banded together to try to eliminate my husband. They have even gone so far as sending willing students to Lanchaster to complain about my husband. He's particularly vulnerable because he's an unorthodox personality, even for Fountain, and because existentialism is viewed with some contempt by most professional American philosophers.

"Professor Lanchaster was to announce his decision to the members of the department, individually, at his home, on Thursday evening. He asked Lord to come at 7:00, Stout at 7:30, my husband at 8:00, and Trilling at 8:30. This schedule has been confirmed by the departmental secretary.

"Lord says he arrived at 7:00 and left at 7:30. He claims that Lanchaster told him that he, Lord, would be retained and that my husband was to be fired. Of course, Lord maintains that Lanchaster was alive when he left. There was no one else in the house to confirm this or to tell of any arrivals or departures. Professor Lanchaster's children are grown, and his wife had been out of town for several weeks visiting a sick sister. The only other visitor that we know of was Lanchaster's niece, Lisa Williams, who stopped by the house at 7:25, with a friend, to pick up some books. Her friend, apparently, can confirm her presence at the library for the rest of the evening. When Lisa arrived, Lord answered the door at Professor Lanchaster's request, he says, and gave her a bundle of books that was on the table in the hallway.

"Stout says that he did not come to the house at 7:30. He arrived instead at 8:30 and found Beatrice Trilling outside the door. Stout has produced a typewritten note that he claims was put in his mailbox at the college that day asking him to come at 8:30 rather than 7:30. The note had apparently been typed on a departmental typewriter and was unsigned. Stout says he assumed that one of the secretaries had typed it at Lanchaster's direction.

"Stout and Trilling say that they rang the bell for several minutes and then entered the house. They say the door was slightly ajar. They found Lanchaster's body and called the police. After the police arrived, Trilling told them she had passed my husband in Lanchaster's neighborhood as she was going to her appointment.

"My husband, I regret to say, has acted stupidly. He now claims that he got back late from an out-of-town lecture, arrived at the Lanchaster house at 8:15, discovered the body, but left without reporting the murder. He has an elaborate rationale for leaving the scene, but the plain fact is that he panicked. When the police questioned him, he first denied being in the Lanchaster neighborhood, then denied being in the house, before telling the police what he now says is the truth.

"The police asked my husband how he thought he could get away with denying his presence at the house, since his appointment was part of a schedule known to the whole department. My husband said that he knew of no schedule. Apparently, Lanchaster did not make a point of telling each person that he was seeing the others. Stout, Trilling, and Lord knew about the schedule because they had talked with one another. My husband was not in on their conversations.

"Unfortunately, my husband's admission makes plausible the assumption that he went to Lanchaster's house with a gun, killed him, and then left, all with a reasonable expectation that no one would ever know he had done it.

"The police have not arrested my husband. They are obviously aware of the other possibilities. The medical examiner places the time of death between 7:45 and 8:15. Trilling or Lord could have faked the note to Stout and killed Lanchaster during Stout's appointment time. Or Stout could have kept his appointment and typed the note himself.

"But my husband is the prime suspect. The police are suggesting that Lanchaster might have typed the note to Stout and asked my husband to come at 7:30 so that they would have an hour to discuss my husband's dismissal. Lord says Lanchaster told him that my husband was to be fired, and Stout and Trilling say that they had hints of this.

"I don't like the situation at all. The police are obviously antagonistic toward my husband, as are the other professors in the department. And one of those others is the murderer. If some piece of planted evidence should show up—well, it would certainly be all over for my husband. I want you to clear him by finding the murderer for us."

Mrs. Bergmann had moved forward in her chair during this recital. Now she let out a breath and leaned back. After a pause, Hulk began to speak. He was scowling.

"I must admit, Madame, that I can't help sharing the negative attitude of the police. Whether or not we assume your husband is the killer, his ineptitude is amazing. Is he an utter idiot? This is a man has been employed to teach reason to the young. I find myself astounded."

Mrs. Bergmann stared at Hulk for a moment, and then, much to my surprise, she laughed.

"Mr. Hulk, you may have heard the story of how Thales, the Greek philosopher, fell into a ditch while gazing at the stars. My husband is like that. He can develop very impressive arguments concerning the existence of God, free will, and the nature of the unobservable world. But ask him which foot fits his left shoe, and he is lost. It is part of his charm for me, but I must admit that I'm less than charmed with him at the moment. However, I'm not asking you to like him. I'm asking you to prove him innocent."

"Are you so sure of his innocence?" said Hulk. "Obviously you don't have any evidence in his favor that the police will accept."

"True. But I know my husband. He is not a violent man. And, quite frankly, he wouldn't have the courage."

"Mrs. Bergmann, you should know that I do not shield murderers. I do not, in the end, hide evidence from the police. If I go after a murderer, I find him, and if it turns out to be your husband, the police shall know about it. Nor will I return your retainer. Are you sure you want to engage me on those terms?"

"I'm quite certain."

"Satisfactory. Tell me, what do the police know about the murder weapon?"

"Lanchaster did not own a gun, and none of the suspects is

known to have owned one. It seems that Lanchaster was shot with one of those handguns you can order by mail. As far as I know, the police have not found it."

"You said that the three other suspects disliked your husband. How did the deceased feel about him?"

"They weren't close, but I think Professor Lanchaster was quite fond of him. A case of opposites attracting, perhaps. Lanchaster was a very precise, proper person, but not dogmatic. I think he enjoyed my husband's flamboyance. Of course, there was no question of competition. My husband posed no threat to Lanchaster's position at the college."

"And Mrs. Lanchaster? How does she feel about you and your husband?"

"Mrs. Lanchaster has always been very kind to both my husband and me."

"Do you think you could persuade her to admit Mr. Crocker to the house?"

"To the house, yes. But I'm afraid questioning Mrs. Lanchaster would be unadvisable. The doctor has ordered her to rest. Lisa Williams, the niece, who is a friend of ours, is staying with her. She could show Mr. Crocker around. Professor Lanchaster was quite a fan of yours, as a matter of fact. He used some of your cases as exercises in his introductory classes. He referred to you as a fellow logician doing battle outside the ivory tower. That's how I happened to think of your name. Yes, I'm quite sure that Mrs. Lanchaster would admit a representative of you."

Hulk glanced at the clock and noticed that it was time to do battle in the plant rooms. He rose from his chair.

"Very well. Please arrange it, and call Mr. Crocker. If you will excuse me now, I have an appointment. But please stay a few more minutes. Mr. Crocker will need some more information from you."

Mrs. Bergmann arranged to have me visit the Lanchaster house the next afternoon. Before visiting the house, I made inquiries at police headquarters and at the philosophy department of Fountain College.

Inspector Shultz wasn't very philosophical about my visit. He loses any composure he has at the sound of Hulk's name or at the sight of me. I suppose I can't blame him. It never makes him look good when Hulk solves a case that Shultz can't. Shultz let me cool my heels for an hour outside his office before letting me know the only thing he was planning to show me was the door.

Professor Stout, who was now acting chairman of the department, showed me into his office immediately—once he realized I was questioning a secretary about a certain typewriter. He was soon joined by Professors Lord and Trilling. Stout looked like a radical from the sixties who had lost his causes but had managed to hang on to his faded jeans. Lord looked like the professors you see in cartoons: balding head, glasses, sport coat with patches on the sleeves, a slightly confused look on his face. Professor Trilling was a Bella Abzug look-alike: heavy-set, with a booming voice.

Even though you know it does no good, you never get out of the habit of looking into eyes, trying to find the guilt there. Stout looked cynical, Lord nervous, and Trilling ferocious, but no one looked guiltier than the others. I told them what I'd found, but, when it became apparent that they intended to ask all the questions, I left. One thing was clear to me: they were all happy to have Bergmann on the hot spot and weren't about to help him.

My next stop was the Lanchaster house. Lisa Williams opened the door seconds after my first ring. She was a nice-looking girl, about eighteen. She greeted me with a finger to her lips and signaled me to follow her to the study, which was at the back of the house. Once we were inside the room, she shut the door carefully.

"Betty—Mrs. Lanchaster—is sleeping. You are Mr. Crocker, aren't you?"

"That's right. I appreciate this."

"Gloria and Heinrich are my friends."

I looked around the study. It was mostly old mahogany and old books. There was a large desk on the far side of the room, facing the door, with a chair behind it, and two other chairs to the side and front of it.

"Your uncle was sitting in the desk chair when he was shot?"

"Yes. The police say he was shot by someone sitting in that other chair, there, in front of the desk."

I walked over to the desk and found the bullet hole in the padded back of the desk chair. I looked quickly at the papers and books scattered on the desk.

"Is the room the same as it was that evening? Did the police take anything?"

"As far as I know, everything is here."

I inspected the area around the desk and noticed that the cord of the desk phone had been torn from the wall. I held up the frayed cord.

"Was this done on the evening of the murder?"

"Yes. At least, this phone was working that afternoon when I called my uncle. I know he was on this line, because he was looking for the books I wanted while holding the phone."

"Those were the books you came by to get that evening? Why don't you tell me about that."

"There's nothing much to tell," she said. "I needed some books for a paper I'm writing. My uncle said he'd be busy and wouldn't be able to see me, but he would put the books on the hall table and leave the front door unlocked. When I rang the doorbell, Lord answered the door and handed me the books. Then I left. I was with a friend all evening at the library, as I told the police."

"Did Lord say anything when he gave you the books?"

"No. He just met me at the door with them and handed them to me before I could say a thing. He obviously knew I was coming for them."

"Did you think it strange that Lord should answer the door?"

"No. My uncle was lame and often asked people to do little things for him so that he wouldn't have to move around too much. And Lord was always anxious to please him."

"How did Lord seem to you?"

"The same as always."

I looked more closely at the items on the desk. There were some books on logic, including one written by Lanchaster, some journal reprints, a draft of a paper on some logical controversy, and notes on a logic exam he'd been preparing. I also went through the desk drawers. There was nothing among the papers that seemed to bear on the murder.

"I assume the police found nothing that indicated which professor was to be fired?"

"No."

"Professor Lanchaster didn't tell his wife?"

"No. The police asked her that."

"All right. Is there a working phone around here I can use? I'm supposed to call Hulk for instructions."

She took me to the kitchen, which was at the front of the house, and I dialed Hulk from there. Hulk didn't want a report on my entire day, just on what I had found in the house. That took only a few minutes.

"I'm heading back now, unless you want me to do something else here," I told him.

There was a long pause. "Photographs," he said finally. "I want photos of every paper, of all writing on or in that desk. When you are finished, take the film to Lew's shop. Tell Lew I want the photographs developed tonight. Offer him the usual bonus."

"Will do," I said, wondering what Hulk could be after.

They were all in place in the office by 4:00, when Hulk came down from the plant rooms: Stout, Lord, and Trilling seated together on Hulk's right, Lisa Williams in the center, Heinrich and Gloria Bergmann on Hulk's left, and Inspector Shultz and Sergeant Joe Kurz in the back row. I'd never seen an existentialist before, but had I imagined one, he would have looked just like Heinrich Bergmann. His long hair and beard, jeans, and shirt were all black. The only contrasts were the brown eyes and the nicotine-colored skin at the center of all that hair.

"All right, Hulk, they're all here," said Inspector Shultz. "They have been told that you have no official standing and that they are not legally obligated to answer any of your questions. However, we have asked for their cooperation. What do you have?"

"I don't have any questions," said Hulk. "What I have is something to show all of you. Arnie, if you please."

$D \supset B$
$D \supset (B \supset W)$
$B \supset (W \supset S) / \therefore D \supset S$

$M \equiv N / \therefore \sim N \vee M$

$\sim R \vee \sim S$
$A \supset (R \cdot S) / \therefore \sim A$

$A \supset B$
$C \supset D$
$(B \vee D) \supset E$
$\sim E / \therefore \sim (A \vee C)$

$\sim (M \cdot N)$
$(O \cdot T) \vee (M \cdot N)$
$(M \cdot N) \vee (R \cdot L)$
$O \supset (I \cdot D)$
$D \equiv S / \therefore$

Ont. Arg.

I gave each person in the room a copy of the photograph of a sheet of paper shown here.

"The reason I have no need to ask questions," said Hulk, "is that Professor Lanchaster has given us the answer we are looking for."

Puzzled exclamations burst out all over the room.

"What kind of nonsense is this?" said Shultz. "What is this picture?"

"This is a picture of a page from Professor Lanchaster's desk pad," said Hulk. "And it is not nonsense. Quite the opposite. Before he died, Lanchaster wrote on his desk pad all that we need to solve his murder."

Switching parodies, in mid-mystery, from Rex Stout to Ellery Queen, I interrupt the story to issue:

A CHALLENGE TO THE READER

You now have all the clues necessary to solve the mystery. A little deduction will indicate "whodunit." Some additional re-

flection should enable you to give a full explanation of the crime. (For instance, when and why was the phone torn out of the wall?) For those readers who have had no philosophy or logic, the following information should suffice:

The relevant logic problem is the one at the lower right-hand side of the paper, the one without a solution filled in:

$$\begin{gathered} \sim(M \cdot N) \\ (O \cdot T) \vee (M \cdot N) \\ (M \cdot N) \vee (R \cdot L) \\ O \supset (I \cdot D) \\ D \equiv S / \therefore \end{gathered}$$

The conclusion you want is a conjunction of all the letters that can be deduced from the premises, without any letter being repeated. The conclusion should not contain "not," "or," or "if–then." The conclusion should have the following form: A and B and C, and so on. *The letters you can deduce from these premises can be rearranged to form a message.* If this appears to be a formidable task, it won't be if you take a moment to read the following instructions:

A, B, C, and so on, stand for distinct statements. But you could not know which, if any, specific statements these letters symbolize. Therefore, you have to concern yourself with the letters themselves.

Here are the meanings of the symbols:

"$\sim A$" means "not A"
"$A \cdot B$" means "A and B"
"$A \vee B$" means "A or B"
"$A \supset B$" means "If A, then B"
"$A \equiv B$" means "If A, then B, *and* if B, then A"
"$/\therefore$" means "therefore" (having the same meaning as a line drawn under the premises)

The parentheses group symbols together, acting as a kind of punctuation. For instance:

"$(A \cdot B) \vee (C \cdot D)$" means "either both A and B, or both C and D"

Start by deducing what letters you can; put those in the conclusion. Then use those letters to deduce others; add those to the conclusion.

Symbolic logic simply formalizes the logic we use every day, and you can do the logic informally. For instance:

$$\frac{\begin{array}{c}A \cdot B \\ (A \cdot B) \supset (C \cdot D)\end{array}}{A \cdot B \cdot C \cdot D}$$

REASONING: The first premise gives us both A and B; these can be put in the conclusion. The second premise says that, if we have both A and B, we can get both C and D. Since we have A and B, we also get C and D. These are added to the conclusion.

$$\frac{\begin{array}{c}\sim A \\ A \vee B\end{array}}{B}$$

REASONING: The first premise says we don't have A; therefore A cannot be put in the conclusion. But the first premise is helpful in conjunction with the second premise, which says we have either A or B. Since we don't have A, we have B.

Also: "Ont. Arg." = "Ontological Argument" = Descartes's proof for the existence of God (originally from Anselm).

The people in the room began to study the photograph intently. No one came up with the answer. Shultz was the first to speak.

"We're not here to play games, Hulk. If you've got an answer, let's have it."

"What's this written at the bottom of the page?" asked Lisa. " 'Ont. Arg.' "

"Ontological argument," said Stout.

"Is that some kind of clue?" asked Mrs. Bergmann.

"Indeed it is," said Hulk. "Ladies and gentlemen, consider the taxing, not to mention frightening, predicament of a man who knows he is going to die and wants to leave a clue as to the name of his murderer. If it is too obvious, the murderer will remove it. If it is too obscure, no one will notice it. Professor Lanchaster got his clue past the murderer but almost erred on the side of subtlety. I have been told that Professor Lanchaster admired my work, and I flatter myself with the supposition that he took a chance that someone, perhaps his wife, would bring me into the case. In any event, it is fortunate that I did get involved. Had the situation been left to the police department, the clue would have gone undetected."

"All I've gotten so far is talk," said Shultz.

"You will also get a murderer, Inspector. A man wants to leave a clue as to the identity of his murderer. He would hardly write out the name. So what would he do instead? He'd devise some word association, perhaps. Here the abbreviation 'Ont. Arg.' stands out on a sheet otherwise devoted to logic exercises. As Professor Stout has noted, this abbreviation stands for 'ontological argument.' None of the books and papers on Lanchaster's desk had any connection with the ontological argument. Perhaps a clue lay there.

"What is the ontological argument? The four professors here can tell you better than I, but, briefly, it is an argument that claims that the actual existence of God is necessarily implied by the mere definition of God. It is a proof concerning God. God . . . why not *Lord?* A good association. I thought: Lord is the killer."

"Hulk, you're an idiot," said Professor Trilling.

"How so, Professor?"

"The proof you refer to is Anselm's ontological proof, also used by Descartes. But it is not the only ontological proof. Sartre has another, a proof for the existence of Being, independent of consciousness. In fact, Bergmann has written an article on it. Perhaps Lanchaster was indicating Bergmann."

"More likely it is only a random scribble," said Stout. "If it isn't, it might as well be. No, Hulk, that gets you nowhere."

"I doubt very much that it was random," said Hulk. "I believe it was written intentionally as a clue. But it was invented in haste, and Lanchaster saw the ambiguity. So he came up with something else, a clue hidden among the logic exercises on his desk pad. Fortunately, that clue is not ambiguous.

"The philosophers here know how introductory logic courses proceed. Students learn to translate normal sentences into symbols that express their logical form. Look." Hulk lifted up a large sheet of paper on which he had printed the symbols and pointed to them as he explained. "Letters like A and M replace basic sentences. Other symbols stand for the logical connectives: $\sim$ means 'not'; $\cdot$ means 'and'; v means 'either . . . or'; $\supset$ means 'if–then'; and $\equiv$ means 'if either, then the other.' For example, 'If Joe gets paid, then Joe buys groceries' can be symbolized as $A \supset B$. Or, 'Either Joe goes to work, or he does not go to work' can be symbolized as $M \vee \sim M$.

"Having learned such symbolization, the students are then taught a series of valid argument forms. A valid argument is an argument such that, if the premises are true, then the conclusion must be true. For example, '$A \supset B$; A; therefore ($\therefore$) B' is a valid argument form, and any argument having that form is valid. 'If the sun shines, then the grass will grow; the sun shines; therefore, the grass will grow' is a valid argument having that form.

"Students then analyze more complex arguments. If the conclusion of an argument can be derived from the premises by employing a series of valid argument forms, then that more complex argument is valid. If not, then there are definite procedures for showing the argument to be invalid.

"Consider the example at the center of Lanchaster's desk pad. This is a typical example of a logic exercise at a point in the course where the ability of the student to translate from English to logical symbolism is assumed. Only the symbolized argument is given. The conclusion of the argument is given. The student is asked to determine whether the argument is valid.

"Now consider the example at the lower right-hand side of the desk pad. No conclusion is given, as if one were being invited to draw a conclusion. Of course, it could be that Lanchaster was simply interrupted there, but a little work shows that such was not the case. The solution to the murder is there.

"Of course, in a sense, there is no single answer to any logic problem. '$\sim(M \cdot N)$,' for example, can be deduced from the premises and would be a 'solution.' Also, since any letter can be deduced from itself, any letters in the conclusion could be repeated indefinitely. But, presumably, a message would be a conjunction of all the individual letters that could be deduced from the premises, with no repetition of any letters. Such, indeed, is the case.

"Let us work out this solution. Since the argument is fairly simple, we can do it informally.

"The second premise says, 'Either both O and T or both M and N.' The third premise says, 'Either both M and N, or both R and L.' Since the first premise says 'not M and N,' we can deduce the other pairs of letters. That gives us O and T and R and L. The fourth premise says, 'If O, then both I and D.' Since we already have O, we can deduce I and D. The last premise says that whenever we have D, we have S, and vice versa. Since we have D, we can deduce S. The conclusion, then, is O and T and R and L and I and D and S.

"Appropriately, Lanchaster, professor of logic, used his own tools to name his murderer. He gave us a problem whose solution is an anagram, giving us his statement: ITS LORD."

Lord was staring at Hulk without speaking, his fingers playing at his lips. Everyone else was staring at Lord. Shultz motioned Sergeant Kurz to move in Lord's direction and then turned to Hulk.

"I don't get it, Hulk. Lanchaster died instantly and obviously didn't write his message after the killer left. Do you mean to tell me that Lord was stupid enough to sit there while Lanchaster jotted down notes that would convict him?"

"Inspector, it would not be the first time that one of this group of supposedly educated people has exhibited blatant stupidity. But, no, Lord wasn't that stupid.

"Presumably Lord had some early hint from Lanchaster that he would be dropped from the department, and Lord planned to kill Lanchaster should that be the decision. He was taking an awful chance, killing him when he did. But he did not want to act before the final decision had been confirmed. Had he waited longer, others would have learned of his dismissal.

"Of course, the time of his appointment was known to the others, so he had to commit the crime in such a way that another would be blamed or, at the very least, that others would be suspected. He sent a note to Stout and perhaps even verified that Stout would be coming late. Would you care to comment, Professor Stout?"

Stout glanced quickly at Lord. "Yes," he said. "He knew I had gotten the note. We discussed it."

"Thank you," said Hulk. "Lord had also decided to kill fairly close to 8:00. That way, both Stout and Bergmann would be suspects. He did not know, of course, that Professor Bergmann would be so helpful with his panic and his bumbling stories.

"Lord arrived at 7:00, learned that he was to be fired, pulled a gun on Lanchaster, and waited. But then a problem arose. The doorbell rang. It was Lisa Williams, who had come to pick up her books. No doubt Lord had locked the door upon entering the house. But he did not dare let the doorbell go unanswered. Miss Williams knew Lanchaster would be there, the lights in the house were on, and the car was in the driveway. For his part, Lanchaster had to cooperate or jeopardize the life of his niece. He told Lord that she had come for the books and told him where they were.

"Lord did not dare let Lanchaster go to the door: he might pass a message to his niece. He saw only one danger in leaving a lame man alone in the room—the phone. So he pulled the phone cord from the wall. It was the broken cord that first made me suspect that there might be a message among the things on the desk.

"Perhaps Lord quickly searched for a message when he returned to the room. Perhaps he didn't think of that possibility. In any case, Lanchaster had hidden his message well. It would not have been spotted by someone afraid and in haste, even a colleague who knew his symbolic logic.

"Lord then waited in the study with Lanchaster for another fifteen or twenty minutes before killing him. All of you know the rest. I am certain that a jury will find the accusation, 'ITS LORD,' in the deceased's own handwriting, sufficient evidence to convict, especially given the cogency of the hypothesis I have outlined. Would you care to comment, Professor Lord?"

"No," said Lord, still rubbing his lips.

"Rest assured, sir, that you will be convicted and sent to prison for the rest of your life. Perhaps the prison authorities will let you teach Plato and Aristotle in prison. If so, I hope that the inmates enjoy your courses. I suspect, from Professor Lanchaster's decision, that your students at Fountain did not. But in prison, at least, you will have tenure."

"Damn you, Hulk, damn you!"

Many men have tried to get at Hulk in that office and none has succeeded yet. Lord certainly didn't, though he made quite a try for a man of his size. I intercepted him, wrestled him to the floor, and held him while Sergeant Kurz put on the cuffs.

Hulk refuses to talk business at dinner, so I waited until we were drinking coffee in the office to tell him.

"While you were in the plant rooms, a messenger arrived with a package from Mrs. Bergmann. It was the second check for $5,000 we'd expected. It has been put in the safe and will be deposited tomorrow. Mrs. Bergmann also sent you a present. It's a copy of an article by her husband on Sartre's ontological proof. The major question seems to be: Is the phenomenon of Being itself the Being of the phenomena, or is it merely a phenomenal representation, nonidentical with, but indicating the nature of, the Being of the phenomena? I haven't quite made up my mind. Perhaps we could discuss the matter after you've read the article."

"Rubbish. They should fire the whole department at Fountain and hire four logicians. At least that is a sensible subject."

"You're just prejudiced because you are a fellow logician, even if you are doing battle outside the ivory tower. But that reminds me, sir. There is one point about the case that hasn't been cleared up to my satisfaction—something you said when you were disclosing the murderer."

"Yes? What was that?"

"You said, 'If Joe gets paid, then Joe buys groceries.' What I want to know is: Did Joe get paid?"

"Pfui. Go amuse yourself elsewhere."

It is a shame to be living with a genius and yet have to do without intellectual conversation. Fortunately, my interests are not purely intellectual. I grabbed my hat and headed for the Starlight Lounge.

Questions

1. Trace the steps in Hulk's reasoning from his first search for evidence to his proposed solution to the crime.

2. Is it implausible to suppose that the exercise yielding the message, "ITS LORD," was written prior to Lord's appearance in the study? Explain.

   If one assumes that it was, what account might one give of the crime?

3. Compare your preliminary solution with those of Hulk and of the other students. (Don't simply assume that Hulk's explanation must be correct.) Are these various explanations equally reasonable? Discuss.

4. Do the following logic exercise as you did the exercise in the mystery story. Here you will need to derive some negative statements in the course of your reasoning (for example, $\sim O$), and you may find it convenient to put these in the conclusion as you proceed. But when you have completed your reasoning, cross out any negative statements in the conclusion. The remaining conjunction of letters can be arranged to form a one-word admonition. As before, there should be no double letters in the conclusion.

   In reasoning out logic problems, one does not usually follow the written order of the premises. In this case, it would be a mistake to begin with the first one. Look over the premises, and choose a reasonable starting point.

$$
\begin{array}{l}
(K \cdot I) \supset \sim O \\
\sim O \supset T \\
I \cdot \sim A \\
(K \cdot N) \vee A \\
H \vee (B \cdot L) \\
\sim (B \cdot L) \\
\hline
\quad ?
\end{array}
$$

Discussion

ARGUMENTS, DEDUCTIVE AND INDUCTIVE

Philosophers, indeed all "rational" individuals, should be able to give arguments for their beliefs. An *argument* consists of a statement that is the conclusion and one or more additional statements that are the premises. The premises are offered as evidence in support of the conclusion.

There are deductive and inductive arguments. It is convenient to define these types of arguments in terms of their valid forms.

A *valid deductive argument* is an argument such that if the premises are true, then the conclusion *must* be true. Two examples of valid deductive arguments are:

(1) All students are human.
All humans are mortal.
―――――――――――――
All students are mortal.

(2) All students are human.
All humans have three heads.
―――――――――――――
All students have three heads.

A *valid inductive argument* is an argument such that if the premises are true, then the conclusion is *probably* true. Two examples of valid inductive arguments are:

(3) All human beings observed have lived less than 500 years.
―――――――――――――
All human beings live less than 500 years.

(4) All human beings observed have lived less than 20 years.
―――――――――――――
All human beings live less than 20 years.

Questions of validity and invalidity concern only the relation between the premises and the conclusion. To show that an argument is valid is not to show that the premises are true. It is to show that one should rely on the conclusion *if* the premises are true. Thus, with any argument you need to know two things:

Is it valid?

Are the premises true?

A valid argument with true premises is called a *sound argument*. Arguments "1" through "4" are all valid. But only "1" and "3" are sound.

Note that if a deductive argument is valid and the premises are true, then the conclusion must be true. However, if an inductive argument is valid and the premises are true, then the conclusion is probably true, but not necessarily so. What accounts for this difference?

The conclusion of a valid deductive argument contains no information that is not contained, at least implicitly, in the premises. In a sense, the conclusion of a valid deductive argument is merely a repetition of the premises. Thus the conclusion could not possibly be false if the premises are true.*

On the other hand, the conclusion of a valid inductive argument does contain information not contained in the premises. Thus, it is conceivable that the premises of such an argument could be true and the conclusion false. In the examples of induction given above, the premises contain information about the human beings who have been observed, whereas the conclusions are statements about *all* human beings. What is true of the human beings we have observed is likely to be true of all human beings, but it need not be. In a valid inductive argument, the premises provide good evidence for the conclusion, but they do not guarantee its truth absolutely.

ASSESSING DEDUCTIVE ARGUMENTS

In assessing deductive arguments, one examines argument forms. "Philosophy Is Murder" has already introduced you to how arguments are formalized. The letters "A," "B," "C," and so on, stand for distinct statements. These letters are merely place markers, and it does not matter which one is used to represent a particular statement. However, within a single argument, a particular letter should be used for only one particular statement whenever that statement occurs.

Other symbols are used to represent what are called "logical connectives": "and," "or," "if–then," and so on. "$\sim$ A" means "not A." "A $\cdot$ B" means "A and B." "A v B" means "A or B." "A $\supset$ B" means "if A, then B." "A $\equiv$ B" means "if A, then B, *and* if B, then A." Parentheses group symbols together, acting as

---

* Note that this is an explanation of deductive validity, not a definition of it. The definition was given earlier. Also, this explanation holds true for *virtually all* valid deductive arguments. There are a few "paradoxical" exceptions, one of which is noted in a later discussion of inconsistency.

punctuation marks. For instance, "(A · B) v (C · D)" means "either both A and B or both C and D."

The premises are separated from the conclusion by a line drawn under the premises or by a slash mark and three dots in triangular form. The line or the dots mean "therefore." "These premises, *therefore* this conclusion."

The following arguments have the same form:

It is raining It is cool	It is snowing It is warm
It is raining and it is cool	It is snowing and it is warm

The form of these arguments is:

$$\frac{\begin{array}{c}A\\B\end{array}}{A \cdot B}$$

(Or, "R; S; therefore R · S." Remember that the letters are merely place markers.)

Every argument of this form is valid. How do we know that this is a valid argument form? Our knowledge of validity is based on our knowledge of the meanings of the logical connectives. The word "and" implies that the statement "A and B" will be true if, and only if, "A" is true and "B" is true. Given this definition, it is impossible for "A and B" to be false if "A" is true and "B" is true.

There are technical methods for determining which basic argument forms are valid. With any complex argument, if the conclusion can be derived from the premises by employing a series of valid argument forms, then the complex argument has been shown to be valid. Consider, for example, the argument used in solving the mystery in "Philosophy Is Murder":

$$\frac{\begin{array}{l}\sim(M \cdot N)\\(O \cdot T) \vee (M \cdot N)\\(M \cdot N) \vee (R \cdot L)\\O \supset (I \cdot D)\\D \equiv S\end{array}}{O \cdot T \cdot R \cdot L \cdot I \cdot D \cdot S^{*}}$$

* For the benefit of those who have had, or may later have, a course in formal logic, it should be noted that this, and not the exercise with the

"R and L and O and T" can be deduced from the first three premises by employing the valid argument form: "A v B; ~A; therefore, B."

"I and D" can be derived from "O" and the fourth premise by employing another valid argument form: "A ⊃ B; A; therefore, B."

The fifth premise has the same meaning as: "(D ⊃ S) · (S ⊃ D)." "D ⊃ S" can be derived from that statement by employing the valid argument form: "A · B; therefore, A." Then "S" can be derived from "D" and "D ⊃ S," by employing a valid argument form already mentioned: "A ⊃ B; A; therefore, B."

In this case, formalization may seem to complicate the obvious. But in the case of more complex arguments, these symbolic techniques make precise and mechanical a process of evaluation that would be difficult, if not impossible, to do informally.

There are formal techniques for proving deductive arguments to be either valid or invalid. There are no simple, informal techniques for demonstrating validity, but there is one such technique for demonstrating invalidity, and you may find it useful on occasion.

Consider the following argument:

> If I am Superman, then I can leap tall buildings.
> I am not Superman.
> ---
> Therefore, I cannot leap tall buildings.

Here the premises are true, and the conclusion is true. Perhaps the argument seems to be valid; perhaps the conclusion seems to follow from the premises. But this argument is, in fact, invalid.

Remember that if an argument is valid, then every argument

---

conclusion omitted, would typify a logic exercise. As Hulk says: "This is a typical example of a logic exercise . . . the symbolized argument is given . . . the conclusion of the argument is given . . . the student is asked to determine whether the argument is valid." As Hulk also states: ". . . there is no single answer to any logic problem. '~(M · N),' for example, can be deduced from the premises and would be a 'solution.' Also, since any letter can be deduced from itself, any letter in the conclusion could be repeated indefinitely." This mystery story employs a special, and rather limited, "logical game" that would not be found in any logic textbook.

having that form is valid. Also, if an argument is valid, that means that it is impossible for an argument of that form to have true premises and a false conclusion. Thus, if we can construct an argument that has the same form as the above and that has obviously true premises and an obviously false conclusion, we will have shown that argument to be invalid.

First, we determine the form of the argument. In the above case, it is:

$$\begin{array}{l} A \supset B \\ \sim A \\ \hline \sim B \end{array}$$

Now we construct an argument of this form, having obviously true premises and an obviously false conclusion. For example:

If I am Superman, then I am a man.
I am not Superman.
___
I am not a man.

The premises are obviously true: Superman is male, and I am not Superman. The conclusion is obviously false: I *am* male. Thus, we have shown the initial argument to be invalid—it does not have a form such that the truth of the premises guarantees the truth of the conclusion. Every argument of the form "$A \supset B$; $\sim A$; therefore, $\sim B$" is invalid.

Note that the manufactured argument used to demonstrate invalidity need not have the same subject matter as the original argument. It is only necessary that it have the same form and that it have obviously true premises and an obviously false conclusion. The following argument would do just as well:

If this is 1942, then this is the 20th century.
This is not 1942.
___
This is not the 20th century.

Another argument is given below as an exercise. Try to prove it invalid using the techniques we have discussed. That is, first determine the form of the argument, and then construct a "counter-example," an argument having the same form with obviously true premises and an obviously false conclusion. Compare your proof with that given in the footnote on p. 203.

> If I am nice to people, then people are nice to me.
> People are nice to me.
> ___
> I am nice to people.

Evaluating inductive arguments

Evaluating inductive arguments is a much trickier business than evaluating deductive arguments. It is difficult to say precisely how the premises and conclusion are related in valid inductive arguments. It is often difficult to determine the degree of support that certain premises give a certain conclusion. This is not to say that we ought to disdain induction: most of us trust induction and use it quite well; indeed, we must use induction if we are to gain any new knowledge. This is only to say that induction is difficult to formalize.

If we know that we have examined ninety-nine out of a hundred beans in a jar, and that all the ones we have examined have been green, we can conclude that the probability that all the beans in the jar will be green is ninety-nine percent. But when we make a judgment about all human beings based on the ones we have observed, we have no idea how many human beings there have been and will be. In such cases, we say our conclusions are "highly probable" or "fairly probable," and even these vague probability assessments can be matters of dispute. When we come to assessing the probability of, say, Einstein's general theory of relativity, the issue becomes enormously complex. Nonetheless, we do seem to come to considerable agreement on our inductive judgments.

Perhaps the simplest way to explain the nature of inductive reasoning is to consider its use in "Philosophy Is Murder." Detectives are often called "masters of deduction." In fact, however, most of their reasoning is inductive. On the basis of certain facts, they form conclusions concerning other matters; and where conclusions contain more information than is contained in the premises, such reasoning is inductive. Furthermore, the guilt of a criminal is never established with absolute certainty. The law requires only that guilt be proved "beyond a reasonable doubt"—which is to say, with a high degree of probability. And where we are dealing with probabilities, we are dealing with induction.

The instances of induction in the story, as in everyday life, are numerous. For instance, to conclude from Lanchaster's wound and from the bullet hole in the back of his chair that Lanchaster had been shot with a gun is to use induction. This conclusion is not the only one theoretically compatible with those premises. The premises would be true if the bullet had been thrown into the air somewhere across town, had landed and bounced erratically through the streets, had bounced into the Lanchaster house, and had struck the deceased. But induction tells us that such a theoretical possibility is so unlikely that we need not consider it seriously. In such an instance, the conclusion seems so obvious that we may not think of ourselves as reasoning at all, but we are. And the reasoning is inductive.

Hulk learns that the phone was torn from the wall on the evening of the murder. He concludes that there is a possibility that Lanchaster had been left alone by the murderer at some point, and a more remote possibility that he had left some kind of message. True, Hulk is dealing with mere possibilities here, but induction tells him that such possibilities are at least worth investigating. He isn't going to tell Crocker to search the bedroom or the lawn for a message.

Hulk finds the logic exercise and deduces the message, "ITS LORD." Conceivably, it is pure coincidence that these letters can be deduced from this logic exercise. But inductive reasoning would convince all of us that this coincidence is unlikely beyond a reasonable doubt.

However, in preliminary readings of the story, some students have taken issue with Hulk's "total hypothesis." Some have favored an alternate account:

The logic exercise was constructed before Lord ever arrived at the house. It was not constructed as a message. Rather, it was a sort of doodle by a logician who was preoccupied with the unpleasant task of having to fire an associate. Lord arrived and argued his case until 7:30. At the time Lisa Williams arrived, Lord had not yet drawn the gun, nor had he torn out the phone.

A bit later, Lanchaster started to phone Stout to find out what was keeping him. At that point, Lord tore out the phone and drew his gun.

There is no difference of opinion here over "whodunit." But this does provide an interesting example of an inductive controversy. Which hypothesis is the more reasonable, and how much more reasonable is it? This I shall leave to your consideration.

Re: the exercise on pp. 200–201.

If I am nice to people, then people are nice to me.
People are nice to me.
____
I am nice to people.

The form of the argument is:

$$\begin{array}{c} A \supset B \\ B \\ \hline A \end{array}$$

Here is an argument having that form which has obviously true premises and an obviously false conclusion.

If I am Superman, then I am a man.
I am a man.
____
I am Superman.

Or:

If this is 1942, then this is the 20th century.
This is the 20th century.
____
This is 1942.

Any argument of the form, "$A \supset B$; B; therefore, A," is invalid.

Another Pilgrim's Progress

CONDITIONS IN THE TOWN OF STATUS QUO WERE RAPIDLY DETERIORATING. First had come the drought, parching the crops; then the winds, filling the air with dust; then the fires, destroying the dwellings in twos and threes. Within the last month, many of the townspeople had departed, driven away by fear and drawn elsewhere by hope. Rumors spread of a Heavenly City somewhere to the north—a city, so it was said, where there was never drought, wind, fire, or famine. Pilgrim had been inclined to leave Status Quo long ago. She was an optimistic soul and had never doubted that there was a Heavenly City. But she was also a kindly soul, her brothers' keeper. She had twin brothers, Skeptic and Caution, who thus far had refused to leave. There was no hope of convincing Skeptic: he could never be convinced of anything. However, he wouldn't offer much resistance if simply pushed down the road. It was Caution who must be convinced.

That day, as on most others, Pilgrim and her brothers were sitting in the tavern. There was no work to be done any longer, and even if there had been, the fierce, choking winds would have made it impossible. The only sensible thing to do was to seek shelter, and the tavern was the only shelter left with space and refreshment enough for a large gathering. The talk, as on other days, concerned the wisdom of leaving the town.

"My family has lived here for generations," Provincial was saying. "This has always been my home. How can any other place be better?"

Caution looked up. He had heard this particular speech too many times.

"What nonsense, Provincial! The crops are destroyed. The rich soil is gone. Most of our town has burned or is burning. The air is so filled with dirt and heat that one can scarcely breathe. Our provisions are dwindling, and soon we may starve. How can you maintain that this is the best place on earth?"

"I didn't say it was perfect," said Provincial. "Anyway, it's always easy to be critical."

"Yes. And it's getting easier all the time."

Provincial crossed the room to Caution's table.

"Speaking man to man, Caution, you've got no right to criticize. I've lived here all my life and you've lived here only five years."

"That's true," said Caution. "But what has that to do with what I say?"

"Why should we listen to you, anyway?" said Provincial. "You're the one who says he doesn't believe in anything. Frankly, I think someone ought to beat some sense into you. Or maybe just beat the stuffing out of you."

With that, Provincial leaned across the table, lifted Caution by the coat, and began to shake him violently.

"Stop, Provincial, stop!" cried Pilgrim. "You'll hurt him. He's not made of straw, you know."

"I—might—as—well—be," stuttered Caution, between shakes.

"Anyway," said Pilgrim, "you're mixing up my brothers again. Skeptic's the one who doesn't believe in anything."

"He is?" said Provincial, pausing. "Then he's a troublemaker, too."

Dropping Caution, Provincial swung his huge fist and sent Skeptic sprawling on the floor. Other men started to join the fight, but the tavern keeper stepped in and stopped the brawl. He picked Skeptic up from the floor, brushed the dust off his clothes, and sat him back on the chair.

"There, he's all right," said the tavern keeper. "Don't hurt my friend Skeptic. He never causes any trouble. How about something to drink, Skeptic? I suppose it doesn't matter what."

"No," said Skeptic with his usual quiet smile. "Just as long as it seems to taste good."

"That's the spirit," said the tavern keeper. "As for the rest of you, I don't know what all this quarreling is about. The whole thing is no dilemma to me. As I see it, either you go out there in the dust and die, or you stay in here and drink my fine ale. That doesn't take much thought, does it?"

"But then again," said Caution, "if we leave here, we might find the Heavenly City. Or, if we stay, you might run out of ale, and we would die of thirst."

"You know, Caution," said the tavern keeper, "I'm beginning to lose patience with you myself. Careful you don't get me angry, or I'll toss you out there in that dust and make the choice for you. How would you like that?"

As the tavern keeper walked away, Pilgrim leaned toward Caution.

"The Heavenly City is there, Caution. I'm sure of it. Won't you make up your mind to go?"

"I'm considering it, Pilgrim. Give me time."

"You, Skeptic. Please come with me."

"But Pilgrim," said Skeptic, "I don't know whether there's a Heavenly City out there. And I don't know whether things here are as bad as they seem."

"But you don't know that there *isn't* a Heavenly City," said Pilgrim. "And you don't know that things here *aren't* as bad as they seem. If you don't know anything, what difference can it make to you whether you stay or go?"

Skeptic looked thoughtful.

"I don't know much," he said. "But I think I know that it seems to be more trouble to seem to walk than to seem to sit still."

"But doesn't it seem to you that while sitting here you've been troubled by a fist in your face? Doesn't it seem to you that your jaw hurts very much?"

"Hmmm," mused Skeptic. "You might just have a point there . . . perhaps."

So they talked until late that night, when it was time for the tavern to close. As was his custom, the tavern keeper did not try to convince Skeptic that it was time to close; that would have been a hopeless task. Instead, he pulled Skeptic to his feet, guided him out the door, and pushed him in the direction of his home. Like a billiard ball, Skeptic would never move until pushed, but, once pushed, he would continue in a straight line until someone or something stopped or turned him. His brother and sister followed behind him. In former days, Pilgrim would have stayed by Skeptic's side, ready to pull him out of the way of wagons coming down the road. But there had been no traffic on that road for some days. And tonight Pilgrim was intent on trying to convince Caution that they should leave. So it was that Skeptic walked some distance ahead of them. They noticed this only when a loud, cracking sound caught their attention. They looked ahead and saw a huge oak tree beginning to topple toward the road. Skeptic was moving toward the spot where the tree would fall.

"Skeptic, stop!" cried Pilgrim. "The tree is falling!"

"How do you know that?" said Skeptic.

"Don't be stupid!" said Caution. "Look overhead."

Skeptic did look up, but he did not alter his stride.

"I will grant you that the tree seems to be falling on me. But appearances can be deceiving."

Pilgrim and Caution began to run as the tree came crashing down on their brother. They found Skeptic lying under the huge tree; only his feet and head protruded from beneath the trunk.

"You know," groaned Skeptic, "it may be that you were right. It seems to be the case that a tree has fallen upon me. It seems to be the case that my body is broken and that I am dying. Perhaps I am jumping to conclusions, but it certainly seems to me that I hurt a great deal."

And with that, Skeptic died.

"Oh, my brother," moaned Pilgrim.

"The poor fool," said Caution.

"At least he died honorably," said Pilgrim. "Whether or not one agrees with him, one must admit that he stood up for what he believed . . . or what he thought he believed . . . or what he thought he didn't believe."

"Well, he's not standing now," said Caution. "Pilgrim, I may be careful, but I'm not a fool. Tomorrow we shall get some friends to help us bury our brother. After we have mourned him, we shall leave this place. I doubt that we shall find any Heavenly City. But whatever becomes of us, it cannot be worse than this."

And so it was that two days afterward, carrying on their backs what provisions they had been able to obtain, Pilgrim and Caution left Status Quo on the road north. The morning's walk was difficult, but the weather began to clear. Pilgrim took this as a promising sign. Caution refused to be optimistic. Perhaps this was but a brief respite from the bad weather. Or perhaps the weather was now clearing all over the land, and they had been fools to leave their town. As they talked, they came upon a fork in the road. In front of them was a sign, done in a crude hand.

THIS ROAD IS HEAVENLY ⟶
⟵ THIS ROAD IS HELLISH

Automatically, they took the right fork as they continued to talk. Then Caution stopped.

"I'd like another look at that sign."

"Why?" said Pilgrim. "It was quite plain."

"Perhaps," said Caution, walking back to the sign.

Reluctantly, Pilgrim followed him. Together they read the smaller lettering, which they hadn't noticed before, at the bottom of the sign.

> The heavenly road, which is the scenic route, leads to the Great Pitfall; the hellish road, which is in disrepair, leads to the Heavenly City.

As they took the left fork, Pilgrim said:

"I must admit you *were* right that time. Perhaps I am not always careful enough."

The road was hellish indeed: pitted, cut by gullies, overgrown with brush. But Pilgrim was quite cheerful about this inconvenience. No longer were they simply guided by rumor. They had now seen a sign that proved that there was a Heavenly City and that this was the road to it. Caution was not so optimistic. After all, he argued, no one, as far as was known, had ever seen the Heavenly City and returned to verify its existence and location. So what if they had seen a sign? The sign, which had been done in a rough hand, might have been placed there by some fool who was merely guessing about the way.

"Now you are being ridiculous," said Pilgrim.

Some time later they came upon a ragged figure seated by the side of the road. They recognized him at once as Circles, a beggar who had left their town a few days before. Caution, knowing that Pilgrim would want to give the beggar something and fearing that they might not have enough for themselves, tried to dissuade his sister from charity. But Pilgrim would not hear of it.

"We must help our friends, Caution. Anyway, we are on the road to the Heavenly City, and certainly we shall reach it soon enough. Hello there, Circles! We don't have much, but we can give you a little."

Circles took the coin and the piece of bread Pilgrim offered and thanked her warmly.

"Bless you, Pilgrim, bless you. I may be a beggar now, but I shall not be one for long. They say there is plenty for everyone in the Heavenly City. When I get there, I shall gladly repay you."

"Don't be foolish," said Pilgrim. "If there is plenty for everyone, I shall no more need your repayment than you shall need my charity. It is enough that we shall all be happy in the Heavenly City."

"*If* there is a Heavenly City," grumbled Caution. "*If* this is the right road. *If* it is not too far for us to reach it."

"But this is the right road," said Circles. "I know it."

"How do you know that?" said Caution.

"Didn't you see the sign back there?" said Circles.

"Yes, yes. But how do we know that the sign is correct?"

"That's easy," said Circles. "I know that the sign is correct because this is the right road."

"Very helpful," said Caution, with disgust.

"But Caution, I have more evidence," said Circles, anxious to please his benefactors.

"Not more of the same, I hope."

"No," said Circles. "Here, look at this."

Circles pulled a crumpled piece of paper out of his pocket and unfolded it on the ground before them. It was a sizable sheet, apparently torn from a larger one, scribbled with lines and letters. Pilgrim and Caution peered at it.

"A map?" said Pilgrim.

"Indeed," said Circles. "It is a map of the way to the Heavenly City."

"Oh happy day!" exclaimed Pilgrim. "Caution, let us memorize the map so that we shall know the way."

"I'm afraid it won't help you there," said Circles. "It has been torn off at just this spot. Apparently the owner discarded the portion that wasn't needed any more."

"What a shame," said Pilgrim.

"Still, it's important," said Circles. "It tells us that we are headed in the right direction. See here: there is Status Quo and the road heading north. There is the fork in the road, with the heavenly road heading toward the Great Pitfall and the hellish road leading toward the Heavenly City. Here we are, right at the edge of the map where it has been torn. Caution was worried that we might be on the wrong road. He ought to feel better now."

But Caution did not feel better.

"This map looks even less official than the sign we saw back there. How do we know this is not merely some travelers' guesswork, based on where they've been and where they *think* they're going? How do we know this map is correct?"

"That's easy," said Circles. "Read what it says at the bottom."

Pilgrim bent over first and read the statement aloud: " 'This is an accurate map of the way to the Heavenly City.' "

"There, you see?" said Circles.

"Come on, Pilgrim," said Caution. "I've had quite enough of this."

Pilgrim protested as Caution dragged her away, but Caution was insistent.

"Really, Caution, this is a bit too much," said Pilgrim. "That was awfully rude, you know. And I don't know what you are making such a fuss about. I swear, sometimes you seem exactly like our poor dead brother, Skeptic. When we walk through the gates of the Heavenly City, will you still be doubtful?"

"No, Pilgrim. *If* I see it with my own eyes, I'll believe it."

"Well, that's something. In any case, I feel much relieved. We got a lot of valuable information from Circles. You certainly can't say we didn't get our money's worth."

"On the contrary," said Caution. "It seems to me that Circles has taken our money and made beggars of our questions."

When night fell, they made camp by the side of the road, ate a modest meal, and, exhausted by the day's walk, fell asleep at once. At the first light of day, they continued on their way. After they had walked for two hours, Caution came to an abrupt stop and groaned. Ahead the road ended, forming a T with another road.

"Not another junction!"

"I'm sure the way is marked," said Pilgrim. "In any case, there are some people standing about. If there is any doubt as to the way, I'm sure they can advise us."

At the end of the road, the travelers were faced with another crudely lettered sign:

HEAVENLY CITY TO THE RIGHT⟶
⟵HEAVENLY CITY TO THE LEFT

"Well, that is certainly clear enough," said Pilgrim, starting to the right.

"Pilgrim, wait a minute. Why are you going that way?"

"The sign says 'Heavenly City to the right.' "

"It also says 'Heavenly City to the left.' "

"So?"

"Pilgrim, you don't suppose there are two Heavenly Cities, do you?"

"I wouldn't suppose so," said Pilgrim. "I've always heard there was only one."

"Do you imagine that one city could be way off in that direction and, at the same time, way off in that other direction?"

"I don't know."

"Pilgrim, you're hopeless."

"On the contrary, I'm full of hope."

"Pilgrim! We do not know which way to go. That sign is no help at all."

"Well, if you really think we are lost, why don't you ask those people for advice?"

Standing next to the sign were three people. One was a fat man who was talking animatedly. Another was a young boy, who seemed quite amused by the fat man and who was trying, unsuccessfully, to keep from laughing. The third man was a skinny fellow who kept fidgeting about, apparently impatient with the conversation. Caution politely greeted the men, introduced himself, and asked them if they were lost.

"Not lost, son," said the fat man. "Just resting."

"Then you know the way to the Heavenly City?" said Caution.

"Of course," said the fat man.

"But the sign . . . ."

"Oh that," said the fat man. "The work of some trickster, I would imagine."

"Then how . . . ?"

"When you run across a problem, son, you've got to look around. You've got to use your eyes, use your head. It didn't take me long to figure it out."

Caution smiled.

"It certainly is a relief to meet a man like you," he said. "A man who uses his head is a man after my own heart."

The fat man chuckled.

"I like you, son. Call me 'Pop.' All my friends do."

"How did you figure out the way to go?" asked Caution.

"Really, it was easy," said Pop. "Look at the road to the right. See all those footprints? Now look at the left road. Hardly any footprints at all. The road to the right is the road that most of the people took. That's got to be the way to go."

Caution frowned.

"Unless they all made a mistake."

"Unlikely," said Pop.

"Perhaps they were all together and just had to take a guess," said Caution. "Or perhaps the first ones took a guess, and the rest just followed the crowd."

The skinny man interrupted.

"I thought of that. Didn't I say that, Pop? But look here, Caution. The footprints all go one way. Surely, if this were the wrong road, there would be some footprints coming back."

"Unless they haven't discovered their mistake yet," said Caution. "Or unless they all encountered some great pitfall and couldn't return."

"Thought of that, too," said the skinny man. "But you can see that some of these footprints are very old and that the others have been made over a span of many days. If this were the wrong road, you'd think that someone would have returned by now. Even if there is a great pitfall up ahead, you'd think that someone toward the rear would have gotten some warning."

"You do have a point there," said Caution. "But let's not be hasty."

"But I am Hasty."

"I know. But I'm saying . . ."

"His name's Hasty, son," said Pop. "He can't help his name."

"Well, Hasty," said Caution, "what about the other road? Are there any footprints coming back from that direction?"

"I don't know," said Hasty, glancing toward the other road. "No, I guess not."

"It seems to me," said Pop, "that anybody who's fool enough to take the wrong road would be fool enough not to come back."

All the while they were talking, the boy continued to snicker. Caution was beginning to get annoyed.

"What is he laughing about?" said Caution.

"He's always like that," said Pop. "He just enjoys himself. His name is Suppressed."

"Because he tries to hold back his laughter? Why does he do that?"

"He's shy," said Pop.

Caution studied the boy for a moment and then caught a glimpse of something over the boy's shoulder. Caution pushed the boy aside and discovered a small sign.

THESE ROADS ARE ONE-WAY. NO TURNING BACK.
THIS ORDINANCE STRICTLY ENFORCED.

"So much for your argument, Hasty," said Caution. "Those people were forbidden to return no matter what. As for you, Suppressed, I'm going to give you such a . . ."

"Stop it, Caution!" said Pilgrim. "Don't hurt him. This isn't like you at all."

"But he was trying to trick us," said Caution.

Suppressed was no longer snickering; he was whining.

"Didn't mean anything by it. It was just a joke. Don't hurt me."

"I still don't know what all this fuss is about," said Pop. "If that's the road that most people took, then . . ."

"Really, I didn't mean anything by it," said Suppressed. "I'll make it up to you. I have an idea. If you're lost, why don't you appeal to the authorities?"

"The authorities?" said Caution. "What authorities?"

"Over there. That little house. The man in charge of the junction is inside."

There was indeed a small building by the side of the road. Caution had noticed it before, but it was so run-down that it hardly looked habitable, let alone official. Still, perhaps it had suffered much damage in the recent storms. Pilgrim was already heading for the hut, and Caution followed. Pilgrim called inside, and in a moment an official appeared, wearing an impressive uniform.

"Are you in charge here?" asked Pilgrim.

"I sure am."

"Which way to the Heavenly City?"

"Take the road to the right," said the official.

"See, Caution?" said Pilgrim. "That was the direction I was going to go in the first place. That was the road those men told you to take. You are always making such a fuss about nothing."

Caution didn't reply, but turned to go. However, Pilgrim had another question.

"Sir, how long ago did the last people come through here? Perhaps some of our friends are among them. Perhaps we could still catch up with them."

"I don't know," said the official. "I just got here an hour ago. I'm working for my brother. He's ill."

"Oh," said Pilgrim.

"But you've worked here before?" said Caution.

"No," said the official. "My brother's never been sick before."

"But he did leave you instructions?" said Caution.

"He sure did."

"Well, that's a relief," said Caution.

"And I'm sure I'll find them just as soon as I get that mess in there cleaned up."

"But he did tell you the correct road to take, didn't he?" said Pilgrim.

"No," said the official. "He doesn't talk much about his work."

"This is absurd," said Caution, throwing up his hands. "You're no authority."

"What do you mean, I'm no authority? You see this badge? It says, 'Authority.' See it?"

"Just because you wear a badge . . ."

"Look here, you," said the official. "I'm going to speak to you man to man."

"I wish you wouldn't," said Caution.

"You're a troublemaker. I heard you arguing with those people over there. That was one thing. But when you start to argue with an authority . . . then *you're* the one in trouble."

"But why should we take your word?"

"That does it," said the official. "You like to argue, don't you? Well, here's an argument that should appeal to the likes of you."

With that the official grabbed Pilgrim and Caution by their collars, turned them around, and marched them to the road that led to the right. He pushed Pilgrim ahead and then gave Caution a kick in the pants that sent him sprawling in the dust.

"There. That'll fix you. You keep going now, and don't let me see you again. That road is strictly one-way, and if you try coming back, you'll get more of the same."

Caution got slowly to his feet, and Pilgrim helped him brush the dust off his clothes.

"Come on, Caution," said Pilgrim. "I think we'd better do what he says."

They walked along in silence for a while. Then Pilgrim spoke again.

"Caution, please don't be so glum. I'm sure everything will be all right."

"Pilgrim, you're hopeless."

"On the contrary, I'm . . ."

"Never mind!"

"I'll admit that there has been some confusion," said Pilgrim. "And it certainly was unfortunate that that official should have abused us so—you especially. But you must admit that there have been many indications that we are on the right road."

"There have been none," said Caution. "Or almost none. Let us *suppose* that the first sign, the map, and even the rumors do count for something. Still, we gained nothing useful at that junction."

"On the contrary," said Pilgrim. "The sign pointed this way, and so did the footprints. And those men at the junction told us this was the way. And that official did seem quite sure of himself. Perhaps he was really doing us a favor by forcing us to take the correct road."

"Pilgrim, you're . . . incorrigible. Can't you see that none of that means a thing?"

As they were talking, they came upon two other travelers. There was a tall man who moved very mechanically and slowly, never turning his head, as if he had to concentrate all his attention on the simple act of walking. Holding his arm was a shorter man who glanced at his companion constantly, as if with concern. As Pilgrim came alongside the other travelers, she bid them good day. The tall man did not respond, but the shorter man returned the greeting in a most pleasant manner. He introduced himself as Faith, and asked about their welfare. Pilgrim decided that, under the circumstances, an offer of help would not be amiss.

"I don't mean to intrude," said Pilgrim. "But could you use some help? Is your friend all right?"

"All right?" said Faith. "He's wonderful!"

"I'm certainly happy to hear that," said Pilgrim. "It appeared to me that you were guiding your friend, and I thought perhaps he might be ill."

"I guiding him?" said Faith, laughing. "It's quite the opposite. He's guiding me."

"Well," said Pilgrim, "as my poor departed brother used to say, 'Appearances can be deceiving.' "

"My friend here knows the way to the Heavenly City."

"He does! Do you hear that, Caution? This may be our lucky day. Faith, would you mind if we accompanied you? We are not sure of the way."

"Please do."

"Just a minute," said Caution to Faith. "This friend of yours—has he been to the Heavenly City before?"

"Many times."

"That's a relief," said Caution.

"There now, Caution," said Pilgrim. "I hope you are satisfied for once."

What satisfaction Caution did feel soon gave way to irritation. No matter how slowly he and Pilgrim tried to walk, they kept getting ahead of Faith and the guide. They were moving at a snail's pace.

"Can't we go a little faster?" said Caution.

"Don't be rude to our friends," said Pilgrim. "You are certainly in no position to complain about someone who takes great care. It is quite obvious that our guide is going slowly so that he will make no mistake."

At that, Faith laughed.

"You are a charitable soul, Pilgrim, but I'm afraid that in this case your charity is misplaced. My friend knows the way to the Heavenly City as well as I know the streets of my town. He has no need to take care."

"Then why is he moving so slowly?" said Pilgrim.

"It's just his habit," said Faith. "And no doubt he is being considerate of me. I'm quite a clumsy fellow, likely to trip over things or go wandering off in the wrong direction. He wants to make certain that I can keep up."

"I must say that your friend is wonderful indeed," said Pilgrim. "It would certainly be unfair to complain about him, wouldn't it, Caution?"

Caution just mumbled, and Pilgrim paid him no attention. Instead, Pilgrim began to daydream about the Heavenly City; but she found her images quite vague.

"Faith," she said, "do you suppose that your friend might describe the wonders of the Heavenly City to us as we walk? That would certainly be a delightful way to pass the time, and it would encourage us on our journey."

"I'm sure that my friend would be more than happy to do that," said Faith. "Unfortunately, he cannot speak at all. He is mute."

"Oh, I'm so sorry," said Pilgrim, blushing, lowering her voice to a whisper.

"Why are you whispering?" said Faith, and then he laughed. "Oh, don't worry about embarrassing my friend. It's quite all right. He's deaf."

"Is he blind, too?" said Caution.

"Of course not," said Faith. "How could he be guiding me if he were blind?"

"Well, that's something," said Caution.

"Perhaps, Faith," said Pilgrim, "you could communicate with your friend in whatever way you do and then translate for us. I'd love to hear his stories. He must have many."

"I'm sorry," said Faith. "We have no way of communicating. I'm afraid we will just have to wait until we get to the Heavenly City to find out what it's like."

"What a shame," said Pilgrim, but then she brightened. "Oh, well. We shall be there soon enough. I suppose our delight will be all the greater for the surprise of it."

"Hold it!"

Caution had moved out in front of them and now turned to face Faith and the guide. Caution put out his hands to stop them but then realized they were moving so slowly that there was hardly any point. Caution walked backward as he spoke.

"Just a minute, Faith. First you tell us that your friend has been to the Heavenly City and knows the way quite well. Then you tell us that he's mute . . . and deaf. Now you tell us that you cannot communicate with him in any way. Just how do you know that he knows the way?"

"Stop it, Caution," said Pilgrim. "It is quite obvious that our guide had some credentials, or that he and Faith were introduced through some mutual acquaintance who knew our guide's abilities quite well."

"No," said Faith. "My friend carries no credentials. Nor were we introduced. When he came walking through my town one day, walking just as he is now, I had never seen him before, nor had I heard of him."

"What made you follow him?" said Pilgrim.

Faith thought for a moment.

"I think . . . I think it was his eyes. They had that special look about them. Yes, his eyes convinced me."

"Ah!" said Pilgrim. "You had seen that look before."

"Are you joking?" said Faith. "How could it be special if I had seen it before? And would I follow a man on an exceptional journey like this one if he looked like any other person?"

"I've had enough of this," said Caution. "You say that your wonderful friend knows many wonderful things. But for all I know, his head may be as empty as yours. Come on, Pilgrim, we're going."

As Caution turned and hurried away, Pilgrim hesitated. Then she said to Faith:

"I'm sorry. I would like to accompany you. But I should stay with my brother. He may need me."

"I understand," said Faith. "It's quite all right. In any case, if you get confused, just stop and wait for us. We'll be along eventually."

Pilgrim hurried after her brother but could not see him as she rounded the next bend, nor the one after that. She had almost decided that some misfortune had befallen Caution when she came upon him at last. Caution was standing midway down a path that sloped toward the plains, holding his hand to his forehead, shaking his head slowly. Pilgrim was perplexed until she also saw. Then she clapped her hands in delight. At the base of the hill, their road met another road that stretched from the other side of the hill; the roads joined and headed straight across the plains. At the junction of the roads was a sign that was visible from where they stood: Heavenly City Straight Ahead.

"I'm sorry, Caution, if I must laugh at you," said Pilgrim. "But surely you must laugh at yourself as well. After all your fussing! After all your talk about how one city couldn't be in two different directions! It is quite obvious now that the sign was no trick. Both roads were leading to the Heavenly City. Though they seemed to go in entirely different directions, it turns out that each curved northward around a different side of the hill, and here they meet."

Caution grumbled, "A competent sign maker would have said, 'Both roads lead to the Heavenly City.' Then there would have been no confusion."

"Caution, must you always quibble? In any case, we're on the right road. Be happy for that."

"I will admit that I'm a bit relieved," said Caution. "But as for being happy, I shall wait awhile for that. We *may* be on the right road. That's all I know at the moment."

"Caution, *you* are hopeless."

"There's some truth in that," said Caution. "But what reason have I to be hopeful? We do not really know that there's a Heavenly City or, if there is one, that this is the right road to it. If we do find the Heavenly City, it will be mere luck."

"Suppose it is luck?" said Pilgrim. "Does that matter, as long as our luck is good?"

That night, the brother and sister made camp on the plains. In the morning, they were awakened not by the light but by a terrible wind that roared in their ears and threw dust in their eyes. Far in the distance, a whirlwind could be seen. They gathered the lightest of their belongings and hurried along the road.

"Pilgrim," said Caution, "let us hope that the luck you speak of finds us a Heavenly City very soon. We shall certainly not survive if that whirlwind comes upon us while we are unsheltered."

For two hours, they stumbled along the road, buffeted by the wind and nearly blinded by the dust. Then they both stopped abruptly. Pilgrim had noticed a sign; Caution had noticed what lay ahead of them.

"Caution, the sign says, Heavenly City One League Ahead Through the Valley. We shall surely make it."

"But look at the valley, Pilgrim! Look and listen. Even smell."

Before them the road dipped sharply into fog and darkness. Threatening forms moved about in the fog, and there were howls like those of wild beasts. The stench was that of a swamp.

"It does look quite fearsome," said Pilgrim. "But the sign would not be here if we could not pass through unharmed."

"What I see before me convinces me more than any sign," said Caution. "Go if you will. I shall not."

Pilgrim pleaded, but Caution sat down by the side of the road and refused to move. Sitting down next to him, Pilgrim was determined to stay until Caution changed his mind. There they stayed for the rest of the morning and part of the afternoon. Pop and Hasty and Suppressed passed by, and Circles the beggar, and Faith and his wonderful friend, and others as well. All urged the brother and sister to come with them, but Caution refused and Pilgrim remained with her brother. Through the day, the dust and wind became more and more terrible.

"By now, Caution," said Pilgrim, "all those people are safe and happy in the Heavenly City."

"Or they are dead, devoured by the swamp."

"I doubt it," said Pilgrim. "But if we stay here much longer, we shall surely die. I can barely breathe now. And that whirlwind should be upon us at any moment."

"All right, Pilgrim," said Caution. "I don't know if there is a Heavenly City. I certainly don't believe that we shall get through that terrible valley in any case. But it is clear now that there is little to gain by staying here. Were I alone, I believe I would prefer to die out here in the wind. But I will not have you die believing that I kept you from the Heavenly City. For your sake, we shall go."

They got to their feet and approached the edge of the dark valley. Pilgrim was cheerful.

"In a little while, Caution, we shall be in the Heavenly City, and I shall enjoy seeing you happy for the very first time."

"Good-bye, Pilgrim."

"Don't be so pessimistic, Caution. Here goes."

"Here goes nothing," said Caution.

And into the valley they went.

Questions

1. Explain, in context, the reasoning of the following characters:

    Provincial
    the tavern keeper
    Circles the beggar
    Pop
    Hasty
    Suppressed
    the official at the junction

    What, if anything, is wrong with the reasoning of each character?

2. What is confusing about the sign on p. 208?
3. What bothers Caution about the claims made by Faith? Do you feel that Caution's attitude is justified? Explain.
4. Explain the differences in outlook among Skeptic, Caution, and Pilgrim. Do you feel that one outlook is better than the others?

Discussion

EIGHT FALLACIES SKETCHED

In this part of the logic discussion, we shall consider some standard "fallacies": common faults in persuasion, reasoning, or argument that have been given individual names by logicians.* Each fallacy to be discussed here has been exemplified in some form in "Another Pilgrim's Progress." Many of the fallacies, though common in, say, political debate, are not so likely to occur in philosophical argument. I shall sketch eight such fallacies in this section, and, in later sections, I shall give more attention to five other fallacies that are more likely to occur in philosophy.

Appeal to force. One appeals to force when one attempts to persuade through intimidation.

The appeal to force is caricatured in the case of the official who kicks Caution down the road, when the official is unable to demonstrate that it is the correct road. The tavern keeper also appeals to force, though not when he argues that Caution will die if he leaves the tavern; that argument (though exemplifying another fallacy) is directed to the question at issue. The appeal to force occurs when the tavern keeper threatens to eject Caution should he continue to disagree.

Provincialism. The fallacy of provincialism is committed when one accepts or rejects a conclusion on the basis of one's identification with a particular group.

In the story, of course, this fallacy is exemplified by Provincial. In spite of all the disasters that have befallen his town, he says, "This is my home. How can any place be better?"

Like most fallacies, this one bears some resemblance to ways of thinking that are reasonable or admirable. If someone says,

---

* In the selection of labels for the fallacies discussed in this chapter, I am conscious of following Howard Kahane more closely than any other writer on logic. (See Kahane, Howard. *Logic and Contemporary Rhetoric*. 2nd edition. Belmont, Calif.: Wadsworth, 1976.)

"He's done something very wrong, and he's suffering for it; but he's my friend, and I'll stick with him through his ordeal," the person may be exhibiting the virtue of loyalty. But if someone says, "He's my friend, therefore he could not have done something wrong," the person is committing the fallacy of provincialism.

Appeal to authority. If a conclusion is supported by referring to the views of some supposed authority who actually has no expertise relevant to the matter at issue, a fallacy has been committed that comes under the heading of "appeal to authority."

In "Progress," it turns out that the official in charge of the junction has no knowledge of the correct road and is an "authority" only in the sense that he is there to enforce the one-way ordinance. Obviously, it would be fallacious to form a conclusion about the correct road on the basis of what the official says.

It is often necessary and justifiable to rely on the word of experts. But often it is wrongly assumed that expertise in one field implies expertise in general. Thus it is that the views of physicists and football coaches are sometimes invoked in support of some political or religious view.

It would seem irrational to rely on expert opinion in matters about which the experts disagree. Also, it would seem irrational to rely heavily on the views of experts in regard to issues that are of personal importance and that are, or could easily be, within one's own area of competence. There is much disagreement among "experts" on questions of religion and ethics, for instance; these are crucial questions that one ought to try to think out for oneself.

Appeal to popular opinion. This fallacy is often treated as a version of the appeal to authority, where the supposed "authority" is popular opinion.

In the story, this fallacy is exemplified by Pop: "The road to the right is the road that most of the people took. That has got to be the way to go." But it should be noted that this argument is fallacious, because in the story it is not clear that anyone actually knows about the correct road. (And, of course, what we have in the story is not a physical road, but a representation of a quest for Heaven.) However, if a person were a stranger in a town and were looking for, say, the county fair, it might be wise to "follow the crowd."

Philosophers, when discussing very basic premises, sometimes will appeal to "universal conviction." This resembles an appeal to popular opinion and, in fact, the legitimacy of such an appeal is a matter of dispute. But at the very least, one can note that this appeal is generally to a conviction that remains after rational scrutiny; thus it is an appeal to reason as well as an appeal to popular opinion.

Hasty conclusion. This fallacy involves drawing a conclusion from supporting evidence without making a reasonable effort to determine if there is other relevant evidence.

The character named Hasty is guilty of this fallacy. He notes that the footprints show that many people have taken the road going right and that there are no footprints coming back toward the junction. He argues that if that were the wrong road, surely someone would have come back by that time; if there were danger ahead, surely someone at the rear would have been warned in time to return. In the absence of all other evidence, it might be reasonable to accept Hasty's argument. But Hasty has failed to check for further relevant evidence. For instance, he has failed to check the other road, which also has no footprints coming back toward the junction—a bit of information that weakens Hasty's argument.

Suppressed evidence. This fallacy involves presenting only evidence that is favorable to one's conclusion and suppressing evidence that is not favorable. (If one were unaware of the unfavorable evidence and had not tried to seek it out, that would be an instance of hasty conclusion.)

In "Another Pilgrim's Progress," the evidence suppressed is the sign stating the one-way ordinance. Obviously, the evidence of this ordinance further weakens Hasty's argument. The people who took the road to the right were forbidden to return no matter where that road led them.

Straw man. When one misinterprets a position or argument so as to make it seem more vulnerable to criticism, what one is attacking is called a "straw man."

In the story, this is lamely exemplified by Provincial's dismissing Caution as if the latter were a skeptic. But Caution's views are not that extreme; he should not be judged as a skeptic. In fact, Caution is not a skeptic. To characterize a person's political views as "socialist" when those views are only slightly left of center would be an example of the straw man fallacy.

It is always tempting to interpret an opponent's position in an unfavorable manner, and philosophers are not immune to this temptation. It is especially inviting to present a straw man in exposition when one wishes to be brief and when one feels confident of showing the more sophisticated versions of an argument to be fallacious if called upon to do so. For example, in remarks about the philosophical play, *Jumpers*, philosopher A. J. Ayer says of the main character: "For the creator, he relies on the first-cause argument, which is notoriously fallacious, since it starts from the assumption that everything must have a cause and ends with something that lacks one."* Ayer knows better and no doubt felt the constraints of his popular forum. Nevertheless, the argument that he presents is an attack on a straw man. It leads one to believe that there is a single first-cause argument and that it is fallacious for the reason he gives. In fact, there are several arguments that come under the heading of "first-cause argument," and the one Ayer attacks is the crudest of them; not all are vulnerable to that criticism.†

In reading philosophical texts, especially brief secondary texts (like this one), one should be aware of the possibility that the author is sometimes attacking straw men. One obvious way to check on this is to consult other primary and secondary sources.

False dilemma. This fallacy comes about when the possible positions at issue are falsely reduced so as to make the position for which one is arguing seem more reasonable.

In the story, the tavern keeper presents the following false dilemma: "Either you go out there in the dust and die, or you stay in here and drink my fine ale." Caution responds: "But then again if we leave here, we might find a Heavenly City. Or, if we stay, you might run out of ale, and we would die of thirst."

---

* Quoted in a National Theater program for *Jumpers* and referenced as: The Sunday *Times* (London), 9 April 1972.

† For a fuller discussion of the first-cause argument, see pp. 87–88.

Of course, once all the possibilities are explored, the rationality of staying in the tavern or the town is much less clear than the tavern keeper claims.

False dilemmas occur with some frequency in and around philosophical debate. One example is the popular argument, "Either Jesus was the greatest liar (or fool) who ever existed, or he was who he said he was," which leaves out a number of possibilities, one of them being that Jesus was misquoted.

Another example is a skeptical argument that claims that any statement unsupported by argument must be mere assumption. This leaves out the possibility that a statement unsupported by argument might be a "self-evident truth."*

Ad Hominem AND BEGGING THE QUESTION

Ad hominem (to the man). When Person A presents an argument, and Person B responds by discussing irrelevant characteristics of Person A, as if they were good grounds for rejecting the argument, Person B commits the *ad hominem* fallacy. Just as it is sometimes justifiable to rely on the word of supposed experts, so it can be legitimate to "attack the man" by showing that he is no expert. What is fallacious is the arguing from irrelevant characteristics.

In "Progress," this fallacy is committed twice. First, Provincial responds to Caution's criticism of the town by saying that Caution has not lived there as long as Provincial. As Caution correctly complains, "That is true. But what has that to do with what I say?" Second, when the junction official is unable to counter Caution's challenges to his expertise, he attacks Caution as a troublemaker.

The *ad hominem* fallacy that is especially likely to occur on the periphery of philosophy deserves the label "genetic fallacy": this involves the attempt to "explain away" an argument or belief by analyzing the genesis of it, whether psychological, historical, or whatever. For example, a student who has emerged

---

* Several accusations of false dilemma are made in this text, though without that label. See p. 93 and the argument that men without free will would walk about like so many zombies; and pp. 88–90 on the argument that the world came about either by design or by chance.

from a psychology of religion course may be tempted to "explain" to his or her friends why they are religious (through fear of death, the need to sustain the youthful belief in an omnipotent father figure, and so on), with the implication that he or she has just shown the religious belief to be false. This reasoning is absurd. To evaluate the truth or falsity of a belief, one must evaluate the evidence for or against the belief, not the motives behind the belief.

To my mind, historians of ideas often provoke genetic fallacies in their audience, whether or not they actually commit such fallacies themselves. Consider the following passage from Friedrich Heer's famous *The Intellectual History of Europe*. Heer notes the chaos, the irrationalism of Europe at the time of the Thirty Years War and then says this of the philosopher Descartes:

> Descartes had seen these things and was terrified of them. In the famous dream at Ulm on 10 November 1619, Descartes felt himself "hard pressed and frightened" (as he himself says) by ghosts, and nearly overcome by a whirlwind. . . . This dream revealed his mission to Descartes. He would work out a method of thinking that would grant to mankind absolute security against illusions, deceptions, and evil temptations.*

Leaving aside questions of distortion and dubious psychological speculation, the danger of this kind of description is that it may lead some readers to conclude that Descartes's philosophical views are false. But to evaluate Descartes's philosophy rationally, one must evaluate his reasoning, not the (supposed) motives behind his reasoning.†

There is another use of the label *ad hominem* that does not designate a fallacy. One is said to present an *ad hominem* argument when one claims to show an inconsistency in someone's beliefs. Such a claim, if true, does not show which of the beliefs

---

* Friedrich Heer, *The Intellectual History of Europe* (Cleveland: World Publishing Co., 1966), p. 340.

† The silliest passage in Heer's book may be the following (p. 170). "In a sense Newton's theory of the cosmos as a balance of forces was a transference of the political theory of 1688 to the universe as a whole." But this idea is relatively harmless. Few people are inclined to treat physics as a branch of psychology or political history.

is false; what it does show is that one of the beliefs must be false.* (See "Inconsistency," p. 234.)

Begging the question, or *circular argument.* One is begging the question, or arguing in a circle, when one purports to offer only additional statements in support of one's conclusion and then employs the conclusion as a premise of that argument.

All circular arguments are valid: if a statement is true as a premise, it must be true as conclusion. Circular arguments are sometimes sound—when the conclusion is, in fact, true. What makes a circular argument fallacious is that it purports to do something it does not: to offer only additional statements in support of the conclusion. When a person requests an argument for a statement, it is (generally) because the statement is considered questionable. To offer that questionable statement in support of itself is, to say the least, unhelpful.

In the story, of course, it is Circles the beggar who exemplifies this fallacy. Note, however, that he does not commit this fallacy simply by pointing to a sign or map as evidence that the travelers are, indeed, on the road to the Heavenly City. One might criticize the reliability of the evidence he presents, but this would have nothing to do with circularity. He commits this fallacy when, in continuing to argue, he "circles back" and uses as premises the very statements at issue. Circles says, "But this is the right road . . . I know that." How does he know that? He points to the sign as evidence. But how does he know that the sign is correct? "That's easy . . . I know that the sign is correct because this is the right road." He is now using the premise "This is the right road" to support the conclusion "This is the right road."

Again: After Circles produces a map as evidence, Caution

---

* The use of *ad hominem* as designating a fallacy occurs in "Those Who Help Themselves" (pp. 108–109): ". . . they avoided *ad hominem* arguments, addressing themselves to issues. . . ." The other usage occurs in a discussion (p. 92): "For any theist who is tempted to say that an omnipotent God must be able to do contradictory things, one can add a rather powerful *ad hominem* argument: You have just denied yourself any recourse to the traditional explanations for why God might have allowed suffering." (In other words, those explanations presuppose that God cannot do contradictory things.)

asks him how he knows that the map is correct. As evidence, Circles points to a statement on the map that says it is a reliable map. But this statement is not additional evidence that the map is reliable: the statement is only as reliable as the map itself.

Pop also presents a question-begging argument. Hasty has pointed to the one-way footprints on the road to the right, indicating it is the correct road. Caution claims that the one-way footprints on the left road weaken this argument. Pop then says: "It seems to me that anybody who's fool enough to take the wrong road would be fool enough not to come back." But this argument, presented in support of Hasty's contention, begs the question: it simply assumes that the road to the left is the wrong road. (Note that Pop's argument would apply just as well, or as poorly, to the matter of the one-way footprints on the road to the right.)

One is particularly likely to beg the question in arguing philosophy, because very basic beliefs are at issue—beliefs one is not accustomed to arguing—and it is easy to fall back on one of those beliefs in the course of the argument. Some very concise examples:

How do you know that you are not now dreaming? "Well, I've checked with the people around me, and they say that I am awake." This response begs the question. The claim that one has checked with other people (as opposed to merely dreaming one has checked with other people) assumes the conclusion.

How do you know that your principles of reasoning are reliable? "Well, I would argue that. . . ." Already one has begged the question. To offer an argument assumes the reliability of those principles of reasoning that have just been challenged.

One could never complete an argument supporting every statement one believes without begging the question. Even if one had a potentially infinite number of new statements to add, one could never complete an infinite argument. If one has only a limited number of statements to add and one tries to continue arguing indefinitely, one will start repeating statements and begging the question (arguing in a circle). Any system of thought must begin with first premises that are employed without argument.

If you find yourself begging the question in arguing for very basic beliefs, you should stop to consider whether the beliefs are really in need of argument. You should consider the possibility that a particular statement may qualify as a "self-evident first premise." (To avoid begging the question myself, I should note that whether there are self-evident statements, and, if so, which statements are self-evident, are matters of dispute in philosophy.)*

AMBIGUITY, AMBIGUOUS HYPOTHESIS, AND INCONSISTENCY

Ambiguity. The fallacy of ambiguity is committed when a crucial word or phrase shifts meaning from its use in the premises to its use in the conclusion, so that the premises seem to support the conclusion but actually do not.

In "Progress," Pilgrim sees a sign and reasons as follows: According to the sign, the road to the right is heavenly; therefore, according to the sign, the road to the right leads to the Heavenly City. Pilgrim's reasoning would be good if the word "heavenly" in the premise had the same meaning as "heavenly" in her conclusion. But the word "heavenly," as used on the sign, simply means "scenic." Thus, though the inference may seem to be valid, it is not.

John Stuart Mill provided logicians with a classic fallacy of ambiguity in his book *Utilitarianism:* "The only proof capable of being given that an object is visible is that people actually see it. . . . In like manner, I apprehend, the sole evidence it is possible to produce that anything is desirable is that people actually desire it . . . . [Each person] desires his own happiness . . . . happiness is a good."†

It would be valid, if unexciting, to conclude from the premise "happiness is desired" that happiness is "desirable" in the sense of "is desired" or "can be desired." But Mill wants to conclude from "happiness is desired" that happiness is "desirable" in the sense of "is good." That inference is invalid.

---

* For a charge of question begging in this text, see the footnote on p. 121 in regard to the argument on pp. 118–121. Also, the discussion of appearance and reality considers the problem of "assuming what is at issue" when one tries to counter skeptical arguments.

† John Stuart Mill, *Utilitarianism* (Indianapolis, Bobbs-Merrill, 1957), pp. 44–45.

Fallacies of ambiguity are a constant danger in philosophy: writers often use broad terms in restricted senses and then easily shift back to the broader usage as the argument goes on. For example, Descartes claims that one cannot be in error about the belief "I think, therefore I am." It would be fallacious, however, to conclude from Descartes's argument that I cannot be in error about the belief that Tom Davis (the person six feet tall, with brown hair, born 1941, and so on) exists. The "I" in Descartes's argument designates only "this mind." It does not imply a body, a past, and so on.*

Ambiguous hypothesis. This fallacy occurs when a person presents an hypothesis as if it were one type of statement but defends it as if it were another type of statement. For example: A person presents what is supposed to be a straightforward factual hypothesis—one supposedly based on observable evidence and to be judged on observable evidence. Yet, as it turns out, there is no imaginable evidence that would ever lead the person to abandon the hypothesis. In defending the claim, the person unknowingly switches back and forth between a factual claim and another kind of claim. The other kind of claim might be a definitional claim, a value judgment, a purely metaphysical claim, or simply meaningless.

As every philosophy teacher knows, specific versions of this fallacy frequently occur in classroom debate about psychological hedonism. According to one version of psychological hedonism, the underlying motive for a person's every action is the desire for his or her own happiness. This theory does not deny that people desire things other than happiness. But it claims that

---

* Throughout this text, there are constant attempts to clarify terms that are ambiguous in such a way as to confuse the problem at issue—for example, distinguishing between "freedom" as "freedom of action" and "freedom of the will" (pp. 62–63). The problem of ambiguity is particularly troublesome in the discussion of appearance and reality and accounts in part for the "belaboring" and use of jargon there. For instance, "Am I now dreaming?" can be interpreted as "Are these experiences consistent with my normal experiences?" or as "Are these experiences inventions of my mind?"

For further discussion of Descartes's argument above, see Chapter 5, "Appearance and Reality."

other things are desired only as means to happiness; people desire something only insofar as they believe that it will bring them happiness.*

To at least one student in such a classroom debate, psychological hedonism will seem a straightforward factual claim that is indisputably true. When faced with what ought to be at least slightly troubling cases (the artist, the saint), this advocate will quite casually interpret these cases in terms of the theory. (Artists desire art only as a means to happiness; Saints desire virtue only insofar as they believe it will bring them happiness. If someone should construct hypothetical cases, it turns out that there is no conceivable evidence that this advocate would ever accept as disconfirming psychological hedonism.

The staunch advocate, without realizing it, is defending an ambiguous hypothesis—presenting it under one interpretation, but defending it under another. *Part* of the problem is the ambiguity of the word "happiness," which could mean "the sensation of pleasure," "the good," or "whatever is desired as an end." The thesis that happiness is desired only as an end might be interpreted in the following ways:

1. People desire only pleasure as an end (where the desire for pleasure is interpreted in terms of some specific outward manifestations).
2. People desire only pleasure as an end (where the desire for pleasure is conceived as some inevitably hidden unconscious drive).
3. People desire as an end only whatever is desired as an end.
4. People desire only the good as an end.

Interpretation 1 would be a straightforward factual thesis to be decided on the basis of whether all people always exhibit the specified characteristics equivalent to desiring only pleasure as an end. Interpretation 2 would be a purely metaphysical claim in the sense that no observable evidence would decide its truth or falsity. Statement 3 would be a tautology: it is true, but

---

* I should note that I am purposely simplifying here. The psychological hedonist would actually say that one will always choose that course of action that one believes will result in the greatest balance of happiness over unhappiness.

simply because of the meanings of the words in it. Statement 4 would be a value judgment.

The staunch advocate may be claiming to hold the thesis as in 1 and yet defending it as if it were 2—supposing an unobservable desire for pleasure as an end in the troublesome cases. Or the advocate may be claiming to hold the thesis as in 1 and yet defending it as if it were 3—shifting the meaning of happiness from "pleasure" to "whatever is desired as an end" in order to handle the troublesome cases. "For the saint," he might say, "virtue is happiness." By juggling two meanings of a claim, the advocate is committing the fallacy of ambiguous hypothesis. Obviously, any defense of a thesis under one interpretation does not support that thesis under a different interpretation.

The advocate needs to clarify the various possible interpretations and then settle on one. If the advocate wants to hold interpretation 3, fine. But it should be noted that 3 is trivial in the sense of being devoid of factual content: it is true, but it gives us no information about people. Perhaps the advocate wants to hold 2. In that case, it should be noted that while no observable evidence could ever count against that claim, no observable evidence could ever count for it, either. If the advocate holds 1, then it is necessary to specify what conceivable behavior would ever count as not directed toward pleasure as the sole end.

In debates about a thesis like "Happiness is desired only as an end," people will often seem to be "talking past" one another; to one person, the objections of another seem to miss the point. What is often happening is that different people are interpreting the thesis differently. Clarifying the various possible interpretations will help eliminate such confusions.

It should be noted that the dividing line between the factual and the metaphysical is not a clear one, and any attempt to characterize these categories in great detail would beg (or get one involved in) important philosophical questions. Thus, I have hedged by talking about the "straightforward factual" and the "purely metaphysical." One can give examples of each. "That chair can support a person weighing two hundred pounds" is a straightforward factual claim that could be decided on observable evidence. "There are spirits in the universe that are unobservable and have absolutely no effect on anything" would be a purely metaphysical claim; no conceivable evidence could count for or against it. The point here is not to provoke a debate about the labels and characterizations of such categories. The point is that in considering a thesis, one should try to determine roughly what it means and how observable evidence might relate to considerations of its truth or falsity.

In "Progress," Faith puts forth a thesis about his wonderful friend that Caution takes to be a straightforward factual thesis. According to Faith, his friend knows the way to the Heavenly City. Caution assumes that Faith has some evidence for this claim. But then it turns out that the wonderful friend is mute and deaf; that Faith and his friend cannot communicate in any way; that Faith has no testimony that gives evidence of his friend's knowledge; that the friend's "special look" cannot be related to others who had that look and had clearly been to the Heavenly City. Faith's claim, then, is not a straightforward factual one; it is supported by no observable evidence whatsoever. Once it is clarified, it is no longer a misleading claim. Faith simply chooses to believe it; Caution does not.

Inconsistency. Two statements are inconsistent when one asserts what the other denies. An argument may suffer from inconsistency but so may a set of beliefs, irrespective of the arguments for those beliefs. If two statements are inconsistent, one of them must be false. To know that two statements are inconsistent is not to know which one is false—further considerations are necessary to determine that. But to discover an inconsistency ought to provoke a reexamination of those beliefs.

Perhaps most people can spot inconsistencies as they occur in snatches of everyday discourse. But they are less easily detected when they occur in the course of a long argument, especially one that covers unfamiliar material or employs unfamiliar terminology. Inconsistency is a constant danger in philosophy, especially for the beginner.

For example, a student who believes in life after death might nod in agreement when hearing an initial lecture on the identity theory, which claims that the mind is the brain—not realizing that belief in the identity theory is inconsistent with the belief that the mind survives the death of the body. (No doubt that inconsistency would be pointed out in a later lecture.)

A simple example of an argument in which the conclusion contradicts a premise would be the crude version of the "first-cause argument" mentioned earlier. It is not the only form of that argument, but it does occur, as in: "I find it hard to believe that there isn't a Creator. Everything has to have a beginning, and things don't come from nothing." If, as is likely, this person is arguing for the existence of an eternally existing Creator, the premise that *everything* must have a beginning contradicts the conclusion. One reason that the person may not spot the inconsistency is that the conclusion is not fully stated.

Paradoxically, any argument with inconsistent premises will be a valid argument. Let us focus on deduction here. A valid deductive argument, you will recall, is one that has a form such that it is impossible for the premises to be true *and* the conclusion false. Since, in any argument with inconsistent premises, it will be impossible for (all) the premises to be true, such an argument must be valid. But though this seems odd, it should not be of serious concern to you. One ought to rely on sound arguments—arguments that are valid *and* have true premises. Inconsistency of premises may guarantee a valid argument, but it also guarantees an unsound argument: inconsistent premises cannot (all) be true.

"Another Pilgrim's Progress" does not contain examples of inconsistency and has only one example of an apparent inconsistency. It seems to Caution that the sign at the junction implies that there is one Heavenly City that is located in two different places. As it turns out, the statements on the sign may be confusing, but they are not inconsistent. The two roads, though initially heading in different directions, eventually meet.

As you are forming or rethinking your philosophical views, you should be looking for possible inconsistencies. Suppose you are tempted to accept two positions, A and B, on the basis of separate arguments. You should state the positions and the arguments as fully and clearly as possible. You should check each argument to see if some premise is inconsistent with either another premise in that argument or with the conclusion. You should check to see if anything asserted by position A is denied by position B. And you should check to see if a premise in one argument contradicts some premise in the other.

Glossary

The definitions below are convenient simplifications for quick reference; they are not meant to replace the fuller definitions presented in the discussions.

AD HOMINEM FALLACY Attacking the man (or woman) rather than the argument.

AMBIGUITY, FALLACY OF Using a word in different senses in premises and conclusion, with the result that the premises only seem to support the conclusion.

AMBIGUOUS HYPOTHESIS, FALLACY OF Arguing for a statement of one type (factual, metaphysical, definitional, or normative) as if it were a statement of another type.

APPEAL TO AUTHORITY, FALLACY OF Appealing to some supposed authority who has no expertise relevant to the matter at issue.

APPEAL TO FORCE, FALLACY OF Attempting to persuade through intimidation rather than argument.

APPEAL TO POPULAR OPINION, FALLACY OF Appealing to the crowd as authority.

BEGGING THE QUESTION, FALLACY OF Presenting some form of the conclusion as if it were additional support for the conclusion.

BEHAVIORISM A version of materialism, claiming that the mind is nothing but complex, overt, physical behavior.

CIRCULAR ARGUMENT, FALLACY OF (see "Begging the Question.")

DEDUCTIVE ARGUMENT (see "Valid Argument.")

DETERMINISM The theory that all events, including mental events, are governed by causal laws; that every event (every choice) is the inevitable effect of some set of circumstances ("the cause") that necessitated that event.

DUALISM The view that the world is composed of two radically different kinds of things: physical objects and nonphysical minds.

FALSE DILEMMA, FALLACY OF Falsely reducing the possible positions at issue to make one's own position seem more reasonable.

FATALISM The view that some specified events must occur in a person's life, no matter what that person may choose to do.

FREE WILL The concept that not all choices are inevitable, that the individual is the ultimate originator of some of his or her choices.

FREEDOM OF ACTION The ability or opportunity to do what one might choose to do.

HASTY CONCLUSION, FALLACY OF Presenting supporting evidence without a reasonable attempt to determine if there is other relevant evidence.

IDENTITY THEORY A version of materialism, claiming that the mind is nothing but the (physical) brain.

INCONSISTENCY, FALLACY OF Arguing for, or from, statements which contradict one another.

INDUCTIVE ARGUMENT (see "Valid Argument.")

INTERACTIONISM A version of dualism, claiming that the (physical) body and (nonphysical) mind are causally related.

MATERIALISM The view that everything that exists is physical, including minds.

METAETHICAL Relating to the nature of moral judgments, especially their meaning and justification.

MORAL OBJECTIVISM The view that where there is a moral judgment and its negation, one of those judgments must be false; that there is such a thing as *the* moral truth.

MORAL SUBJECTIVISM The view that where there is a moral judgment and its negation, neither judgment need be false; that there is no such thing as *the* moral truth.

PARALLELISM A version of dualism, claiming that the (physical) body and (nonphysical) mind are not causally related.

PROVINCIALISM, FALLACY OF Accepting or rejecting a conclusion on the basis of one's identification with a particular group.

SOLIPSISM The view that, with the exception of the belief in one's own mind, one cannot justify any beliefs about the world.

SOUND ARGUMENT An argument that is valid and has true premises.

STRAW MAN, FALLACY OF Misinterpreting an opponent's position to make it seem more vulnerable to criticism.

SUPPRESSED EVIDENCE, FALLACY OF Presenting evidence favorable to one's position while suppressing evidence that is not favorable.

UTILITARIANISM The moral view that only happiness is good in itself and that one ought to promote the greatest happiness of the greatest number.

VALID ARGUMENT

DEDUCTIVE An argument such that if the premises are true, then the conclusion is necessarily true.

INDUCTIVE An argument such that if the premises are true, then the conclusion is probably true, but not necessarily so.

Further Readings

The Nature of the Mind

PHILOSOPHY

Beardsley, Monroe C., and Elizabeth Lane Beardsley. *Philosophical Thinking: An Introduction.* New York: Harcourt, Brace & World, 1965. Chapter 11, pp. 428–55, on mind and body, and Chapter 3, pp. 92–105, on life after death.

Shaffer, Jerome A. *Reality, Knowledge, and Value.* New York: Random House, 1971. Chapters 11–14.

Taylor, Richard. *Metaphysics.* Englewood Cliffs, N.J.: Prentice-Hall, 1963. Chapters 1–3.

LITERATURE

Asimov, Isaac. *I, Robot.* Greenwich, Conn.: Fawcett World, 1966. A series of robot stories in which the robots get progressively more "lifelike."

Vonnegut, Kurt, Jr. "Epicac" and "Unready to Wear" in *Welcome to the Monkey House.* New York: Dell Publishing Co., 1970. The first story concerns a computer who falls in love, and the second is about a group of people who have learned to step in and out of their bodies.

Freedom, Foreknowledge, and Time

PHILOSOPHY

Beardsley, Monroe C., and Elizabeth Lane Beardsley. *Philosophical Thinking: An Introduction.* New York: Harcourt,

Brace & World, 1965. Chapter 11, pp. 455–67, on freedom and determinism.

Taylor, Richard. *Metaphysics*. Englewood Cliffs, N.J.: Prentice-Hall, 1963. Chapter 4 on freedom and determinism; Chapter 6 on time. The beginner should avoid Chapter 5 on fate, since it is difficult, idiosyncratic, and likely to confuse.

Literature

Borges, Jorge Luis. "The Secret Miracle" in *Ficciones*. New York: Grove Press, 1962. A man facing execution gets his wish that time stop for awhile.

Dostoevsky, Fyodor. *Notes from the Underground*. N.Y.: Dell, 1960. An expression of a man's hysterical insistence on free will.

Heinlein, Robert A. "—All You Zombies—" in *The Unpleasant Profession of Jonathan Hoag*. New York: Berkeley Medallion Books, 1976. The story presents the ultimate in time-travel complexities: a man manages to become the mother and father of himself.

God and the Problem of Suffering

Philosophy

Beardsley, Monroe C., and Elizabeth Lane Beardsley. *Philosophical Thinking: An Introduction*. New York: Harcourt, Brace & World, 1965. Chapter 2, pp. 68–91, on the traditional proofs for God, and Chapter 3, pp. 105–17, on the problem of suffering.

Hick, John. *Philosophy of Religion*. Englewood Cliffs, N.J.: Prentice-Hall, 1963. Chapters 3 and 4. The latter chapter presents a discussion of suffiering that is sympathetic to the theist point of view.

Pike, Nelson (ed.). *God and Evil*. Englewood Cliffs, N.J.: Prentice-Hall, 1964. Of special interest is the essay by H. J.

McCloskey entitled "God and Evil," pp. 61–84, which presents a systematic argument against the possibility of an omnipotent, omniscient, morally perfect God.

LITERATURE

The Book of Job. Does God provide an adequate explanation of suffering?

Dostoevsky, Fyodor. *Brothers Karamazov.* New York: Norton, 1976. Chapter entitled "Rebellion." An outcry against a God who would allow suffering.

Huxley, Aldous. *Brave New World.* New York: Perennial Classics, 1969. Chapters 16 and 17, pp. 147–63. The discussion between Mustapha Mond and the Savage parallels the discussion between the theist and the nonbeliever concerning suffering.

Pope, Alexander. *Essay on Man.* Indianapolis: Bobbs-Merrill, 1965. A poetic defense of God.

Stoppard, Tom. *Jumpers.* New York: Grove Press, 1972. The main character, a philosopher, presents an amusing discussion of the first-cause argument.

Voltaire. *Candide.* Oxford: Oxford University Press, 1968. A satire based on the claim that this is the best of all possible worlds.

Moral Proof and Moral Principles

PHILOSOPHY

Beardsley, Monroe C., and Elizabeth Lane Beardsley. *Philosophical Thinking: An Introduction.* New York: Harcourt, Brace & World, 1965. Chapter 12, pp. 521–44, on metaethics, and pp. 487–521, on normative ethics.

Frankena, William. *Ethics.* Englewood Cliffs, N.J.: Prentice-Hall, 1963. Chapter 6 includes a concise discussion of the "moral point of view."

Literature

Huxley, Aldous. *Brave New World.* New York: Perennial Classics, 1969. Chapters 16 and 17, pp. 147–63, especially pp. 154–5. Mustapha Mond defends a quasi-utilitarian morality, distinguishing between his personal preferences and moral perspective.

Sartre, Jean-Paul. "The Flies" in *No Exit and Three Other Plays.* New York: Vintage, 1965. The "freedom" exalted in this play is not so much free will as the freedom to choose a morality without any possibility of being in error. In other words, the play is primarily concerned with moral subjectivism.

Stoppard, Tom. *Jumpers.* New York: Grove Press, 1972. The characters discuss moral subjectivism with some sophistication.

Appearance and Reality

Philosophy

Descartes. *Meditations.* Indianapolis: Bobbs-Merrill, 1960. This book contains the thoughts of Descartes that are discussed in this textbook.

Shaffer, Jerome. *Reality, Knowledge, and Value.* New York: Random House, 1971. Chapters 1–6 concern skepticism and the problem of the external world.

Literature

Borges, Jorge Luis. "The Circular Ruins" in *Ficciones.* New York: Grove Press, 1962. In this story, a man discovers that he is only an illusion.

Calderon, Pedro. *Life Is a Dream.* New York: Hill & Wang, 1970. The main character has difficulty distinguishing dream from reality.

Logic

Philosophy

Kahane, Howard. *Logic and Contemporary Rhetoric.* 2d ed. Belmont, Calif.: Wadsworth, 1976. An extended discussion of fallacies, employing examples from everyday life, particularly from politics and advertising.

Salmon, Wesley. *Logic.* Englewood Cliffs, N.J.: Prentice-Hall, 1963. A brief introduction to the subject of logic. The beginner may find pp. 22–52 too technical.

Literature

Any "whodunit" can be helpful in the analysis and exercise of reasoning. Agatha Christie's mysteries are, of course, among the more sophisticated, and Rex Stout's are among the most enjoyable. But the Ellery Queen novels containing his characteristic "Challenge to the Reader" provide the most legitimate opportunity to reason out the solution.

As for informal fallacies, after practicing on exercises included in almost any logic textbook, you might try to find other examples in newspapers, newsmagazines, advertisements, and other everyday sources.

Index

About the Author

Thomas D. Davis received his Ph.D. in philosophy from the University of Michigan, where he wrote his dissertation on Sartre. He has taught courses at Michigan, at Grinnell College, and in Austria for the University of Redlands.

A writer of fiction, Davis composed a series of philosophical short stories for use in his introductory classes. *Philosophy: An Introduction Through Original Fiction and Discussion* evolved from his stories and lectures.